WHAT IS TRUTH?

Why I'm a Christian:
An Examination and Refutation of
Opposing Worldviews

DJ Robinson

ISBN 978-1-63874-264-7 (paperback)
ISBN 978-1-63874-591-4 (hardcover)
ISBN 978-1-63874-265-4 (digital)

Christian Faith Publishing, Inc.
832 Park Avenue
Meadville, PA 16335
www.christianfaithpublishing.com

All Bible quotations taken from: the King James Version unless otherwise noted.

All Quran quotations taken from: 'Omar, Amatul Rahman, and 'Abdul Mannan 'Omar, trans. *The Holy Qur'ān: Arabic Text—English Translation*. Hockessin, DE: Noor Foundation International Inc., 2010.

All Book of Mormon/D&C/PoGP quotations taken from: *Book of Mormon; Doctrine and Covenants; Pearl of Great Price*. Salt Lake City, UT: The Church of Jesus Christ of Latter-day Saints, 1981.

All New World Translation quotations taken from: *New World Translation of the Holy Scriptures*. Wallkill, NY: Watch Tower Bible and Tract Society of New York, Inc, 2013.

Printed in the United States of America

But sanctify the Lord God in your hearts:
and be ready always to give an answer to every
man that asketh you a reason of the hope that
is in you with meekness and fear.

—1 Peter 3:15

CONTENTS

PREFACE

I want to thank my family and friends for the encouragement to finish this work. I could not have done it without them. And most importantly, I want to thank the Lord Jesus for offering me salvation and changing my life. I am not speaking officially on behalf of any church; rather, I am giving my own arguments, reasonings, etc. The goal of this work is to persuade the reader to seek the one and only Lord Jesus Christ. Much love and God bless you all!

CHAPTER 1

JUST A KID FROM SIXTH STREET

CHRISTIAN NOMINALISM

Growing up, I had a strong sense for the divine. My mother is Roman Catholic, and my father is a Christian as well (more of a Baptist background). Throughout my childhood, my sister and I went with my mom to mass (Roman Catholic Church service) pretty much every Sunday. I was young, and I did not really understand anything that went on. I can recall at least once or twice actually falling asleep during church. Now, I always believed God existed; I always believed Jesus existed. I would even say I always believed Jesus died on the cross, but I did not really know what that meant. In fact, I did not know much of anything about the faith besides the fact of Jesus dying on the cross, Adam and Eve, Noah's Ark, and Jonah and the fish. That was about as far as my Christian knowledge went. We continued going to church up until I entered the sixth grade. With sports, school, and everything else life threw at my family, we gradually stopped going. Of course, like most people in America, I still called myself a Christian.

SEEING A UNICORN

I remember one day in the sixth grade very well. I was in geography when, for some reason, the people at my table and I began discussing God. Two of the guys and I agreed that God existed, and of course, we were referring to the God of the Bible. Then one of the guys at my table (who became one of my good friends in school) said he did not believe in God. Keep in mind, I live in Oklahoma. My state is very conservative. Most people here are Christian, at least nominally. Hearing my friend say he did not believe in God was like seeing a unicorn. That was the first time I had ever encountered an atheist. In reaction to his words, the other two guys and I tried to convince him of God's existence. Like stated previously, my biblical knowledge was not exactly the best. I just nodded my head in agreement with what the other two said. Even with all that, my friend did not budge. He still rejected God's existence. I do not remember much after that, but that encounter is something I remember to this day.

ELEVEN-YEAR-OLD VERSUS
THE PROBLEM OF EVIL

Later that year, I was playing video games on my PlayStation with some friends I made online. Somehow, we began discussing God. I soon heard something that has echoed in my mind since. One of my friends said, "If God is real, how come my mom died?" Now, what does an eleven-year-old say to this? I did not know what to say. For the first time in my short life, I had been presented with the philosophical concept known as "the problem of evil." I responded to him saying something along the lines of "I know it doesn't make sense, but things happen for a reason." This answer did not satisfy my friend. My face was very red at that point. He continued to curse God. I remained silent after that and so did the whole party chat. I do not remember much after that.

ALL IS VANITY

I started playing online video games in fifth grade, and I was addicted. Fast forward a year or two. I was still in middle school, but I cannot remember whether I was in seventh or eighth grade. One day, I had been binging video games. Late in the day, after I had been playing for hours, I suddenly stopped and started thinking. From a young age, I was always a thinker. I was a kid who wanted to know why. I was quiet, so I did not always ask why out loud. But I always asked why in my head. So this day, I began thinking about what I was doing. I started to feel ashamed and guilty for playing video games all day. Remember, I was a kid. It is not like I had a job I needed to be at or a family to take care of. But even with that being the case, I still felt like what I was doing was wrong. I knew it was not playing the games in and of itself that was wrong, but I knew something about it was wrong.

Of course, now I know my conscience convicted me that day because I was being idolatrous by making video games my god. In short, I felt ashamed because I was *sinning*. The Bible shows that sin brings shame and guilt (Gen. 3:9–10), and our conscience accuses us when we do wrong (Rom. 2:14–15). I can very strongly resonate with these verses in Romans because my whole life, I have had an extremely sensitive conscience. I remember in kindergarten going to a sleepover at a friend's house. They were all playing a game that was rated "mature" (seventeen and up). I sat there and really wanted to play, but my conscience was telling me no. My mom said I was not allowed to play those types of games, and I would have been breaking the commandment (honor thy father and mother) by doing so. One of the other kids handed me the controller, and I took it. I stared at it for a couple seconds, looked down, and then said, "No I can't." I could have done it. My mom would have never known. But I knew it was wrong, and my conscience did not allow me.

Now, continuing from the day in middle school. In that moment, I realized that all I did was play video games. I played them when I got home from school all the way until I went to sleep. On the weekends, I played them all day. That was all I really did outside of school. I started to contemplate the future. I envisioned myself binging video games the next day and the next day and the next day and so forth. Thinking about that made me realize how empty life seemed. It all seemed pointless. It was in that moment I believe that I felt depression for the first time. It was not debilitating depression or anything like that, but it was my first experience with it, as far as I can remember. Looking back on my emotions at that moment, I felt like the author of Ecclesiastes when he said, "I have seen all the works that are done under the sun; and, behold, all is vanity and vexation of spirit" (Eccles. 1:14). Life seemed like it did not matter. I, once again, felt like the author of Ecclesiastes when he said, "Then I commended mirth, because a man hath no better thing under the sun, than to eat, and to drink, and to be merry: for that shall abide with him of his labour the days of his life, which God giveth him under the sun" (Eccles. 8:15).

In this moment, it truly felt like there was nothing better in life than to eat, drink, and be merry; nothing better than to seek pleasure. But with the help of my conscience, I knew there had to be more to life. There just had to be.

GLASS BONES AND PAPER SKIN

I did not get much playing time in middle school sports. A lot of this was because of my elementary school. In elementary, I was the star player (mainly because there was not much competition). If you asked me what I wanted to be when I grew up, it was an NBA or NFL player. When I got to middle school, I was not ready for the competition. Before I was the fastest and most skilled, but at that point, I was mediocre at best. I honestly believe that was one of the main reasons I played video games as much as I did. As a child, I really put my whole identity into being the athletic kid, so when I was no longer the best, it messed with me a lot. I mean, what can you do? Everybody must put their identity somewhere. And if you do not have your identity in God, you'll put it in something or someone else.

Once I entered high school, God was the least of my thoughts. I was focused on trying to fit in and be successful in sports. My freshman year, I was finally catching up to my peers. I was getting better in football and ended up starting in basketball. Things were on the up for me. Everything changed the following summer. I was about five feet eight my freshman year. That summer I grew to about six feet one. Because of that, I developed Osgood Schlatter Disease, which is basically a condition that causes a bump under the knee-caps as well as severe pain from inflammation. I did not know I was developing this, but one day at a summer workout, my knees and shins were feeling a bit achy. I did not know what was wrong, but I could barely pick up my legs or plant when running and changing directions. While doing a cone drill, I planted and felt a strange feeling in my knee. I do not remember if I finished that workout or not, but the pain was severe. There are different degrees of the condition, but when I went to the doctor, he told me I had one of the most severe cases he had ever seen. I had major inflammation. Most people would probably just suggest taking some ibuprofen and moving on. I wish it were that simple.

Once again, my whole identity was in sports. Not to mention, I was extremely excited for the seasons because I was improving in both sports. So when this happened, I was devastated—not only was my body in pain, but my mental health suffered as well. Once my sophomore school year started, I was not practicing. I got treatment on my knees and did rehab for weeks. I could barely walk up and down the stairs, let alone run. My knees were so inflamed that nothing helped for long. It felt as if somebody was stabbing me in the knees with every step I took. I remember barely being able to get up when I kneeled at my bottom locker because of the pain. I continued to rehab. My coaches kept asking me every day when I was coming back.

"I'm not sure," I would say. Every time they saw me, they would ask, "How are your knees?" I would respond with something like "They still hurt." I could tell they were frustrated (not because I was good or anything, but because they did not want their players out), and I was frustrated too. Many people thought I was lying or milking it, but the truth is, I was in extreme pain. Over this time, I started to feel depressed. I truly did not enjoy life at all. Around week 4 of my sophomore season, I returned to practice. I returned with massive knee sleeves and knee bands to try to mask as much pain as possible. Some people even called me "robot knees." It is funny now, but it just added to my depression back then. One thing should be noted: there is no way I should have been playing that season.

Like stated previously, I could barely walk, let alone run; let alone take physical contact from testosterone-filled teenagers running at me full speed. What made things worse was that I was a sophomore, which meant most of the players were way bigger than me. So not only did I have to take hits while in excruciating pain, but I had to take them from people fifty to a hundred pounds heavier than me. Because of the pain practice caused me, I fell into deeper depression. I could not enjoy any day because I constantly thought about the pain I would have to endure at practice. And even on the weekends, the next week's practices haunted me. I really did not know who I was or what the purpose to life was.

But thankfully, after football season and the first semester of school ended, my knees were completely healed, and I began to enjoy some days again. I ended up not playing basketball because I wanted to focus on getting my body stronger and healthier. Because I was not in basketball, I was in powerlifting for football. I was a lanky kid. My legs were decently strong, but my upper body was very scrawny. I began to increase my numbers in powerlifting. I was getting strong for my body weight, and I was also increasing my speed and agility. Things were once again looking up, and I expected to see the field and the court my junior year. That summer, I was continuing to get stronger and faster. I was also feeling happier because, once again, my identity was in sports, so how I was doing in them dictated my mood.

One day at a seven-on-seven scrimmage, I was running a post route when I felt something pop and fell. I could barely move. I laid there on the field until our coach and trainer came over. They examined me, and I guess did not notice anything. I could barely walk. This pain was more excruciating than the Osgood Schlatter. They drove me back to the training room to be looked at some more. The coaches concluded that I pulled a muscle and just needed some rest. I had pulled plenty of muscles in my life. I knew for a fact that I did not have a pulled muscle. This was something much more severe.

Once again, I could barely walk. I called my parents to come get me and that it was an emergency. They came. and I hobbled to the car. I laid down in the backseat and was crying out in agony. They drove me to the emergency room where we waited for about five hours. The whole time I could barely sit down because it hurt so bad. If I moved the wrong way, it felt like I was being stabbed. Eventually I went in for an x-ray, and it turns out I fractured my pelvic bone. I left the emergency room on crutches. At this point, I fell back into depression. And this time, it was worse, because it was the second time in a row something like this happened. Every time I became injured, I lost my worth. I suited up for the first time around week 5 of my junior season. Shortly after returning, I developed shin splints. Because I was sitting around for about three months, my body could not handle the immediate intensity of practice. So once again, I was in pain every single day at practice. That was not as bad as Osgood Schlatter, but some days, it got close. Instead of feeling like a knife was stabbing me in my knees, the pain moved slightly lower. My mood just got worse and worse.

WHY ME?

Toward the end of the season, when we were preparing for the playoffs, my shins finally started to heal, and I felt almost normal for the first time in a long time. Right after this, something else occurred.

One night, I was lying in bed when I remembered I had some reading to do for school the next day. I started reading in my bed with the lights off. Next thing I know, I opened my eyes to three or four men standing above me. I did a double take and started to freak out. My mom was crying, and my dad was saying it was going to be okay. Keep in mind, nobody told me what was going on. I thought I was being kidnapped to be tested on by the government or something of the sort. My mind was racing to all sorts of things. They put me on a stretcher and wheeled me out to the ambulance.

While I was riding in the back of the ambulance, I did not ask anybody what was happening. I was still in a daze. Finally, one of the EMTs was on the radio and said, "African American male, seizure." Apparently, I had a seizure. I had never had one in my life before this, nor did I have any conditions that caused them. While I was in the ER, I had another seizure. When I finally woke up, I was confused and could barely walk. Once I got home, I fell right asleep. Seizures make your body exhausted. The doctor put me on seizure medication, and I took it for about six months. Because of this, I could not get my license, and I also couldn't suit up for the remainder of the football season. I had come back to football for only five weeks and was out again. This was all so confusing to me. I knew people had things a lot worse, but at the same time, I was asking God why. I felt as if I was being punished.

Around this time, I began talking to girls. I was always a quiet kid, but junior year is when I started to become more confident in myself. I shifted my worth from sports to girls. I put my whole value as a human into these girls, and when it ended up not working out, I would be devastated and fall deeper into depression. Not only was I putting my worth into them, but I was deep in lust. That was my main sin. I even remember praying to God to help me sin. That is one of my more shameful moments. I knew my lust was wrong, yet I prayed for God to help me lust. My depression was not much better because I kept having failed relationships with girls. And since I was putting my worth in them, it was no different than how I felt when I got injured. I had no purpose—or at least I thought.

BETRAYAL

That summer going into senior year, I was deep in lust. All I thought about and worried about was girls and video games. Sure, I still played sports, but honestly, my focus was not on them as much. With that being said, I was still looking forward to the sports seasons. My body was feeling healthy and strong, and I thought I would be seeing the field. In fact, a coach pulled me aside personally after seeing my progress and hard work and promised me a spot in the starting lineup. I was ecstatic. This is what I had been working so hard for all these years through all the setbacks—the injuries and seizures and everything else. That summer, I got my first girlfriend. She was a nice young lady. As the school year started and went on, I fell deeper and deeper into lust. It was truly a problem. When the first day of practice came around and the lineups were being announced, I was expecting that promised spot I had been told about.

Spoiler alert: I did not get it. I thought maybe the coaches just wanted to see me practice a little bit first since I did not really play much at all the past two seasons. It was no big deal to me at first. After about three weeks passed and I still received no word from any of the coaches about my position, I started to get upset. Nonetheless, I kept trying my hardest. By the time week 4 of the season came around, I still was not seeing the field and was not hearing anything from any of my coaches about that promised spot.

That week, I officially gave up. I stopped trying in practice from that point on. I no longer cared. I shifted my focus off sports and back to lust. I was hurt from being lied to by my coaches. I felt disrespected as a man. It was not just the fact that I was not playing that bothered me, but the fact that none of the coaches took the time to speak to me as a man and tell me what was going on and why I wasn't getting the opportunity I was promised. I have nothing against them now, but at that time, I became bitter at life. From that point on, all I cared about was gratifying my flesh whether that be lust, gluttony, etc. I adopted the humanist philosophy of "Whatever feels good, do it." I was truly depraved and carnal (Rom. 8:5–8).

LUST IS NEVER SATISFIED

With all cares removed from sports, I began to shift my focus back to lust. Lust made me feel good. Lust made me forget about all the people who did me wrong and all the stresses in life. Lust was my friend—or so I thought. After a while in my relationship, I started to feel down. It wasn't because of her, but because of me. I was full of lust. One day, I became that same kid from middle school sitting in his room, binging video games. I became that kid; except this time, my video game was lust. I thought about the nature of lust. You gratify your flesh, and then it is over. Then your flesh craves it again, and you repeat the process.

Just like I had thought about binging the video games; in this moment, I was thinking about how I was binging lust. I was binging it, yet it did not fulfill me. Every time I lusted, my flesh just craved more. I was never satisfied (Prov. 27:20). I wanted to feel satisfied. I wanted to feel fulfilled. It was at that moment too that I realized I was not right with God. I did not know the extent of my sinfulness, but I knew I was living wrong. It was at that moment that I began to put the pieces together. I felt as if the reason I was not happy was because I did not know God. After reflecting on all these things, I realized I needed to end my relationship, grow as a person, and find God. A month or so later, my girlfriend and I broke up. She was a wonderful young lady, but I had a lust problem. And she could not fulfill the void in my soul. Only God could do that.

BACK IN CHURCH

A few months later, prom time was approaching. It would be my one and only prom, so I wanted to go and make it a memorable time. I asked a girl to prom, and she said yes. Soon after, this girl and her friend both invited me to church. Here I was, wanting to find God a few months prior, and here were two angels sent from God to help me. I avoided the offer at first. While I wanted to find God, I could not bring myself to go to church. For one, I had not been to church since the fifth or sixth grade. Secondly, like stated previously, I have always had a sensitive conscience. And after all the lusting I had been doing, I had a deep understanding of my sinfulness. I did not know any Bible verses or anything like that, but my conscience testified that I was in trouble with God. I felt like a child who just broke something in the house. I was not scared of God in the sense that I thought He was an evil dictator, but because of my conscience, I knew He was holy—which was something I was far from.

After they kept asking me, I eventually went. It was a mega-church. It was quite different from the Roman Catholic Church I grew up attending. This church had colorful lights and a band. Roman Catholic Church is very formal and filled with things like incense and even singing in foreign languages (Latin). It was different, but I liked it. I began going every week. I ended up graduating high school in May of 2018, and little did I know that my life was about to change drastically.

A NEW CREATION

In June of that summer, I confessed Jesus as Lord and believed that God raised Him from the dead (Rom. 10:9–10). Because of this, I made it my goal to read the Bible. I read it nonstop. I could not put it down. I used to read a lot in elementary school, but once I got to middle school and high school, I hated reading. But for some reason, I could not put the Bible down. There was just something about it that fulfilled me. It was as if every verse I read filled that void in my soul a little more. In October of 2018, I finished reading the Bible from Genesis to Revelation for the first time, and in that same month, I got baptized.

WHAT IS TRUTH?

Around this time, while I was not as lustful (although I still struggled with it), I was still chasing girls and putting my worth in them. I was very insecure. I had a few failed relationships from the summer after my high school graduation (2018) to January of the next year (2019). All through that time, I was reading my Bible, and I was growing in my faith, but I was still putting my worth into girls. Another thing I was putting my worth into was fitness. I got heavily into powerlifting as well as bodybuilding. If I did not hit a certain number on my lifts, I would feel down and purposeless. If I did hit my goal numbers, I would feel happy. That is a dangerous game to play.

Every time I would get an injury and be forced to take time off from the gym, I would fall into depression. I was extremely insecure. I stopped focusing on girls and tried to focus on God, but I was still very hurt and insecure. I kept studying the Bible and watching YouTube videos about Christianity. I was growing in my faith rapidly. Like stated before, I could not put my Bible down. Often, I did not even want to do my college work because I wanted to study the Bible.

It just amazed me that I could read the very words of my Creator. At this time, I began thinking about other worldviews. Many people are not Christians. Not to mention, even many that claim to be Christians have quite different worldviews from one another. Look at this passage from the gospel of John:

> Pilate therefore said unto him, Art thou a king then? Jesus answered, Thou sayest that I am a king. To this end was I born, and for this cause came I into the world, that I should bear witness unto the truth. Every one that is of the truth heareth my voice. Pilate saith unto him, **What is truth?** And when he had said this, he went out again unto the Jews, and saith unto them, I find in him no fault at all. (John 18:37–38)

There are atheists and agnostics. There are polytheists. There are Jews. There are Muslims. There are Mormons and Jehovah's Witnesses. There are Hebrew Israelites. There are many worldviews different from my own. I did not doubt Christianity necessarily, but I had many questions. These questions consumed my thoughts. And so, returning to those deep thoughts that had so consumed me since my youth, I began asking the same question Pontius Pilate asked the Lord Jesus Christ—namely: *what is truth?*

CHAPTER 2

ATHEISM/AGNOSTICISM

INTRODUCTION

As discussed previously, my first encounter with atheism was in the sixth grade. While I was not always right with God, I always knew God existed. There is too much evidence for there not to be. The word of God discusses atheism a good number of times. The Bible says, "The fool hath said in his heart, There is no God. They are corrupt, they have done abominable works, there is none that doeth good" (Ps. 14:1). According to God, it is foolish to be an atheist. Many atheists mock Christians and say they believe in the "flying spaghetti monster."

The truth is, I would much sooner believe in the flying spaghetti monster than be an atheist. Just looking at creation proves to me there is a God. So it is much more logical to believe in the flying spaghetti monster than to believe we all evolved from a primordial soup. With that being said, it should be known that I do not believe in "atheists." There are people who call themselves atheists, but there are no true atheists. Everybody believes in God. Every person has at least two proofs given to them for the existence of God. The first evidence they have is creation. The Bible says,

> For the wrath of God is revealed from
> heaven against all ungodliness and unrighteous-

ness of men, **who hold the truth in unrigh-teousness**; [19] Because that which may be known of God is manifest in them; for God hath shewed it unto them. [20] **For the invisible things of him from the creation of the world are clearly seen, being understood by the things that are made, even his eternal power and Godhead; so that they are without excuse:** [21] Because that, when they knew God, they glorified him not as God, neither were thankful; but became vain in their imaginations, and their foolish heart was darkened. [22] **Professing themselves to be wise, they became fools**. (Rom. 1:18–22)

Everybody believes in God. The reason many profess to be "atheists" is because they "hold the truth in unrighteousness." This means that the reason people *identify* as atheists is not because they do not know God exists, but rather because they suppress the truth; they hold down the truth because they love their sin. Atheists do not want God to exist because if He does, that means they have to submit to Him and give up their sins like drunkenness, premarital sex, etc. That is the real reason we have people called atheists. God's handprint is "clearly seen" when looking at creation. The second proof of God that every person has is their conscience. The Bible says, "For when the Gentiles, which have not the law, do by nature the things contained in the law, these, having not the law, are a law unto themselves: [15] **Which shew the work of the law written in their hearts**, their conscience also bearing witness, and their thoughts the mean while accusing or else excusing one another" (Rom. 2:14–15).

Even somebody who has never heard of God or the Bible still has the moral law written on their heart. Every single person has a conscience that tells them right and wrong. Every person inherently knows it is wrong to murder because God has written His law on every human being's heart. With that being said, it is also possible to *corrupt* your conscience (1 Tim. 4:2). Every human is born with a pure conscience given by God to know right from wrong, but many people corrupt their conscience through continuous sin, and that is why a small minority of people think things like murder are morally acceptable. So creation and conscience are two different proofs of God that every person in the world, no matter where they are, has. Atheists say they do not believe in God, but the truth is, God does not believe in atheists. Nonetheless, I will provide some arguments for why a person should believe in God.

COSMOLOGICAL ARGUMENT

The question that always seems to arise in a back and forth between theists and atheists is the first cause. What caused the universe to begin? Some atheists will even go as far as to say the universe is eternal. Notice how they simply replace God with "the universe." God is eternal and He is the first cause. The formal argument looks as such,

1. Everything that begins to exist must have a CAUSE for its existence.
2. The universe began to exist.
3. Therefore, the universe must have a CAUSE for its existence.[1]

The world could not have caused itself; therefore, something must have caused it. The question is, *what* caused it? Atheists have been trying to answer this question for centuries, but maybe they are asking the wrong question. A better question would be, *who* caused it? This first cause can either be a natural cause or a supernatural cause. Everything that has been caused is either time, space, or matter. The Bible speaks about this in the first sentence of the Bible—which happens to be the creation story, "In the beginning God created the heaven and the earth" (Gen. 1:1). Within this verse, time, space, and matter are present. God is the first cause. The "beginning" is time. The "heaven" is space. And the "earth" is matter. Thus, in the

---
[1] Hunter, Braxton. *CORE FACTS*. Bloomington, IN: AuthorHouse, 2014, 5.

first sentence of the Bible, there is an answer for creation. Braxton Hunter says,

> [T]ime, space nor matter could cause the universe to come into existence because they are a part of what was created. Thus, the cause of the universe must not be in time. It must, instead, be eternal. The cause cannot be material, but non-material. Whatever brought the universe into being must not occupy space, it must be spaceless. For these reasons, it is clear that the cause of the universe must be an eternal, non-material, spaceless something.[2]

Since the universe consists of time, space, and matter, the first cause must be timeless, spaceless, and immaterial. Not only this, but the first cause must also have a mind because without mind there will be no way of creating. The Christian easily identifies this as God. The atheist cannot come up with anything to fit this description.

TELEOLOGICAL (INTELLIGENT DESIGN) ARGUMENT

Some people believe the universe came together by random chance. The problem with that is the uniformity we see in nature. I find true amazement when examining the intelligence behind creation. The formal argument is such,

1. The fine-tuning of the universe is due to either, physical necessity, chance, or design.
2. It is not due to physical necessity or chance.
3. Therefore, it is due to design.[3]

---

2   Hunter, 7–8.
3   Hunter, 28.

There is an obvious design to the universe, yet some will claim everything happened by random chance. But is that logical? Braxton Hunter refers to Paul Davies who says, "Chance will not do as a fitting explanation. The chances of the universe being life permitting has been estimated by Davies to be one in 10 to the 100th power."[4] Like discussed previously, I'd much sooner believe the flying spaghetti monster created the universe than nobody at all. The intricacies in nature cry out "Abba, Father" (Rom. 8:15)!

MORAL ARGUMENT

During my summer job, I had an interesting conversation with an agnostic. Somehow, he brought up God. I immediately was moved by the Spirit of God to engage with him. A bit into the conversation, I asked him if he believed in objective morality. He told me there is no such thing as right and wrong. I responded and asked, "So would it be wrong if I killed you right now?" Of course, everybody knows murder is wrong, but I knew he could not answer properly as an agnostic. He looked at me for a second and then responded, "Technically no."

I started laughing, and he did as well. He knew it was an absurd worldview to hold, but nonetheless, he tried to explain himself further. Atheists/agnostics must either say there is no objective right or wrong, or they must reduce themselves to even more absurdity by saying there's no right and wrong at all! A while back, I was watching a preacher speak to college students on their campus. That was when Black Lives Matter protests were at their peak. The preacher asked, "Why do you believe black lives matter?" Naturally, many students got angry, but that was only because what he was saying went right over their heads. He explained himself, further saying, "I know black lives matter because I'm a Christian and every person is made in the image of God. But as an atheist or agnostic, why is murdering black people wrong?"

---

4 Hunter, 31.

A few of the students started to catch on to what he was saying, and they were shaken. Everybody can explain *what* they believe. But explaining *why* you believe something is a whole different story. Everybody believes it is wrong to kill black people, but *why* is it wrong? Even unbelievers know things like murder and rape are objectively wrong because, as discussed before, God has given everybody a conscience and has written the moral law of the universe on their hearts (Rom. 2:14–15). When it comes to morality, the question always circles back to this: by what standard? You may know things are wrong, but you also need to know *why*. Here is the moral argument:

1. If God does not exist, objective moral values and duties do not exist.
2. Objective moral values and duties do exist.
3. Therefore, God exists.[5]

I have never met anybody that thought rape was acceptable in any circumstance. Yet the atheist/agnostic worldview cannot say rape is objectively wrong. They might *think* it is wrong personally, but that would just be their *opinion*, not a *fact*. See, the Christian can say rape is *always* wrong because we have an *objective* standard of right and wrong—God and His word. Some atheists argue that morality is relative. This means they believe everybody determines what is right and wrong in their own minds. This means, according to the atheist worldview, Hitler did nothing wrong in the Holocaust; because Hitler did what he believed to be right! He believed it was right to murder Jews! But obviously, we know that believing something to be right does not make it right. Still, the atheist/agnostic cannot condemn Hitler! Some atheists/agnostics claim that morality is based on what society says is right and wrong. Now let us apply their logic.

In colonial America, most whites said it was just and morally right to enslave black people. That is a wicked act! Yet according to the atheist/agnostic, what they did is not wrong because society said

---

it was okay! Some atheists/agnostics say morality is based on whatever is best for the progression and preservation of society. Consider their logic. Say there is only one woman left in the world. The only way to progress/preserve the world is to procreate. The problem is the woman does not want to have sex with anybody. If she will not have sex with any of the men, the society and the whole human race would die out. Would it be morally right for the men to rape her? According to the atheist/agnostic worldview, it would be since that is the only way to progress/preserve society! How wicked! In atheism/agnosticism it is just one man's opinion versus another. There is no objectivity. As a Christian, I appeal to God and His word (the Holy Bible) to know what is objectively right and wrong. It does not matter what I *feel* is right or what I *want* to be right. All that matters is, "Thus saith the LORD"!

THE RELIABILITY OF THE BIBLE

It never fails to hear an atheist/agnostic declare, "The Bible was written by men!" My response is pretty much always the same. "Yes, that's what the Bible says about itself." This response seems to catch them off guard, but it is true. The Bible says,

> We have also a more sure word of prophecy; whereunto ye do well that ye take heed, as unto a light that shineth in a dark place, until the day dawn, and the day star arise in your hearts: [20] Knowing this first, that no prophecy of the scripture is of any private interpretation. [21] For the prophecy came not in old time by the will of man: but **holy men of God spake as they were moved by the Holy Ghost**. (2 Pet. 1:19–21)

The Bible is clear that God used "holy men" to declare His word. God used men as the instrument in His hand to write His word. Athenagoras writing in the second century said, "Moses or of Isaiah and Jeremiah, and the other prophets, who, lifted in ecstasy above the natural operations of their minds by the impulses of the Divine Spirit, uttered the things with which they were inspired, **the Spirit making use of them as a flute-player breathes into a flute.**"[6]

When somebody plays a flute, they are the author of the notes, but the flute is the instrument by which those notes come forth. And likewise, God is the author of the Bible, but He used holy men as His instrument to write down the Bible. Second Timothy says, **"All scripture is given by inspiration of God**, and is profitable for doctrine, for reproof, for correction, for instruction in righteousness: [17] That the man of God may be perfect, thoroughly furnished unto all good works" (2 Tim. 3:16–17).

All the Bible is inspired by God. A lot of people think this just means that men were inspired in the same way that we might be inspired by an athlete to begin working out or something of the sort. The English language makes this confusing. In the original Greek, the word Second Timothy terms as "inspiration of God" is *theopneustos*. This word literally means "God-breathed," and this is the only place in the whole Bible that it's used. All Scripture is God-breathed. This means every single word in the Bible is directly from God.

Archaeological evidence has further authenticated the validity of the Bible. Ron Rhodes says, "Over 25,000 sites in biblical lands have been discovered, dating back to Old Testament times, which have established the accuracy of innumerable details in the Bible."[7] Rhodes goes on to give many examples of evidence: The Hittites are spoken of in the Bible and were thought to be a myth for a long time, but now it is widely known that the Hittites were a real group of people! Many atheists/agnostics have claimed that Moses could not have written the first five books of the Bible because there was no handwriting back then.

This claim has been debunked by written inscriptions found and thus proves that Moses very well could have written the Pentateuch.

---

[6] Athenagoras. *The Ante-Nicene Fathers: A Plea for the Christians.* Chapter IX. Edited by Alexander Roberts, James Donaldson, and Arthur Cleveland Coxe. II. Vol. II. X vols. New York, NY: Cosimo Classics, 2007, 133.

[7] Rhodes, Ron. *Answering the Objections of Atheists, Agnostics, & Skeptics.* Eugene, OR: Harvest House Publishers, 2006, 130.

The cities of Sodom and Gomorrah have also been found. In fact, if you go there, you can find sulfur balls on the ground from when God rained fire and brimstone on them (Gen. 19:24)! There are also groupings of fossils that attest to Noah's flood. The tomb of Abraham's wife Sarah was found in Israel.[8] Probably one of the most authenticating finds for the validity of the Bible was the Dead Sea Scrolls in 1945. Speaking of the validity of the Bible, Henry Morris says,

> This fact has been further confirmed by the discovery of the famous Dead Sea Scrolls, beginning in 1945 and continuing on to the present. These manuscripts actually date from the time of Christ or earlier and are the oldest actual manuscripts of any parts of Scripture found to date. Many scrolls have been found and these include, in one scroll or another, practically the entire text of the Old Testament. The agreement of all these with the received Masoretic text is remarkable, such variations as exist being insignificant.[9]

There are many more archaeological finds that validate the Bible but would take much longer to list.

The Bible is the most authentic and reliable historic document of all time. It beats any and every ancient document in reliability. Henry Morris says, "Altogether there are probably available today over 5,000 manuscript copies of portions of the New Testament in Greek and at least 15,000 more in other languages. Nothing remotely comparable to this abundance exists for any other ancient writing."[10]

This work from Henry Morris is a bit old, and there are now closer to twenty-five thousand manuscripts in total. Ron Rhodes

---

[8] Rhodes, 131.
[9] Morris, Henry M. *Many Infallible Proofs: Evidences for the Christian Faith*. El Cajon, CA: Master Books, 1974, 41.
[10] Morris, Henry M. *Many Infallible Proofs: Evidences for the Christian Faith*. El Cajon, CA: Master Books, 1974, 23.

gives the following data: The writings of Caesar were written in the first century BC, but the earliest copy we have is from AD 900, and there are only ten copies. The writings of Livy were written in the first century BC, and there are only twenty copies. The writings of Tacitus were written in AD 100, but the earliest copy we have is from AD 1100, and there are only twenty copies. The writings of Thucydides were written in the fifth century BC, but the earliest copy we have is from AD 900, and there are only eight copies. The writings of Herodotus were written in the fifth century BC, but the earliest copy we have is from AD 900, and there are only eight copies. The writings of Demosthenes were written in the fourth century BC, but the earliest copy we have is from AD 1100, and there are only two hundred copies. The writings of Homer were written in the ninth century BC, and there are only 643 copies.

I want the reader to keep all these numbers from historic documents in mind. **Now compare these numbers to that of the New Testament, written in the first century AD; the earliest copy we have is from the second century AD; there are five thousand copies.**[11] Lee Strobel quotes Daniel B. Wallace who said, "If you stacked the works of other ancient writers on top of each other, they'd be about four feet tall. Stack up copies of the New Testament, and they'd reach more than a mile high and, again, that doesn't include quotations from the church fathers."[12]

Not only that, but the New Testament manuscripts line up within 99 percent accuracy of one another![13] The only reason it is not 100 percent accuracy is because of something called "textual variants." Textual variants are slight differences in some of the manuscripts. This is because human scribes were used to copy the manuscripts. The original writings penned by the inspired writers like Paul, Peter, John, and the rest were completely inerrant because they were being used directly by God to write them (as demonstrated previously with the flute player). But the scribes who copied the man-

[11] Rhodes, 146–147.
[12] Strobel, Lee. *The Case for the Real Jesus*. Grand Rapids, MI: Zondervan, 2008, 60.
[13] Rhodes, 147.

uscripts were not inspired. This means, every once in a while, they copied something wrong.

With that being said, we have all these manuscripts and can compare the minor differences. It is widely agreed amongst scholars (Christian and secular) that none of the textual variants (differences) change any Christian doctrine. In other words, these differences that happened because of scribal/copyist errors are so minute that they do not affect the religion at all. Ron Rhodes gives an example of common textual variants:

> MANUSCRIPT #1: Jesus Christ is the Savior of the whole world.
> MANUSCRIPT #2: Christ Jesus is the Savior of the whole world.
> MANUSCRIPT #3: Jesus Christ s the Savior of the whole world.
> MANUSCRIPT #4: Jesus Christ is th Savior of the whle world.
> MANUSCRIPT #5: Jesus Christ is the Savor of the whole world.[14]

These minute differences make up most textual variants. Lee Strobel quotes Daniel B. Wallace who says, "Somewhere between 70 to 80 percent of all textual variants are spelling differences that can't even be translated into English and have zero impact or meaning."[15] There was no printing press back then and the process of copying manuscripts was a long and strenuous process. After hours of copying, the scribes could easily skip a line in the text or skip a word or something like that. Our eyes can be easily deceived when staring at something for hours on end. That is what often happened with scribes. But the scribes took the process and the handling of the word of God very serious.

---

[14] Rhodes, 144.
[15] Strobel, Lee. *The Case for the Real Jesus*. Grand Rapids, MI: Zondervan, 2008, 62.

If the writers messed up, they would throw the manuscript away and start over. But often, they did not notice their mistakes and thus we recognize there are "scribal/copyist errors" present in many manuscripts. But because of the massive number of manuscripts available, we can compare all of them and see the small differences. Once again, these minute differences do not change any doctrine of the faith, so there's no valid conspiracy theory about not knowing God's word. Daniel B. Wallace also says, "Only about 1 percent of variants are both meaningful—which means they affect the meaning of the text to some degree—and viable, which means they have a decent chance of going back to the original text."[16]

That 1 percent that can slightly change the understanding of a specific passage, still do not change any doctrine. The three verses/passages that are the most meaningful textual variants are John 7:53–8:11, Mark 16:9–20, and 1 John 5:7. Some Christians accept these passages as authentic, and some do not. An argument can be made that these passages are authentic since Mark 16:9–20 was quoted by the early church writers Irenaeus, Justin Martyr, Tatian, and Hippolytus. First John 5:7 was quoted by the church father Cyprian in his treatise titled *On the Unity of the Church* in the mid-third century (long before the Council of Nicaea). He said, "The Lord says, 'I and the Father are one;'" and again it is written of the Father, and of the Son, and of the Holy Spirit, "And these three are one."[17] But whether these few passages are authentic or not does not matter.

Every Christian doctrine can be defended without these textual variant passages. Knowing all that, it is clear that the manuscripts of the Bible beat every other historic writing in validity and reliability! And not only do we have the actual manuscripts, but we also have all the early church writings. The early church writers quoted the Bible extensively. If one were to just use the writings of the early church

---

[16] Strobel, Lee. *The Case for the Real Jesus*. Grand Rapids, MI: Zondervan, 2008, 64.

[17] Cyprian. *The Ante-Nicene Fathers: On the Unity of the Church*. Section 6. Edited by Alexander Roberts, James Donaldson, and Arthur Cleveland Coxe. V. Vol. V. X vols. New York, NY: Cosimo Classics, 2007, 423.

fathers, we could write all but eleven verses of the New Testament![18] That is an amazing, might I say *divine*, feat to accomplish! That is the power and influence of the holy word of God! So the Bible must be accepted by any honest person as historically accurate—unless of course they also want to throw out the validity of the writings of Julius Caesar, Homer, Tacitus, etc.

THE PROBLEM OF EVIL

Relating to morality, many atheists/agnostics object to Christianity, claiming that God is a monster. "How could a good God allow evil to happen?" they ask. First, like discussed previously, the atheist/agnostic has no objective moral standard and therefore cannot say anything is right or wrong; good or evil. Because like discussed before, in atheism/agnosticism morality is just one man's opinion versus another man's opinion. There is no objectivity or absolute standard. So it is illogical for any atheist/agnostic to claim God is immoral when they have no objective standard of morality to make such a claim. Secondly, God did not bring evil into the world. Humans, specifically Adam and Eve, brought evil into the world through their sin. Once the first sin occurred, sin entered the world causing everybody and everything to suffer corruption. Romans says,

> For I reckon that the sufferings of this present time are not worthy to be compared with the glory which shall be revealed in us. [19] For the earnest expectation of the creature waiteth for the manifestation of the sons of God. [20] For the creature was made subject to vanity, not willingly, but by reason of him who hath subjected the same in hope, [21] **Because the creature itself also shall be delivered from the bondage of corruption into the glorious liberty of the children of God.** [22] **For we know that the whole creation**

---

[18] Rhodes, 140.

groaneth and travaileth in pain together until now. ²³ And not only they, but ourselves also, which have the first fruits of the Spirit, even we ourselves groan within ourselves, waiting for the adoption, to wit, the redemption of our body. ²⁴ For we are saved by hope: but hope that is seen is not hope: for what a man seeth, why doth he yet hope for? ²⁵ But if we hope for that we see not, then do we with patience wait for it. (Rom. 8:18–25)

Us human beings and the creation itself are both waiting to be redeemed. We are waiting for this corruptible to put on incorruption and this mortal to put on immortality (1 Cor. 15:53). We are waiting to be perfected apart from sin, where there will be no more pain, suffering, or evil (Rev. 21:3–4). Evil is not a result of God, but rather a result of us. There are a couple types of evil. The first is called natural evil which consists of things like natural disasters (hurricanes, tornadoes, wildfires, etc.) and the other is moral evil, which is sin (murder, stealing, etc.).[19] Moral evil is the evil we do directly as humans and natural evil is a result of the original sin in the garden. A simple example of moral sin from the Bible is Jesus being murdered (John 19:17–24). Here is an example of natural evil: "And as Jesus passed by, he saw a man which was blind from his birth. ² And his disciples asked him, saying, Master, who did sin, this man, or his parents, that he was born blind? ³ Jesus answered, Neither hath this man sinned, nor his parents: but that the works of God should be made manifest in him" (John 9:1–3).

In this passage, the disciples assumed this man was blind because of his personal sin or maybe the sin of his parents. Jesus refuted both of those concepts. The man was not blind because of his sin or even his parents', but rather sin entering the world in the beginning. In the book of Job, God allowed Satan to do evil to Job to test his faith.

---

[19] Wright, N. T. *Evil and the Justice of God.* Downers Grove, IL: InterVarsity Press, 2006, 17.

Job's friends, like the disciples, assumed Job had done something to deserve this evil that came upon him (Job 4:7). The truth was, he did not do anything. God was just testing his faith—and God does this to all of us at different times in our lives. Other times, because evil is in the world, it affects those who did nothing to deserve it. That is the reason people get cancer and other sicknesses. It is not always because God gave it to them, but rather because sin entered the world and corrupted everything.

One thing that atheists/agnostics also do not understand is that suffering is not necessarily a bad thing. Most atheists/agnostics think suffering is inherently bad because their good in life is doing whatever is pleasing to their flesh. That is what the Bible calls the carnal mind (Rom. 8:5–8). It is called the carnal mind because it is beastly. That is how animals function. An animal's whole goal in life is to please their flesh. Us humans have souls. We are not supposed to live like animals. Suffering helps growth. The Bible says, "And not only so, but we glory in tribulations also: knowing that tribulation worketh patience; [4] And patience, experience; and experience, hope" (Rom. 5:3–4). Suffering builds character. James says, "My brethren, count it all joy when ye fall into diverse temptations; [3] Knowing this, that the trying of your faith worketh patience. [4] But let patience have her perfect work, that ye may be perfect and entire, wanting nothing" (James 1:2–4).

Suffering produces patience. Christians also practice other forms of "suffering." Christians practice fasting. Fasting is not pleasurable, but we do it anyway. Christians practice abstinence. It would be much more pleasurable to indulge in fornication, but nonetheless it betters us. Christians practice sobriety. Getting drunk may be pleasurable or fun but abstaining from drunkenness betters us. Not only this, but much more serious forms of suffering can seem like a good thing to Christians as well. Paul said,

> And lest I should be exalted above measure through the abundance of the revelations, there was given to me a thorn in the flesh, the messenger of Satan to buffet me, lest I should be

exalted above measure. [8] For this thing I besought the Lord thrice, that it might depart from me. [9] And he said unto me, My grace is sufficient for thee: for my strength is made perfect in weakness. Most gladly therefore will I rather glory in my infirmities, that the power of Christ may rest upon me. [10] Therefore I take pleasure in infirmities, in reproaches, in necessities, in persecutions, in distresses for Christ's sake: for when I am weak, then am I strong. (2 Cor. 12:7–10)

Prior to this passage, Paul explained how he had been receiving revelations. He went on to say in this passage that God gave him a "thorn in the flesh" to keep him humble. God does not cause everything, but He very well can give one of His children some sort of suffering to be their "thorn in the flesh." Most atheists/agnostics would say all suffering is wrong. But once again, that is a presupposition. Not everybody believes all suffering is bad, and especially not Christians. Suffering builds us up and makes us stronger. That is why Paul concluded at the end of the passage saying, "For when I am weak, then I am strong." Suffering is not always bad. How you respond to suffering will build you as a person. Trials and tribulations can be greatly beneficial.

With all that being said, the most important truth in understanding the problem of evil is free will. From the beginning, God has given all His creatures free will. God desires a genuine, loving relationship with each human being and without free will, there can be no love. Timothy ware says, "God will not force us to love Him, for love is no longer love if it is not free; how then can God reconcile to Himself those who refuse all reconciliation?"[20] Besides that, without free will, no person could be praised for good or condemned for their bad. For example, if Hitler were predetermined to kill six million Jews, we could not condemn him. But since he had free will,

---

[20] Ware, Timothy. *The Orthodox Church: An Introduction to Eastern Christianity.* Newed. Penguin Books, 1963, 254.

we can say he was wrong for what he did. The early church apologist Justin Martyr wrote in the mid-second century saying,

> Since it be not so, but all things happen by
> fate, neither is anything at all in our own power.
> For if it be fated that this man, e.g., be good,
> and this other evil, neither is the former meri-
> torious nor the latter to be blamed. And again,
> unless the human race have the power of avoid-
> ing evil and choosing good by free choice, they
> are not accountable for their actions, of what-
> ever kind they be. But that it is by free choice
> they both walk uprightly and stumble, we thus
> demonstrate.[21]

Without free will, we cannot call anybody's actions good or evil. Since we have free will, there is a chance that people will freely choose to do evil. And this is where moral evil comes into play. Thieves freely choose to steal. Murderers freely choose to murder. Natural evil is a result of the first free will decision in the Garden. Free choices can also lead to natural evil for us today. For example, if a person freely chooses to eat an unhealthy diet, they may develop health problems. The health problems are natural evil because they are a result of the original sin in the Garden, but this natural evil can be brought about by a person's free will choice. Free will is necessary for love and for genuine choices to be made.

Little do most atheists/agnostics realize that they must answer the flipside of the problem of evil—which can be referred to as "the problem of good." The problem is presented as such: "If the world is the chance assembly of accidental phenomena, why is there so much that we want to praise and celebrate? Why is there beauty, love and laughter?"[22]

---

[21] Martyr, Justin. *The Ante-Nicene Fathers: The First Apology of Justin.* Chapter XLIII. Edited by Alexander Roberts, James Donaldson, and Arthur Cleveland Coxe. I. Vol. I. X vols. New York, NY: Cosimo Classics, 2007, 177.
[22] Wright, 19.

If the world is just a result of random chance and none of us have any inherent value or purpose, why are there good things? Why do people enjoy food and the sun on their skin? Why is there good if the world is a result of chance? The atheist/agnostic would need to answer this just as much as the Christian must answer the problem of evil. At the end of the day, God has promised a day in which all evil and suffering would be removed. God will destroy this corrupted earth one day (2 Pet. 3:10). Revelation says,

> And I saw a new heaven and a new earth: for the first heaven and the first earth were passed away; and there was no more sea. ² And I John saw the holy city, new Jerusalem, coming down from God out of heaven, prepared as a bride adorned for her husband. ³ And I heard a great voice out of heaven saying, Behold, the tabernacle of God is with men, and he will dwell with them, and they shall be his people, and God himself shall be with them, and be their God. ⁴ And God shall wipe away all tears from their eyes; and there shall be no more death, neither sorrow, nor crying, neither shall there be any more pain: for the former things are passed away. (Rev. 21:1–4)

After God destroys this earth, He will give us a new earth and a new Jerusalem. This is the awaited redemption spoken of (Rom. 8:18–25). In that day, there will be no more evil (moral or natural), but everybody will love God and love their neighbor perfectly, apart from all suffering.

EPISTEMOLOGY, TRUTH, EMPIRICISM, AND THE SCIENTIFIC METHOD

In my time of studying apologetics, I have heard many things. The most common objection of the unbeliever is something like, "I don't believe in God! I believe in science!" I believe in science too. Bodie Hodge says,

> If science is a strictly secular endeavor without any need for a biblical worldview, then why were most fields of science developed by Bible-believing Christians? For example, consider Isaac Newton, Gregor Mendel, Louis Pasteur, Johann Kepler, Galileo Galilei, Robert Boyle, Blaise Pascal, Michael Faraday, James Joule, Joseph Lister, and James Clerk Maxwell. Were these "greats" of science not doing science? Francis Bacon developed the scientific method, and he was a young-earth creationist and devout Christian.[23]

Isaac Newton! Ever heard of that guy? You know the guy that discovered the laws of motion? He was just a dumb ol' Bible-believing Christian! This whole list is full of some great names that were all Christians! Science is a *word*, not an *argument*. The word "science" means "knowledge." So the question is, how do you get knowledge? Epistemology is defined by *Merriam-Webster* as "the study or a theory of the nature and grounds of knowledge especially with reference to its limits and validity."[24]

In lay terms, epistemology is how you know what you know; what a person appeals to for knowledge. Regarding epistemology, most atheists/agnostics are empiricists. Empiricism is defined as "the practice of relying on observation and experiment especially in the natural sciences."[25] In other words, empiricism is the belief that everything a person knows is through the five senses—taste, touch,

---

[23] Hodge, Bodie. *Glass House: Shattering the Myth of Evolution.* Edited by Ken Ham and Bodie Hodge. Green Forest, AR: Answers in Genesis, 2018, 49.

[24] *Merriam-Webster.* "Epistemology." In *The Merriam-Webster Dictionary.* Merriam-Webster, 2016.

[25] *Merriam-Webster.* "Empiricism." In *The Merriam-Webster Dictionary.* Merriam-Webster, 2016.

smell, hearing, and sight. There was a man in the Bible who was an empiricist (or at least appeared to be by what he said). His name was Thomas:

> But Thomas, one of the twelve, called Didymus, was not with them when Jesus came. [25] The other disciples therefore said unto him, We have seen the LORD. But he said unto them, **Except I shall see in his hands the print of the nails, and put my finger into the print of the nails, and thrust my hand into his side, I will not believe.** [26] And after eight days again his disciples were within, and Thomas with them: then came Jesus, the doors being shut, and stood in the midst, and said, Peace be unto you. [27] Then saith he to Thomas, Reach hither thy finger, and behold my hands; and reach hither thy hand, and thrust it into my side: and be not faithless, but believing. [28] And Thomas answered and said unto him, My LORD and my God. [29] Jesus saith unto him, Thomas, because thou hast seen me, thou hast believed: blessed are they that have not seen, and yet have believed. (John 20:24–29)

The disciples told Thomas that Jesus had risen from the dead and appeared to them. He did not believe them. Instead, he said he would only believe if he saw Jesus and touched Him; in other words, Thomas would only believe something based on his senses—which is what most atheists believe today. Lucky for Thomas, Jesus did appear to him. But Jesus is not going to appear to everybody. Notice what Jesus said in the last verse. Those who believe without seeing are blessed! "But how can it be true if it can't be tested with my five senses?" the atheist might object. There are many problems with the worldview of empiricism. First, to test things using your five senses, they must be reliable.

The problem is, if God does not exist and there is no intelligent design, there is no reason to believe your five senses are working properly. The reason a Christian can trust their five senses is because we believe we are intelligently designed by an intelligent Creator. But if we are all the result of random chance, the atheist has no reason to believe his senses are working properly. The scientific method requires uniformity in nature, which only exists if God exists. For example, if a person wants to do an experiment, they will likely have more than one test. To discover the difference between the constant and variable, the universe must be the same at the time of each test.

But if God does not exist and there's no uniformity in nature, that means there's no reason to trust that the universe will be the same during the two tests; if God doesn't exist, there's no reason to expect the law of gravity to continue to work in the next second, and the second after that, and the second after that, and so on. There is no ground for it. But obviously, everybody lives like there's uniformity in nature whether they believe in God or not; if people really believed there was no uniformity in nature, they would not walk outside for fear of the laws of gravity ceasing to work properly and carrying them into the sky! Science, and specifically the scientific method, necessitates uniformity in nature; and uniformity in nature necessitates God! Secondly, the senses are different for different people. Some people are color blind. If a person with twenty-twenty vision examines the same thing as a person that's color blind, they will come to different conclusions.

Lastly, there are things that exist that cannot be tested with the five senses. The laws of logic and numerical law are both prime examples. The laws of logic and numerical law are both eternal and immaterial; they have always existed, and they cannot be touched, tasted, smelled, heard, or seen. The laws of logic and numerical law were never created. Before there were any humans, the law of noncontradiction (a law of logic) was true. For example, even before humans existed and started discussing the laws of logic, a rock could not be a rock and not a rock at the same time—that would violate the law of noncontradiction.

Likewise, even before humans existed, one rock plus one rock would make two rocks. No humans had to create the laws of logic or numerical law. They always existed. Thus, there are two examples of things that are real and believed by everybody but cannot be tested with the five senses, and those two things make the world go round (words and numbers)! Another example is the brain. Nobody can see, taste, touch, smell, or hear their brain. They can see *images* of their brain using technology, but that is not the same as seeing it itself. Even though we cannot see our brain, we still know it exists, because we do not have to see something for it to be true or real. God does not have to be seen to be real (although God in the flesh was seen two thousand years ago). It is unreliable to appeal solely to your five senses for knowledge.

SCIENCE AND EVOLUTION

We have already demonstrated that doing science relies on the uniformity in nature and intelligent design of God. Most atheists/agnostics say they are not Christians because they "believe in science." I believe in *science* too, but I do not believe in *science fiction*. There are two main types of evolution: microevolution and macroevolution. Ron Rhodes says,

> Microevolution refers to changes that occur within the same species, while macroevolution refers to the transition or evolution of one species into another. Macroevolution "consists of changes within a population leading to a completely new species with genetic information that did not exist in any of the parents." There is no question, even among creationists, that microevolution has taken place, for all the different races of human beings have descended from a single common human ancestor (Adam). Likewise, all kinds of dogs have "microevolved" from the original dog species created by God. In

no case, however, has macroevolution ever been observed by scientists.[26]

In short, microevolution refers to adaptation in creatures while macroevolution refers to one species changing into another. Microevolution is science and macroevolution is science *fiction*. Within macroevolution, there are three main types: cosmological, geological, and biological (chemical).[27] Cosmological evolution argues that "from the singularity of the big bang, all space, matter, and energy gradually formed the universe and all the galaxies, stars, and planets in it."[28] Geological evolution argues that the "earth formed from the debris spinning around our sun as it gathered into a ball. Over time, the earth cooled, the atmosphere formed, and the seas accumulated. The surface of the earth was shaped and reshaped over billions of years."[29] And lastly, biological evolution argues that "the first life formed as chemicals spontaneously formed every component needed for life. From this first organism, all life on earth has gradually developed into the variety we see today."[30]

In summary, macroevolution teaches "from goo to zoo to you." Macroevolution teaches that all humans evolved from animals like apes and apes evolved from aquatic animals and those aquatic animals came from cells. That is a laymen's explanation. This theory sounds little like science and more like an episode of the Teenage Mutant Ninja Turtles. They came from goo! On the contrary, the Bible teaches that God created the world in six days (Gen. 1:1–31). Yes, this means six literal days. The Hebrew word for "day" is the word *yom*. While it is possible for this Hebrew word to stand for a

---

[26] Rhodes, Ron. *Answering the Objections of Atheists, Agnostics, & Skeptics*. Eugene, OR: Harvest House Publishers, 2006, 79.

[27] Patterson, Roger. *Glass House: Shattering the Myth of Evolution*. Edited by Ken Ham and Bodie Hodge. Green Forest, AR: Answers in Genesis, 2018, 25.

[28] Patterson, 25.

[29] Patterson, 25.

[30] Patterson, 25.

period of time rather than just a twenty-four-hour day, the context makes the meaning clear. Exodus says,

> Remember the sabbath day, to keep it holy. **⁹ Six days shalt thou labour, and do all thy work: ¹⁰ But the seventh day is the sabbath of the Lord thy God**: in it thou shalt not do any work, thou, nor thy son, nor thy daughter, thy manservant, nor thy maidservant, nor thy cattle, nor thy stranger that is within thy gates: **¹¹ For in six days the Lord made heaven and earth, the sea, and all that in them is, and rested the seventh day**: wherefore the Lord blessed the sabbath day, and hallowed it. (Exod. 20:8–11)

The reasoning that the book of Exodus gave for the Sabbath day of rest (Saturday) was the example of God who worked six days in creation and then rested the seventh day. Now if one wants to argue that the word "day" in Genesis really means billions of years like some people do, they will have to also argue that the Jews worked for around six billion years and then rested. That would make no sense. The Jews worked for six literal days and then rested on the seventh literal day (Saturday).

And likewise, God created the world in six literal days and then rested on the seventh. If a person reads the text normally, they will never conclude that Genesis is allegorical. The book of Genesis is historical narrative, not poetic literature. This is one of the key rules in biblical interpretation. Always know the genre of the book being examined. Atheists/agnostics like to attack Creation calling it a fairy tale, but which makes more sense? That intelligent beings came from goo or that intelligent beings came from an intelligent Being? I will let the reader decide.

There are many problems with macroevolution. Supposedly, we are descendants of apes. I have one question. Where are all the transitional fossils? How come there are zero fossils of an ape-human hybrid? Or how about animals. Evolutionists claim that land animals evolved from aquatic animals, but how come there are no transitional/hybrid fossils of these? If macroevolution is so prominent, why is there no evidence of it? I want to ask the reader, have you ever seen a dog turn into a cat? How about a cat turn into a dog? You might say, "There are many different kinds of dogs so macroevolution must be true!" But this premise is false. Having many *kinds* of a species is what the Bible teaches. Genesis says, "And God said, Let the earth bring forth the living creature *after his kind*, cattle, and creeping thing, and beast of the earth *after his kind*: and it was so" (Gen. 1:24). Creationists strongly affirm that there are different "kinds" of a species. That is *microevolution* not macroevolution. What we deny is that one species can change into another species. That is impossible.

Evolutionists try to argue for macroevolution with "natural selection." Natural selection is not macroevolution. Georgian Purdom says,

> From a creationist perspective natural selection is a process whereby organisms possessing specific characteristics (reflective of their genetic makeup) survive better than others in a given environment or under a given selective pressure (i.e., antibiotic resistance in bacteria). Those with certain characteristics live, and those without them diminish in number or die.[31]

In other words, natural selection is *adaptation*. What happens when you stay in the sun too long? Most people get darker. That is why people groups who are in hotter environments are darker skinned. Melanin allows one to stay in the sun for longer periods without being harmed. One of the cases that evolutionists use to support their case of macroevolution is the case of the peppered moth. In the 1800s, during the industrial revolution, trees became darker

---

[31] Purdom, Georgia. *The New Answers Book 1: Over 25 Questions on Creation/ Evolution and the Bible.* Edited by Ken Ham. Green Forest, AR: Answers in Genesis, 2006, 272–273.

due to soot. Because of this, the population of moths turned to a dark color. In other words, they *adapted* to their environment. These moths did not turn into a different species. All they did was adapt. This is *microevolution*, not macroevolution.

Perhaps the biggest flaw in evolutionary theory is the understanding of origins. You see, there are two different types of science: observational and historical.[32] Observable science has to do with experimentation while historical science attempts to reconstruct past events through experimentation. Historical science is problematic because it assumes what happened in the past. This is what evolutionists do. They *assume* that macroevolution is true, and they carry that presupposition with them into experimentation. Let the reader understand, the origin of the universe is a historical question, not a scientific one. In other words, the question is what *did* happen, not what we *think* happened based on present-day experimentation. Henry Morris says, "Scientists may speculate about the past or the future but they can only observe the present. The study of origins— whether by creation or evolution—is necessarily outside the scope of science in its real sense. Therefore, the theory of evolution is not science but is rather a belief, a religious philosophy of origins."[33]

The scientific method (put in place by a Christian named Francis Bacon) requires observation and testing. You cannot test history. That is impossible. This means you cannot use science to determine the origin of the universe. Macroevolution has never been observed nor will it ever be. The law of biogenesis states that life must come from life. Macroevolution teaches that life comes from nonlife (abiogenesis). That is not science. Never in the history of the world has life been observed to come from non-life. Some evolutionists will refer to a study in which scientists did in fact create a living organism from nothing and they say this proves macroevolution. Think about the experiment they refer to. An intelligent being (the scientist) created life from nothing. My friends, this proves creationism, not mac-

---

[32] Rivera, Jennifer Hall. *Glass House: Shattering the Myth of Evolution*. Edited by Ken Ham and Bodie Hodge. Green Forest, AR: Answers in Genesis, 2018, 38.

[33] Morris, Henry M. *Many Infallible Proofs: Evidences for the Christian Faith*. El Cajon, CA: Master Books, 1974, 249.

roevolution! Creationists believe an intelligent being (God) created the world from nothing (ex nihilo)!

One major flaw in the evolutionary theory is carbon 14 dating. Many atheists/agnostics have claimed that carbon 14 dating has proven the Earth to be billions of years old. Carbon 14 decays into nitrogen 14 over time, which means the amount of carbon 14 in a dead organism becomes less and less over time. The decay rate (half-life) of carbon 14 is 5,730 years. To determine the starting amount of carbon 14 in an organism, scientists use carbon 12 (a stable isotope of carbon). The ratio of carbon 14 and carbon 12 is one carbon 14 atom for every one trillion carbon 12 atoms. This ratio becomes less and less when an organism dies, which means the smaller the ratio is observed to be, the older the organism is. Carbon 14 dating has multiple assumptions. Mike Riddle says,

> A critical assumption used in carbon-14 dating has to do with this ratio. It is assumed that the ratio of ^{14}C to ^{12}C in the atmosphere has always been the same as it is today (1 to 1 trillion). If this assumption is true, then the AMS ^{14}C dating method is valid up to about 80,000 years… In other words, the amount of ^{14}C being produced in the atmosphere must equal the amount being removed to be in a steady state (also called "equilibrium"). If this is not true, the ratio of ^{14}C to ^{12}C is not a constant, which would make knowing the starting amount of ^{14}C in a specimen difficult or impossible to accurately determine. **Dr. Willard Libby, the founder of the carbon-14 dating method, assumed this ratio to be constant. His reasoning was based on a belief in evolution, which assumes the earth must be billions of years old.**[34]

---

[34] Riddle, 82.

Carbon 14 dating *assumes* that the ratio of carbon 14 to carbon 12 has always been the same! And this assumption was based on another assumption—namely that macroevolution is true! That is why scientists who use this method come up with such high numbers for the age of the earth. Those who use this method are not looking for their minds to be changed about macroevolution. They already assume that macroevolution is true and then conduct experimentation based on that assumption, which is why their dating is so flawed. Evolutionists cannot see past their presuppositional blinders. Another assumption has to do with the magnetic field of the earth. Because of the decay of the magnetic field as years go by, the ratio of carbon 14 to carbon 12 also increases. This means the age found for the organisms when using carbon 14 dating will be way higher than it really is! Mike Riddle quotes D. R. Humphreys who says, "Though complex, this history of the earth's magnetic field agrees with Barnes's basic hypothesis, that the field has always freely decayed... The field has always been losing energy despite its variations, so it cannot be more than 10,000 years old."

When taking all these evolutionary assumptions out of the equation, it is evident that the earth is much younger than macroevolution says it is.

So as demonstrated, macroevolution is not science at all. Atheists/agnostics like to claim that Christians are blinded by our belief in the supernatural, but they are guilty of carrying their presuppositions about the earth into experimentation. Macroevolution is nothing more than a theory and it will remain a theory. It has never been proven, nor will it ever be because it is not possible. Macroevolution is not science. It is science fiction. I believe Henry Morris put it perfectly when he said,

> In the real world, tales about fishes and frogs turning into men are found only in books of fables and fairy tales; they have no proper place in books purporting to be textbooks of science. When a beast is transformed into a man in a moment, it is called magic; when the beast

becomes a man over a million years it is called evolution. The factor of time becomes the fairy's magic wand! It seems that for a person to believe in evolution, he must "turn his ears from the truth and be turned unto fables." (2 Tim. 4:4)[35]

EVOLUTION AND RACISM

Before Charles Darwin came around to formulate his evolutionary theory, people were not really separated by "race." Before Darwin, people were often identified by nationality. We see this all through the Bible with the "Jews and Gentiles." Identification almost always had to do with nationality and not skin color. But this all changed with Darwin and his theory of evolution. So it is evident that distinguishing people by "race" is a social construct. That is why I am completely and utterly opposed to people identifying as their skin color. I do not identify as black or white. I am just a Christian. My identity is in Christ.

I will never separate myself from my fellow humans by distinctions that are meaningless (like skin color). There is only one race and that's the human race. God made us all from one blood (Acts 17:26). The theory of evolution is inherently racist because it claims that some "races" are under evolved. According to Darwinian evolution, there is always a race that's the most evolved and thus making all the other races inferior. Ken Ham quotes a man named Ernst Haeckel who once said,

> At the lowest stage of human mental development are the Australians, some tribes of the Polynesians, and the Bushmen, Hottentots, and some of the Negro tribes. Nothing, however, is perhaps more remarkable in this respect, than that some of the wildest tribes in southern Asia

---

[35] Morris, Henry M. *Many Infallible Proofs: Evidences for the Christian Faith*. El Cajon, CA: Master Books, 1974, 255.

and easter Africa have no trace whatever of the first foundations of all human civilization, of family life, and marriage. They live together in herds, like apes.[36]

Due to evolutionary theory, Haeckel believed some races were inferior to others! This is ultimately what a belief in macroevolution leads to. Some of the most-evil people in the world were influenced by Darwin's theory of evolution: Karl Marx, Leon Trotsky, Adolf Hitler, Pol Pot, Mao Zedong, Joseph Stalin, Vladimir Lenin, and many others.[37] That's a terrifying list of names. This idea of evolution is most easily seen in the case of Adolf Hitler. Charles Darwin taught,

At some future period, not very distant as measured by centuries, the civilized races of man will almost certainly exterminate and replace the savage races throughout the world. At the same time the anthropomorphous apes...will no doubt be exterminated. The break between man and his nearest allies will then be wider, for it will intervene between man in a more civilized state, as we may hope, even than the Caucasian, and some ape as low as a baboon, instead of as now between negro or Australian [Aborigine] and the gorilla.[38]

You see, in evolutionary thinking, the darker and hairier you are, the closer to an ape you are. This means those that are lighter skinned and have less body hair are more evolved. This means lighter

---

[36] Ham, Ken. *The New Answers Book 1: Over 25 Questions on Creation/Evolution and the Bible.* Edited by Ken Ham. Green Forest, AR: Answers in Genesis, 2006, 221.

[37] Hodge, Bodie. *Glass House: Shattering the Myth of Evolution.* Edited by Ken Ham and Bodie Hodge. Green Forest, AR: Answers in Genesis, 2018, 298.

[38] Hodge, Bodie. *Glass House: Shattering the Myth of Evolution.* Edited by Ken Ham and Bodie Hodge. Green Forest, AR: Answers in Genesis, 2018, 298–299.

skinned people are superior to darker-skinned people (in evolutionary theory)! You can easily see how Hitler viewed the "Aryan race" as the master race. That is why Hitler believed Jews, black people, and many other people groups were inferior. Evolutionary theory gave Hitler all the justification he needed for exterminating the "under evolved races"! This type of evolutionary thinking played a major role in the enslavement of black people as well as the destruction of Native Americans and the idea of "manifest destiny."

Europeans believed they were the superior human beings and thus gave them the right to treat those with darker skin as animals! Because that is what macroevolution teaches! A man in 1925 named George William Hunter said, "The Races of Man. At the present time there exist upon the earth five races...the highest type of all, the Caucasians, represented by the civilized white inhabitants of Europe and America."[39] Not only did Hunter say this, but this is what he taught in his biology textbook *A Civic Biology Presented in Problems*.[40] This was a book that was used for schools in America! This means students in America were being taught that white people were the superior race while all others were inferior. This was all due to evolutionary thinking! In Darwin's theory, some people are extremely close to apes! No wonder darker skinned people were treated as animals!

There is another major act that's influenced by evolutionary thinking—abortion! One of the main arguments in favor of abortion is that the babies are not "fully developed." In other words, the babies are "underevolved." That is why so many nowadays think killing babies in the womb is okay. They do not see them as human—or at least not a fully evolved human. And because of that, many believe killing them is justified! Do you see how Darwin's wicked concept has perverted the whole world? The whole world has been influenced by Darwin's worldview. Now many people think we are just animals with no inherent value from a loving Creator. But the truth is we are

---

[39] Ham, Ken, and A. Charles Ware. *Darwin's Plantation: Evolution's Racist Roots*. Green Forest, AR: Master Books, 2007, 92.

[40] Ham, Ken, and A. Charles Ware. *Darwin's Plantation: Evolution's Racist Roots*. Green Forest, AR: Master Books, 2007, 92.

all made by a loving Creator who formed us in the womb and made us with value. We are not meaningless animals. Psalm 139 says,

> For thou hast possessed my reins: thou hast covered me in my mother's womb. [14] I will praise thee; **for I am fearfully and wonderfully made**: marvellous are thy works; and that my soul knoweth right well. [15] My substance was not hid from thee, when I was made in secret, and curiously wrought in the lowest parts of the earth. [16] Thine eyes did see my substance, yet being unperfect; and in thy book all my members were written, which in continuance were fashioned, when as yet there was none of them. (Ps. 139:13–16)

We were all formed in the womb by a loving Creator. He created us all with inherent value. We are "fearfully and wonderfully made"! That includes every skin color, ethnicity, nationality, etc. That includes men and women! That includes babies in the womb! Every single human being is fearfully and wonderfully made. We are all equal (Gal. 3:28) and come from one blood (Acts 17:26). There is no such thing as a "master race" or "under evolved" races. We are all equal in the eyes of a loving God.

THE BIBLE'S HISTORIC TESTIMONY OF THE RESURRECTION

If God exists, it logically follows that He would leave a revelation of Himself. But even if one does not want to accept the existence of God, they are still not exempt from examining the claimed revelation. One point I always try to convey to unbelievers is that they must deal with the Bible. What do I mean by that? Well since the Bible exists, one cannot just turn a blind eye to it and reject it without studying it themselves. It is the most sold book in the world and has shaped society tremendously, specifically American society which was founded on biblical principles. For a person to truly become a historian in testing the validity of the resurrection, they must research the primary document that speaks of it, whether they believe it is divinely inspired or not.

Many will argue that you cannot use any of the Bible as proof of the resurrection. This argument is very flawed. For one, you do not have to accept the Bible as divinely inspired and/or inerrant to examine it historically. There are claims of a resurrection therefore they must be considered. One does not have to believe the Bible is perfect and void of error (like Christians do) to examine it as a historical document. Secondly, many passages in the Bible are accepted even by skeptics. For example, regarding the most important passage on this topic, 1 Corinthians 15:3–5, it is regarded by scholars as an early church creed: "For I delivered unto you first of all that which I also received, how that Christ died for our sins according to the scriptures; ⁴And that he was buried, and that he rose again the third day according to the scriptures: ⁵And that he was seen of Cephas, then of the twelve" (1 Cor. 15:3–5).

Gary Habermas says, "One of the earliest and most important is quoted in Paul's first letter to the Corinthian church… Several factors mark this as an ancient creed that was part of the earliest traditions of the Christian Church and that predate the writings of Paul."[41] This was written around AD 55, which is only about twenty-two years after the crucifixion of Jesus and many even argue that Paul learned this creed in Jerusalem right after his conversion. That means he would have learned it within five years of the crucifixion. This passage is accepted as a credible source for what early Christians believed. That means we have an extremely early primary source that testifies to the death, burial, and resurrection of Jesus.

EXTRA-BIBLICAL HISTORICAL SOURCES FOR THE RESURRECTION OF JESUS

There seems to be a myth that is kept alive by atheists and skeptics that the Bible is the only source that mentions Jesus. That is

---

[41] Habermas, 52.

simply untrue. The sources I will mention are non-Christian sources. That means they have no bias and pass as enemy attestation, making the life of Jesus and His resurrection even more credible. **Pliny the Younger** was a governor in the Roman Province of Bithynia-Pontus in Asia Minor. He was writing to the Roman Emperor Trajan in AD 112 when he said, "[The Christians] sing hymns to Christ as to a god."[42] **Suetonius** was a Roman Biographer. In his biography of Emperor Claudius of Rome, who reigned from AD 41 to AD 54, he explained how Claudius deported Jews in Rome because of riots that took place during the "instigation of Chrestus [Christ]."[43] **Josephus** was a Jewish historian born in AD 37, which is four years after the crucifixion. He writes arguably the most famous source outside the Bible speaking of Jesus:

> Now, there was about this time Jesus, a wise man, if it be lawful to call him a man, for he was a doer of wonderful works—a teacher of such men as receive truth with pleasure. He drew over to him both many of the Jews, and many of the Gentiles. He was [the] Christ; and when Pilate, at the suggestion of the principal men amongst us, had condemned him to the cross, those that loved him at the first did not forsake him, for he appeared to them alive again the third day, as the divine prophets had foretold these and ten thousand other wonderful things concerning him; and the tribe of Christians, so named from him, are not extinct at this day.[44]

---

[42] Ehrman, Bart D. *Did Jesus Exist?: The Historical Argument for Jesus of Nazareth.* New York City, New York: HarperOne, an imprint of HarperCollinsPublishers, 2013. 51–52.

[43] Ehrman, 53.

[44] Whiston, William. Josephus: The Complete Works. Nashville, Tennessee: Thomas Nelson Inc, 1998. 576.

Eusebius quotes this same passage in his writings, making it even more historically credible.[45] **Tacitus** was a Roman historian born in AD 56. He said, "Nero fastened the guilt [of the burning of Rome] and inflicted the most exquisite tortures on a class hated for their abominations, called Christians by the populace. Christus, from whom the name had its origin, suffered extreme penalty during the reign of Tiberius at the hands of one of our procurators, Pontius Pilate."[46]

Lucian of Samosata was a Greek satirist. He wrote, "The Christians, you know, worship a man to this day—the distinguished personage who introduced their novel rites, and was crucified on that account."[47] **Mara Bar-Serapion** was a philosopher born in AD 50. He was writing to his son from prison when he said, "Or [what advantage came to] the Jews by the murder of their Wise King, seeing that from that very time their kingdom was driven away from them?"[48] **The Talmud** is a Jewish writing compiled in the fourth century that states, "on the eve of the Passover Yeshu was hanged."[49] Jesus's name in Hebrew is widely known as Yeshua. It also says He was hanged. This may seem like it cannot be speaking of Jesus since we know He was crucified, not hanged. One must understand the language of these times. It was common then to speak of being "hanged on a tree." The book of Acts says, "The God of our father raised up Jesus, whom ye slew and hanged on a tree" (Acts 5:30). It is clear that being hung on a "tree" or a wooden "cross" is synonymous. The fact that Jesus existed and was crucified is a historically undisputed fact. Skeptic scholar John Dominic Crossan says, "That he [Jesus] was crucified is as sure as anything historical can ever be."[50]

---

[45] Eusebius, and Paul L. Maier. *Eusebius—the Church History*. Grand Rapids, MI, Michigan: Kregel Publications, 2007. 44.
[46] Habermas, 49.
[47] Habermas, 49
[48] Habermas, 49.
[49] Habermas, 49.
[50] Habermas, 49.

THE APOSTLES TRULY BELIEVED THEY HAD SEEN THE RESURRECTED JESUS

Now that we have seen the historical evidence of Jesus's death by crucifixion, we must turn to the reality of testimony. The Apostles were willing to die for their belief in the resurrection. Not only do we have the obvious accounts of the resurrection in the gospels, but we have outside sources as well. The Apostles were convinced they had seen the risen Jesus in the flesh. Tertullian wrote in the second century saying,

> That Paul is beheaded has been written in their own blood. And if a heretic wishes his confidence to rest upon a public record, the archives of the empire will speak, as would the stones of Jerusalem. We read the lives of Caesars: At Rome Nero was the first who stained with blood the rising faith. Then is Peter girt by another, when he is made fast to the cross Then does Paul obtain a birth suited to Roman citizenship, when in Rome he springs to life again ennobled by martyrdom.[51]

That Peter and Paul, as well as the other Apostles, were martyred is widely known and accepted. It makes no sense for somebody to die for something they knew to be a lie.

CONVERSION OF PAUL AND JAMES

The next two facts that should be examined are the conversions of Paul and James. The Apostle Paul was a persecutor of Christians. He even testifies to this himself saying, "For ye have heard of my conversation in time past in the Jews' religion, how that beyond measure I persecuted the church of God, and wasted it" (Gal. 1:13). Once again, when examining the Bible, one does not have to view

---

[51] Habermas, 58.

it as divinely inspired and inerrant to read it as any other historical document. These verses are just for reference. Continuing, the
fact of Paul's conversion is also attested by Luke, Clement of Rome,
Polycarp, Tertullian, Dionysius of Corinth, and Origen.[52] Next we
should examine the conversion of James. James was the brother of
Jesus which is attested in the gospels (Matthew 13:55) as well as by
sources outside the Bible like Josephus who said, "the brother of Jesus
who was called the Christ, whose name was James."[53]

James did not believe Jesus was the Christ (John 7:5). He was a
devout Jew attested by Hegesippus who said, "He [James] was holy
from his mother's womb; and he drank no wine nor strong drink,
nor did he eat flesh. No razor came upon his head; he did not anoint
himself with oil, and he did not use the [public] bath."[54] He was
later converted after seeing the resurrected Jesus (1 Cor. 15:7). James
later became a leader in the church (Acts 15:13–21). He even wrote
his own epistle calling himself the servant of the Lord Jesus Christ
(James 1:1). So we can see that both Paul and James were devout Jews
who were converted to Christianity.

THE TOMB WAS EMPTY

In his research, Gary Habermas found that 75 percent of scholars believe the empty tomb is a historical fact.[55] Jesus's crucifixion
took place in Jerusalem. That is where the preaching of the resurrection and Christianity began. If it were the case that His body was
still in the tomb, the officials would have displayed the body for all
to see so they could put a stop to the spread of Christianity. The fact
of the matter is they could not do this because the tomb was in fact
empty. In the time of the early church, critics of Christianity accused
the Christians of stealing the body out of the tomb to make it appear
that He rose from the dead (enemy attestation). This is attested in

---

[52] Habermas, 65.
[53] Habermas, 67.
[54] Habermas, 67.
[55] Habermas, 70.

Matthew 28:12–13, but there are also sources outside the Bible that affirm this such as Justin Martyr and Tertullian.[56] This accusation of a stolen body makes it clear that the tomb was in fact empty or else there would be no need for critics to make this claim. Another point to take into consideration is the fact that women were the first to see the empty tomb. Back in those days, women were not viewed as reliable witnesses; they were viewed as lesser than. In his *Antiquities*, Josephus wrote, "But let not the testimony of women be admitted."[57] This ideology is evident in the gospels. In the gospel of Luke, Mary Magdalene and two other women went to the apostles to tell them the tomb was empty, but the disciples did not believe them (Luke 24:11). Because women were considered unreliable witnesses, the gospel accounts are regarded as reliable since we know from history that nobody would lie about women being witnesses to *help* their case. Female witnesses would not help a case, but actually *hurt* a case in those days, making it less credible (to that society). In other words, it would make no sense for the disciples to lie about female witnesses (principle of embarrassment).

ARE JESUS AND CHRISTIANITY COPIES OF PAGAN RELIGIONS?

It is often asserted by atheists and agnostics that Jesus and Christianity are just copies of pagan religions that predated them. This claim has garnered much attention in the twenty-first century. Does this claim hold any weight? When examined further, the answer is an emphatic no.

When it comes to these pagan religions, they were an attempt to explain phenomenon in the world around them. Joel McDurmon says, "Most of the Greek mysteries were tied to the cycle of nature and related to the unpredictable aspects of human life such as reproduction, safety, and food production. Gods, goddesses, and myths

---

[56] Habermas, 71.
[57] Habermas, 72.

were created to explain the continual dying and rebirth of vegetation during the year."[58]

It makes sense that these religions would develop since mankind is always trying to explain the happenings of the world. Ronald H. Nash lists the mystery religions:

> Each region of the Mediterranean world seems to have produced its own mystery religion. Out of Greece came the cults of **Demeter and Dionysus**, as well as their later developments, the **Eleusinian and Orphic** mystery religions. Asia Minor (more specifically, the region known as Phrygia) gave birth to the cult of **Cybele and Attis**. The cult of **Isis and Osiris (later Serapis)** originated in Egypt, while Syria and Palestine saw the rise of the cult of **Adonis**. Finally, Persia (Iran) was a leading early locale for the cult of **Mithras**.[59]

Demeter was the goddess of grain and agricultural fertility. Her daughter Kore was kidnapped by Hades. Zeus made a deal with Hades that Kore would spend eight months with Demeter and the other four months of the year with Hades. That is how the people of the time explained why plants grew at certain times of the year and not others.

Dionysus is also known as Bacchus. Dionysus was the child of Zeus. He saved his human mother from the underworld. Dionysus was associated with vegetation.[60] The worship of Dionysus evolved into that of **Orpheus**. Orpheus was supposedly a priest of the cult that was ripped apart and eaten by female worshippers.[61]

---

[58] McDurmon, Joel. *Manifested in the Flesh*. Powder Springs, GA: American Vision, Inc, 2007, 23.

[59] Nash, Ronald H. *The Gospel and the Greeks*. Phillipsburg, NJ: P&R Publishing Company, 2003, 106.

[60] McDurmon, 24.

[61] McDurmon, 25.

In the story of **Osiris**, he was killed by his brother Set who put his body in the Nile. Osiris's wife (and sister—weird huh) **Isis** found his body. Osiris's brother Set found the body again and cut it into pieces. Osiris then lived in the underworld. There are multiple versions of this story and in some Osiris rules the underworld.[62]

Astarte was the fertility goddess. The original story is a mystery as there is no evidence, but the later story goes as such: Astarte is in love with the deity **Adonis**. Adonis is killed and goes to the underworld. Adonis ends up splitting time between the upper and underworld. Because he was a god of vegetation, this once again helped explain seasons and planting cycles.[63]

Cybele, also known as the Great Mother or the Mother of the Mountain, was in love with the human **Attis**.[64] There are multiple versions of this myth. One says that Attis was rejected by Cybele after somebody else joined to her and this caused Attis to castrate himself. Other versions say that Cybele drove Attis crazy until he finally castrated himself.[65]

Mithra and Mithraism is probably the most prominent of these cults since the emperor of Rome in the late forth century, Julian the Apostate (AD 360–363), tried to make Mithraism the dominant religion over Christianity.[66] Mithra was born by emerging from a rock. He had a knife, a torch, and wore a "Phrygian cap."[67] Ronald H. Nash says, "He battled first with the sun and then with a primeval bull, thought to be the first act of creation. Mithra slew the bull, which then became the ground of life for the human race."[68]

Skeptics love to make the parallel between Jesus and Mithras because Mithras was associated with Sol Invictus or the "Unconquerable Sun," which was celebrated on December 25.[69]

---

[62] McDurmon, 25.
[63] McDurmon, 26.
[64] McDurmon, 27.
[65] McDurmon, 27.
[66] Nash, 133.
[67] Nash, 134.
[68] Nash, 134.
[69] Strobel, 126.

Atheists and agnostics see this fact as a "gotcha" moment against Christianity. Except there is one problem: The Bible never tells us the date of Jesus's birth. That is correct. We do not know the exact date of Jesus's birth. In fact, it is widely understood that Jesus was *not* born on December 25. This date seems to have been associated with Jesus around the fourth century. There's no parallel between the birth of Jesus and the pagan Mithras.

Many will claim that Jesus's virgin birth was copied from religions like these. But is this true? **Dionysus** was not born of a virgin. Lee Strobel quotes Edwin M. Yamauchi who says, "As the story goes, Zeus, disguised as a human, fell in love with the princess Semele (the daughter of Cadmus), and she became pregnant. Hera, who was Zeus's queen, arranged to have Semele burned to a crisp, but Zeus rescued the fetus [Dionysus] and sewed him into his thigh until Dionysus was born. So this is not a virgin birth in any sense."[70]

There are also myths of **Zeus** impregnating **Danae** and giving birth to a child called **Perseus**.[71] This is compared by skeptics to the story of Jesus's birth. The major difference is that the Holy Spirit came upon Mary and she conceived. That is extremely different from Greek mythological religions like that of Zeus. In stories like this, it was understood that Zeus literally and physically had sexual relations with Dane. The Holy Spirit did not have sexual relations with Mary. So there is no parallel. A similar story to that of Zeus circulated regarding **Alexander the Great**. Lee Strobel, once again, quotes Edwin M. Yamauchi who says, "The story about Olympias being impregnated by Zeus [while she slept] was propaganda designed to support Alexander's demand for worship."[72] The birth of **Buddha** is also often compared to the birth of Jesus, but there is no comparison. Yamauchi says, "According to legend, Buddha's mother dreamed that he entered her in the form of a white elephant—fully formed! In

---

[70] Strobel, Lee. *The Case for the Real Jesus*. Grand Rapids, MI: Zondervan, 2008, 132.
[71] Strobel, 132.
[72] Strobel, 133.

addition, she had been married for many years prior to this, so she certainly wasn't a virgin."[73]

Krishna was born to a mother who had seven sons already, so she wasn't a virgin.[74] **Zoroaster** dates before the birth of Jesus. And there's evidence that he was born when his mom drank something, but the evidence of his birth dates to the ninth century AD (nine centuries after Jesus)!

Besides the virgin birth, many will also claim that the resurrection of Jesus was stolen from these pagan religions. This claim is faulty. There are multiple stories of **Osiris**. In some versions, he comes back to life from a baptism in the waters of the Nile.[75] In other versions, he does not come back to life but rather becomes ruler of the underworld.[76] There's no resurrection in the story of Osiris. When it comes to the cult of **Cybele and Attis**, Ronald H. Nash quotes Gunter Wagner who says, "In its various forms, from the oldest traditions right down to the versions received in the fourth century AD, the Attis myth knows nothing of a resurrection of Attis. The Attis of the myth is not a dying and rising god."[77]

When it comes to **Mithras**, Lee Strobel quotes Richard Gordon who says there's "no death of Mithras"—and thus, there cannot be a resurrection."[78] In fact, Strobel says the scholar T. N. D. Mettinger "admits in his book *The Riddle of Resurrection* that the consensus among modern scholars—*nearly universal*—is that there were no dying and rising gods that preceded Christianity. They all post-dated the first century."[79] So it's clear from the evidence that the resurrection of Jesus was not copied from pagan myths. But atheists and agnostics will continue to claim the idea of a "resurrection" was not

---

[73] Strobel, 133.
[74] Strobel, 134.
[75] Nash, 127.
[76] Nash, 128.
[77] Nash, 131.
[78] Strobel, 127.
[79] Strobel, 117.

new to the story of Jesus. But that claim is false when examining the New Testament:

> Now while Paul waited for them at Athens, his spirit was stirred in him, when he saw the city wholly given to idolatry. [17] Therefore disputed he in the synagogue with the Jews, and with the devout persons, and in the market daily with them that met with him. [18] Then certain philosophers of **the Epicureans, and of the Stoicks**, encountered him. And some said, What will this babbler say? other some, **He seemeth to be a setter forth of strange gods: because he preached unto them Jesus, and the resurrection**. [19] And they took him, and brought him unto Areopagus, saying, **May we know what this new doctrine**, whereof thou speakest, is? [20] For thou bringest certain **strange things to our ears**: we would know therefore what these things mean. (Acts 17:16–20)

As Paul began speaking about Jesus and Christianity in Athens, the home of many philosophers and thinkers, the people were astonished. Atheists and skeptics claim the idea of a dying and rising God is copied from other religions, but if that is true, why did these people in Athens ask to know about "this new doctrine" that Paul was speaking of? Why would they say they wanted to know what these things meant? If the atheist claim is true that the story of Jesus is a copy, these people in Athens would have known it! Verse 21 of this passage says, "For all the Athenians and strangers which were there spent their time in nothing else, but either to tell, or to hear some new thing" (Acts 17:21). All these people did was study, discuss, and debate! If the story of Jesus even somewhat resembled another religion, they would have recognized it and called it out rather than call Paul's preaching "new doctrine." Further down in the chapter reads,

> And the times of this ignorance God winked at; but now commandeth all men everywhere to repent: [31] Because he hath appointed a day, in the which he will judge the world in righteousness by that man whom he hath ordained; whereof he hath given assurance unto all men, in that he hath raised him from the dead. [32] **And when they heard of the resurrection of the dead, some mocked: and others said, We will hear thee again of this matter.** [33] So Paul departed from among them. [34] Howbeit certain men clave unto him, and believed: among the which was Dionysius the Areopagite, and a woman named Damaris, and others with them. (Acts 17:30–34)

Once again, the people were astonished at the idea of a resurrection! But if the skeptic claim that resurrections were common in pagan religions, why were the people intrigued? The answer is because the resurrection of Jesus *is not* a copy. It is a unique account that has historical evidence, as documented in previous sections.

Often these false religions developed over time and stole ideas and concepts from Christianity—not the other way around. Justin Martyr wrote extensively about this in the second century. I will provide three long quotations from him because they are extremely relevant to the topic. In chapter 69 of his *First Apology*, he wrote,

> "Be well assured, then, Trypho," I continued, "that I am established in the knowledge of and faith in the Scriptures by those counterfeits which he who is called the devil is said to have performed among the Greeks; just as some were wrought by the Magi in Egypt, and others by the false prophets in Elijah's days. For

when they tell that **Bacchus**, son of Jupiter, was begotten by [Jupiter's] intercourse with **Semele**, and that he was the discoverer of the vine; and when they relate, that being torn in pieces, and having died, he rose again, and ascended into heaven; and when they introduce wine into his mysteries, do I not perceive that [the devil] has imitated the prophecy announced by the patriarch Jacob, and recorded by Moses? And when they tell that **Hercules** was strong, and travelled over all the world, and was begotten by **Jove of Alcmene**, and ascended to heaven when he died, do I not perceive that the Scripture which speaks of Christ, 'strong as a giant to run his race,' has been in like manner imitated? And when he [the devil] brings forward **Aesculapius** as the raiser of the dead and healer of all diseases, may I not say that in this matter likewise he has imitated the prophecies about Christ?"[80]

According to Justin, these pagan religions were satanic imitations of Christianity who stole from the Old Testament. That is one major point that many skeptics forget. The Old Testament is where many Christian ideas/doctrines come from. These pagan religions often stole from the Old Testament for their practices. Justin goes on to say,

"And when those who record the mysteries of **Mithras** say that he was begotten of a rock and call the place where those who believe in him are initiated a cave, do I not perceive here that the utterance of Daniel, that a stone without

---

80 Martyr, Justin. *The Ante-Nicene Fathers: The First Apology of Justin.* Chapter LXIX. Edited by Alexander Roberts, James Donaldson, and Arthur Cleveland Coxe. I. Vol. I. X vols. New York, NY: Cosimo Classics, 2007, 233.

hands was cut out of a great mountain, has been imitated by them, and that they have attempted likewise to imitate the whole of Isaiah's words? For they contrived that the words of righteousness be quoted also by them. But I must repeat to you the words of Isaiah referred to, in order that from them you may know that these things are so. They are these: 'Hear, ye that are far off, what I have done; those that are near shall know my might. The sinners in Zion are removed; trembling shall seize the impious. Who shall announce to you the everlasting place? The man who walks in righteousness, speaks in the right way, hates sin and unrighteousness, and keeps his hands pure from bribes, stops the ears from hearing the unjust judgment of blood, closes the eyes from seeing unrighteousness: he shall dwell in the lofty cave of the strong rock. Bread shall be given to him, and his water [shall be] sure. Ye shall see the King with glory, and your eyes shall look far off. Your soul shall pursue diligently the fear of the Lord. Where is the scribe? where are the counsellors? where is he that numbers those who are nourished—the small and great people? with whom they did not take counsel, nor knew the depth of the voices, so that they heard not. The people who are become depreciated, and there is no understanding in him who hears.' Now it is evident, that in this prophecy [allusion is made] to the bread which our Christ gave us to eat, in remembrance of His being made flesh for the sake of His believers, for whom also He suffered; and to the cup which He gave us to drink, in remembrance of His own blood, with giving thanks. And this prophecy proves that we shall behold this very King with glory; and the very terms of the prophecy declare loudly, that the people foreknown to believe in Him were foreknown to pursue diligently the fear of the Lord. Moreover, these Scriptures are equally explicit in saying, that those who are reputed to know the writings of the Scriptures, and who hear the prophecies, have no understanding. And when I hear, Trypho," said I, "that **Perseus** was begotten of a virgin, I understand that the deceiving serpent counterfeited also this."[81]

And in another place, he said,

"And when we say also that the Word, who is the first-birth of God, was produced without sexual union, and that He, Jesus Christ, our Teacher, was crucified and died, and rose again, and ascended into heaven, we propound nothing different from what you believe regarding those whom you esteem sons of **Jupiter**. For you know how many sons your esteemed writers ascribed to Jupiter: **Mercury**, the interpreting word and teacher of all; **Aesculapius**, who, though he was a great physician, was struck by a thunderbolt, and so ascended to heaven; and **Bacchus** too, after he had been torn limb from limb; and **Hercules**, when he had committed himself to the flames to escape his toils; and the sons of **Leda**, and **Dioscuri**; and **Perseus**, son of **Danae**; and **Bellerophon**, who, though sprung from mortals, rose to heaven on the horse **Pegasus**. For what shall I say of **Ariadne**, and those who,

[81] Martyr, Justin. *The Ante-Nicene Fathers: The First Apology of Justin.* Chapter LXX. Edited by Alexander Roberts, James Donaldson, and Arthur Cleveland Coxe. I. Vol. I. X vols. New York, NY: Cosimo Classics, 2007, 233–234.

like her, have been declared to be set among the stars? And what of the emperors who die among yourselves, whom you deem worthy of deification, and in whose behalf you produce some on who swears he has seen the burning **Caesar** rise to heaven from the funeral pyre? And what kind of deeds are recorded of each of these reputed sons of Jupiter, it is needless to tell to those who already know. This only shall be said, that they are written for the advantage and encouragement of youthful scholars; for all reckon it an honourable thing to imitate the gods. But far be such a thought concerning the gods from every well-conditioned soul, as to believe that Jupiter himself, the governor and creator of all things, was both a parricide and the son of a parricide, and that being overcome by the love of base and shameful pleasures, he came in to **Ganymede** and those many women whom he had violated, and that his sons did like actions. **But, as we said above, wicked devils perpetrated these things**. And we have learned that those only are deified who have lived near to God in holiness and virtue; and we believe that those who live wickedly and do not repent are punished in everlasting fire."[82]

Many atheists and agnostics that love this conspiracy theory of Christianity being a copy of pagan religions seem to believe they make a good case. But it was clear to Justin that these pagan religions were imitations of Christianity and not the other way around. The things that resembled Christianity were actually stolen from the Old

---

[82] Martyr, Justin. *The Ante-Nicene Fathers: The First Apology of Justin.* Chapter XXI. Edited by Alexander Roberts, James Donaldson, and Arthur Cleveland Coxe. I. Vol. I. X vols. New York, NY: Cosimo Classics, 2007, 170.

Testament. This conspiracy theory was debunked in the first and second centuries. This is nothing new. Just an old argument resurfacing in the twenty-first century.

The cult of **Cybele** performed a ritual called "Taurobolium." Joel McDurmon quotes Everett Ferguson who describes it, saying,

> The person receiving the rite entered a deep underground pit that was covered with a wooden lattice work. A garlanded bull was brought to the planks covering the pit and killed with a spear. "The blood ran through the openings and showered the initiate below, who held up his face so that the blood covered it and so that he could drink some. He was then exhibited to the worshipers, who praised him. The rite apparently meant the transfer of the energy of the bull to the person undergoing it or to the one for whom he performed it."[83]

Many have attempted to parallel this to Christian baptism. Now I want to ask the reader, does this heinous and debauched ritual sound like it resembles baptism even a bit? One would have to be intellectually dishonest to claim a parallel here. In the Taurobolium, a person is being showered in blood from a bull. In Christian baptism, one is cleansed by water as a picture of the death, burial, and resurrection of Jesus—or in other words, new life. There is no similarity. And like most of these false religions and rituals, it is a development. Ronald H. Nash explains the development, saying,

> In the first stage of this process (about A.D. 160–250), the taurobolium was primarily a bull-sacrifice in honor of Cybele. Duthoy describes the second stage (about A.D. 228–319) as a period of transition to the third stage.

---

[83] McDurmon, 28.

During this intermediate period, the blood of the bull became increasingly important. The blood was caught in a vessel and given to the dedicator. Duthoy suggests that since the blood came to be associated with the power of purification, the possibility of a Christian influence cannot be ruled out. It was after A.D. 300 that the rite evolved into the blood bath used as a rite of purification.[84]

It was not until the fourth century that the taurobolium began to be viewed as a purification. And the most popular date amongst historians for the first evidence of the taurobolium is AD 160.[85] This would date the taurobolium about one hundred and thirty years after Christian baptism. So who copied who exactly? Looks like, once again, a false religion copied Christianity.

In **Mithraism**, there was a sacred meal of bread and water.[86] Many have tried to make a parallel between this and the Christian communion of bread and wine. However, the date of this sacred meal is far removed from the Christian Lord's Supper. Ronald H. Nash says,

> The sacramental function of the Mithraic ceremony in which initiates ate bread and drank water seems well established. But the major problem with the Mithraic rite is its late date, which precludes its having any influence on Paul. Attempts to find a Dionysiac source for Paul's teaching about the Lord's Supper (1 Cor. 10:14–22; 11:17–34) or the words of Jesus in John 6:53–56 face at least one major obstacle: the chronology is all wrong. As we have seen,

---

[84] Nash, 145.
[85] Nash, 144.
[86] Nash, 149.

many times the belief or practice that is supposed to have influenced first-century Christians is too late; it developed after A.D. 100. In this case, the Dionysiac practice is too early![87]

Evidently, the chronology of the Mithraic meal and the Lord's Supper do not follow. Not to mention, the church fathers rebuked this rite as a satanic imitation of the Lord's Supper. Justin Martyr writing in the second century said,

> Jesus took bread, and when He had given thanks, said, "This do ye in remembrance of Me, this is My body;" and that, after the same manner, having taken the cup and given thanks, He said, "This is My blood;" and gave it to them alone. Which the wicked devils have imitated in the mysteries of Mithras, commanding the same thing to be done. For that bread and a cup of water are placed with certain incantations in the mystic rites of one who is being initiated, you either know or can learn.[88]

Justin recognized that the sacred meal of Mithraism was a satanic imitation of the Lord's Supper.

The Lord's Supper is based on the Old Testament Passover and the manna from heaven which dates to the time of Moses! Shadows to Christian practices can also be seen in other places of the Old Testament like the prophets. This proves indisputably that the Lord's Supper was not derived from pagan religions but rather from the Old Testament!

---

[87] Nash, 141.
[88] Martyr, Justin. *The Ante-Nicene Fathers: The First Apology of Justin.* Chapter LXVI. Edited by Alexander Roberts, James Donaldson, and Arthur Cleveland Coxe. I. Vol. I. X vols. New York, NY: Cosimo Classics, 2007, 185.

Liberal scholarship will go to whatever end possible to discredit the historicity of Jesus. When examined closely apart from atheistic blinders, it is clear that the story of Jesus is unique from these pagan religions and not only that, but the person and work of Jesus is a historical fact (as demonstrated in previous sections) unlike these pagan religions which are myths. Jesus and His story are no myth. The apostle John said,

> **That which was from the beginning, which we have heard, which we have seen with our eyes, which we have looked upon, and our hands have handled, of the Word of life;** [2] **(For the life was manifested, and we have seen it**, and bear witness, and shew unto you that eternal life, which was with the Father, and was manifested unto us;) [3] That which we have seen and heard declare we unto you, that ye also may have fellowship with us: and truly our fellowship is with the Father, and with his Son Jesus Christ. [4] And these things write we unto you, that your joy may be full. (1 John 1:1–4)

The early church had seen Jesus with their own eyes and "handled" Him with their hands. There was no doubt that He was real and that He really died and rose again. Joel McDurmon elaborates,

> We see Peter, for example, urging that, "We have not followed cunningly devised fables…but were *eyewitnesses* of his majesty" (2 Pet. 1:16). The apostle responded to the charge that Christianity was just another myth by referring to a distinct historical event that he had *eyewitnessed*. The New Testament writers always emphasized their physical witness of the Lord (Luke 1:1–3; John 19:35–6; 21:24; 1 Cor. 15:5–8; 2 Pet. 1:16–18; 1 John 1:1–3). By their accounts, the original

Jesus was indeed an historical figure. Likewise, the apostle Paul often speaks of Jesus as the historical person that He was. Paul purposefully warns *against mythology* several times. In fact, the words, "myth" or "fable" (from the Greek word *mythos*) only appear in the New Testament in the context of warning or condemnation (1 Tim. 1:4, 1:14, 4:7; 2 Tim. 4:4; 2 Pet. 1:16).[89]

When examining all the evidence, one can be sure that the story of Jesus was not copied from pagan mystic religions. In fact, these mystic religions often stole from the Bible. The death, burial, and resurrection of Jesus is an attested, historical fact. Jesus is real and Jesus is Lord!

PASCAL'S WAGER

I want to make one last point for the reader to consider. As an atheist/agnostic, what are you risking? We have already seen that atheists/agnostics must give up objectivity and absolute truth, but what else? Let us take the two largest religions, Christianity and Islam, and compare them to atheism/agnosticism. Yes, there are many other religions, but I will just use these two to make a point. If Christianity is right, I go to heaven. If there is really no God, I just cease to exist. If Islam is true, then I go to hell. In math terms, I only have a 33 percent chance of going to hell. Now the atheist/agnostic—since they reject both Christianity and Islam—has a 66 percent chance of going to hell. So by being an atheist/agnostic, not only are you forced into a worldview with no truth, but you also double your chances of going to hell for all eternity. Atheists/agnostics talk to Christians a lot about a "burden of proof," but, my friend, who is the "burden" really on? You have double the chance to go to hell than I do. I have no burden. The burden is on the atheist/agnostic! The Lord Jesus can take that burden from you (Matt. 11:28–30). There cannot be multiple

---

[89] McDurmon, 5–6.

truths. Either one religion is right, or they are all wrong, but they cannot all be right. I choose Christ!

CONCLUSION

I have been friends with many atheists/agnostics and I know most of them are not bad people. In fact, many of them act better than professing Christians. I have a love for these people and desire that they know the love of Jesus and His message. I know how lost I was without Jesus and I want to help others out of that darkness and into the light. I promise you there is more to this life than what we can see. Jesus loves you! I pray for your salvation!

ATHEISM/AGNOSTICISM REFUTED

1. The universe must have an uncaused first cause (God).
2. There is an intelligent design to the universe, pointing to an Intelligent Designer (God).
3. Humans know certain things are objectively right and wrong, necessitating an objective Moral Law Giver (God).
4. The Bible is more reliable/valid than any other historic document in number and antiquity.
5. Suffering is not always a bad thing. Some suffering is a test of faith from God. Other suffering is just a result of sin entering the world. Evil exists because of free will choices made by humans, not because of God.
6. Science necessitates uniformity in nature and uniformity in nature necessitates an Intelligent Designer.
7. Evolution is not science because it cannot be tested and goes against the law of biogenesis. Evolution is a historical question not a scientific one.
8. Evolution is inherently racist because it declares that one race is always inferior (under evolved) to another.
9. The Bible is a first century document that attests to the person and resurrection of Jesus and 1 Corinthians 15:3–5

is accepted even by unbelieving scholars as an early church creed.

10. Historical sources outside the Bible from non-Christians that speak of Jesus: Pliny the Younger, Suetonius, Josephus, Tacitus, Lucian of Samosata, Mara Bar-Serapion, and the Talmud.

11. The Apostles were willing to die for proclaiming the resurrection of Jesus because they truly believed it; they were not lying.

12. Paul and James were both devout Jews who converted to Christianity which proves they truly witnessed the resurrected Jesus.

13. First-century unbelievers spread the rumor that the disciples stole Jesus's body out of His tomb, proving that His tomb was empty.

14. Jesus and Christianity are completely different from pagan religions. Often these pagan religions stole concepts from the Old Testament.

15. Statistically speaking, atheists/agnostics are risking more than religious people.

CHAPTER 3

———— ✑ ————

POLYTHEISM

THE LOGICAL IMPOSSIBILITY
OF POLYTHEISM

The idea that there are multiple gods is not something I have ever genuinely considered, and there are a few reasons why. For one, polytheism is not something common in America. Most people here subscribe to one of the three Abrahamic religions. Secondly, polytheism is illogical. *Merriam-Webster* defines God as "the supreme or ultimate reality: such as: the Being perfect in power, wisdom, and goodness who is worshipped."[90] The main attributes of God are omnipotence (all-powerful), omniscience (all-knowing), and the objective standard of morality (right and wrong). Let us first examine omnipotence. For God to be God, He must be all-powerful. If polytheism is true and there are many gods, they cannot be omnipotent. For example, if there are two gods, each can be powerful, but they cannot be *all-powerful* because they do not have power over each other. If the first god has power over the second, then the second is not all-powerful and thus is not God (and vice versa).

Now let us examine omniscience. If there are two gods, they may both have *almost* all knowledge, but there is one thing they cannot know—the first god cannot know the mind of the second god

———————————

[90] *Merriam-Webster*. God.

(and vice versa). This means they are not omniscient and thus are not God. Or if the two gods somehow did know the mind of the other, they would not be God because nobody can know the mind of God except Himself. Now consider morality. If there are two gods, there can be no objective standard of morality. The first god could disagree with the second god as to what is right or wrong. For example, if the first god says murder is wrong, but the second god says it is right, there is a problem. Since they disagree on morality, there is no objective standard of morality—but God, by definition, must be the objective standard of morality. So with two gods disagreeing on the standard of morality, there are now two objective standards of morality. An objective standard must be absolute. It cannot be absolute if there are multiple standards (in this situation there are two).

Thus, neither god is the objective standard, creating a logical contradiction and impossibility. The early church writer Tertullian wrote around AD 209 against the polytheist Marcion, saying,

> Since then, God is the great Supreme, our *Christian* verity has rightly declared, "God is not, if He is not one." This unique Being, therefore, will be God—not otherwise God than as the great Supreme; and not otherwise the great Supreme than as having no equal; and not otherwise having no equal than as being Unique. Whatever other god, then, you may introduce, you will at least be unable to maintain his divinity under any other guise, than by ascribing to him too the property of Godhead—both eternity and supremacy over all. How, therefore, can two great Supremes co-exist, when this is the attribute of the Supreme Being, to have no equal, an attribute which belongs to One alone, and can by no means exist in two?[91]

---

[91] Tertullian. *The Ante-Nicene Fathers: Against Marcion.* Chapter 3. Edited by Alexander Roberts, James Donaldson, and Arthur Cleveland Coxe. III. Vol. III.

He goes on to say,

> But on what principle did Marcion confine his supreme powers to *two*? I would first ask, If there be two, why not more? Because if *number* be compatible with the substance of Deity, the richer you make it in number the better. Valentinus was more consistent and more liberal; for he, having once imagined two deities, Bythos and Sige, poured forth a swarm of divine essences, a brood of no less than thirty Aeons, like the sow of Aeneas... In short, we feel that reason herself *expressly* forbids the belief in more gods than one, because the self-same rule lays down one God and not two, which declares that God must be a Being to which, as the great Supreme, nothing is equal; and that Being to which nothing is equal must, moreover, be unique."[92]

Tertullian's point is that God, by definition, as the supreme being must be the one and only. If there are multiple, they cannot be properly called God!

One other thing I want to address is the uniformity in nature. In many polytheistic religions, the gods control different parts of nature. For example, there is a god of the trees and the god of water and the god of fire and the god of thunder, etc. If this theology is true, there can be no uniformity in nature. Many polytheists believe that if they upset these gods of nature, they will be punished. If they please the gods, they will reward them. For example, if you upset the sun god, maybe he would decide to not shine any longer. The moon only shines half the day, so that means during the time that is supposed to be day, there will be no light whatsoever—not even the bit

X vols. New York, NY: Cosimo Classics, 2007, 273.
[92] Tertullian. *The Ante-Nicene Fathers: Against Marcion.* Chapter V. Edited by Alexander Roberts, James Donaldson, and Arthur Cleveland Coxe. III. Vol. III. X vols. New York, NY: Cosimo Classics, 2007, 274.

we get from the moon. This would mean half the day it would not just be dark; it would be pitch black and nobody could see anything. This would mean there is no uniformity in nature. But since we know this cannot happen, there cannot be multiple gods.

MORAL PROBLEMS

Besides the logical impossibilities of polytheism, there are major moral problems. One major example is that of Hinduism—the largest polytheistic religion in the world. In Hinduism, one of the major doctrines is karma. Karma has to do with good works. Good works lead to good karma and bad works lead to bad karma. Karma is connected to reincarnation. If a person lives well, they will have good karma and be reincarnated into an elite class of people. If they do not live well, they will be reincarnated at the bottom of the totem pole. This "totem pole" is also known as the caste system. The book *World Religions and Cults 101* says,

> One of the unfortunate effects of the Hindu belief in reincarnation and karma is that it has perpetuated the caste system in India. The only way to move up to a higher caste is to be reincarnated into that caste. And the only way to do that is to be obedient to the rules of the caste you are in. For example, if a Shudra wanted to move up to the level of a Vaisyas, he would have to be a very good Shudra and hope for a promotion in his next life... The reality of karma is that it prevents people from attempting to rise to a higher caste or help members of other castes.[93]

Because of Hinduism's belief about the caste system and reincarnation, people in predominantly Hindu countries will never cease to

---

[93] Bickel, Bruce, and Stan Jantz. *World Religions & Cults 101*. Eugene, OR: Harvest House Publishers, 2002, 156.

be oppressed. To move up in society in your next life (in Hinduism), you must live an obedient life in your current social status. This is the equivalent of telling a black slave in colonial America to be a good, obedient slave to their master, and if they do, they will be reincarnated as a person of higher social status like a slave master. This is ultimately what Hinduism is telling its followers. "Be a good, obedient peasant and when you die and are reincarnated, you will move up in the caste system!"

This is what happens when a society forsakes the objective moral standard of God and does what is right in their own eyes (Judg. 21:25). This is directly related to moral relativism. In polytheistic religions like Hinduism, there are many gods. This means, ultimately, Hindus have a buffet of gods to choose from; whichever ones fit their style, they can choose to worship. This polytheism is ultimately no different from an atheist choosing to do whatever he thinks is subjectively right. There is no objectivity in it. Humans were made to worship so if one does not worship God, they will worship someone or something else. Often, humans worship gods that suit their desires rather than seeking for the God that actually exists. This is the case with polytheism, atheistic moral relativists, and even progressive Christians. The book of Romans says, "Wherefore God also gave them up to uncleanness through the lusts of their own hearts, to dishonour their own bodies between themselves: 25 Who changed the truth of God into a lie, and worshipped and served the creature more than the Creator, who is blessed for ever. Amen" (Rom. 1:24–25). Polytheists worship and serve the creatures rather than the Creator. Isaiah says,

> They that make a graven image are all of them vanity; and their delectable things shall not profit; and they are their own witnesses; they see not, nor know; that they may be ashamed. **10 Who hath formed a god, or molten a graven image that is profitable for nothing?** 11 Behold, all his fellows shall be ashamed: and the workmen, they are of men: let them all be gathered

together, let them stand up; yet they shall fear, and they shall be ashamed together. **¹² The smith with the tongs both worketh in the coals, and fashioneth it with hammers, and worketh it with the strength of his arms**: yea, he is hungry, and his strength faileth: he drinketh no water, and is faint. **¹³** The carpenter stretcheth out his rule; he marketh it out with a line; he fitteth it with planes, and he marketh it out with the compass, and maketh it after the figure of a man, according to the beauty of a man; that it may remain in the house. **¹⁴** He heweth him down cedars, and taketh the cypress and the oak, which he strengtheneth for himself among the trees of the forest: he planteth an ash, and the rain doth nourish it. **¹⁵** Then shall it be for a man to burn: for he will take thereof, and warm himself; yea, he kindleth it, and baketh bread; yea, **he maketh a god, and worshippeth it; he maketh it a graven image, and falleth down thereto**. **¹⁶** He burneth part thereof in the fire; with part thereof he eateth flesh; he roasteth roast, and is satisfied: yea, he warmeth himself, and saith, Aha, I am warm, I have seen the fire: **¹⁷ And the residue thereof he maketh a god, even his graven image: he falleth down unto it, and worshippeth it, and prayeth unto it, and saith, Deliver me; for thou art my god. ¹⁸ They have not known nor understood: for he hath shut their eyes, that they cannot see; and their hearts, that they cannot understand**. **¹⁹** And none considereth in his heart, neither is there knowledge nor understanding to say, I have burned part of it in the fire; yea, also I have baked bread upon the coals thereof; I have roasted flesh, and eaten it: and shall I make the residue thereof an abomination? Shall I fall down to the stock of a tree? [20] He feedeth on ashes: a deceived heart hath turned him aside, that he cannot deliver his soul, nor say, Is there not a lie in my right hand? (Isa. 44:9–20)

Isaiah describes the folly of polytheism/idolatry. People will form an image of something with their hands and then fall down to worship it! How could something you created be your god? A creature is not the Creator by definition! Would a watchmaker praise the watch? Or would the watch praise its maker? The latter makes sense. The former is folly. And so, for many reasons, polytheism cannot be true.

CONCLUSION

Polytheism is not very well known in America, but it is prominent in places like India. It is vital that we send missionaries to evangelize them. We are blessed in America to have a church on every corner, but other places are not that fortunate. We must send help to these polytheistic areas of the world and spread the love and message of Jesus Christ. I pray for their salvation!

POLYTHEISM REFUTED

1. Polytheism is logically impossible because God, by definition, must be omnipotent, omniscient, and the objective moral standard, which is only possible in monotheism.
2. Polytheistic religions like Hinduism lead to moral problems like the caste system because of their beliefs like reincarnation and karma.

CHAPTER 4

⸎

JUDAISM

INTRODUCTION

Judaism is one of the three Abrahamic religions with Christianity and Islam. There are many branches of Judaism, but the main three are Orthodox, Conservative, and Reformed.[94] Jews hold to the inspiration of the Old Testament, known to them as the *Tanakh* and/or *Torah*. Many also look to the *Talmud* and the writings of sages.[95]

IN THE BEGINNING, GOD

Judaism is the oldest religion dating back to the origin of the universe. As it is written, "In the beginning God created the heaven and the earth" (Gen. 1:1). God created the world in six days and rested on the seventh day.[96] God made man (Adam) on the sixth day.[97] God also made woman (Eve) so man would not be alone.[98] While in the Garden of Eden, the serpent came to tempt Eve. Eve

---

[94] Carden, Paul, ed. *World Religions Made Easy*. Peabody, MA: Rose Publishing, 2018, 26.

[95] Carden, Paul, ed. *World Religions Made Easy*. Peabody, MA: Rose Publishing, 2018, 26.

[96] Gen. 1:31, 2:1–3.

[97] Gen. 1:26–28.

[98] Gen. 2:18–25.

gave into the temptation along with Adam.[99] Speaking of this, the New Testament says, "Wherefore, as by one man sin entered into the world, and death by sin; and so death passed upon all men, for that all have sinned" (Rom. 5:12). Because of their sin, death has entered the world and spread to us all. God spoke of the remedy for this problem saying, "And I will put enmity between [the serpent] and the woman, and between thy seed and her seed; it shall bruise thy head, and thou shalt bruise his heel" (Gen. 3:15). This is the first prophecy in the Old Testament of Jesus and how He would crush Satan which He did by resurrecting from the dead.[100]

The fall of man led to the first murder in human history— Cain killing his brother Abel.[101] As sin abounded more and more, the world became exceedingly wicked. The Bible says,

> And God saw that the wickedness of man was great in the earth, and that every imagination of the thoughts of his heart was only evil continually. [6] And it repented the LORD that he had made man on the earth, and it grieved him at his heart. [7] And the LORD said, I will destroy man whom I have created from the face of the earth; both man, and beast, and the creeping thing, and the fowls of the air; for it repenteth me that I have made them. [8] But Noah found grace in the eyes of the LORD. (Gen. 6:5–8)

The world was wicked, and God regretted even creating man. He then decided to destroy all the inhabitants in the earth by a flood and start over. But Noah and his family found grace with God. God told Noah to build an Ark.[102] Noah and his family entered the Ark along with two of every animal to repopulate and seven of every clean

---

[99] Gen. 3:1–6.
[100] Heb. 2:14; 2 Tim. 1:10.
[101] Gen. 4:8.
[102] Gen. 6:14.

animal for food.[103] Genesis reports, "And the flood was forty days upon the earth; and the waters increased, and bare up the ark, and it was lift up above the earth" (Gen. 7:17). It then says,

> And it came to pass in the six hundredth
> and first year, in the first month, the first day
> of the month, the waters were dried up from off
> the earth: and Noah removed the covering of
> the ark, and looked, and, behold, the face of the
> ground was dry. [14] And in the second month, on
> the seven and twentieth day of the month, was
> the earth dried. (Gen. 8:13–14)

After the flood waters dried up, Noah, his family, and the animals left the Ark.[104] Noah and his wife were fruitful and multiplied the earth exceedingly.[105] And yes, Noah's descendants married each other, but it was not a sin at the time. Incest did not become a sin until the time of Moses.[106] At that time on the earth there was only one language.[107] The people joined together and decided to build a tower to reach heaven.[108] Before allowing this to happen, God confused the languages of the people and they scattered throughout the earth.[109] This place is known as "Babel" because God confused the languages.[110] That is why there are so many languages today, instead of one universal language.

God chose a man named Abram (later changed to Abraham)[111] and He promised to bless him and his seed.[112] Abraham's sons were

---

[103] Gen. 7.
[104] Gen. 8:15–19.
[105] Gen. 10.
[106] Lev. 18:6–18.
[107] Gen. 11:1.
[108] Gen. 11:4.
[109] Gen. 11:7–8.
[110] Gen. 11:9.
[111] Gen. 17:5.
[112] Gen. 12:1–3.

Isaac and Ishmael.[113] Isaac's sons were Jacob and Esau.[114] Jacob's name was later changed to Israel.[115] From Israel came the twelve tribes based on his twelve sons: Reuben, Simeon, Levi, Judah, Zebulun, Issachar, Dan, Gad, Asher, Naphtali, Joseph, and Benjamin.[116] These twelve tribes settled in Egypt.[117]

EXODUS AND WANDERING IN THE WILDERNESS

As the tribes of Israel grew in number in Egypt, Pharaoh became worried.[118] He then began to oppress the Israelites, but nonetheless the Israelites continued to grow in number.[119] To prevent this any further, Pharaoh ordered the killing of all male babies.[120] A Levite couple conceived and bore a son.[121] Because of Pharaoh's order to kill all male babies, the woman took her son and put him in a basket in the river.[122] The boy was found by Pharaoh's daughter.[123] He was raised as an Egyptian and named Moses.[124] One day years later, Moses saw a fellow Hebrew being beaten by an Egyptian, so he killed the Egyptian.[125] Moses fled soon after to Midian where he married Zipporah.[126] Meanwhile, the Israelites were being oppressed more and more and God heard their cries remembering His covenant with Abraham, Isaac, and Jacob.[127] God then appeared to Moses in a

---

[113] Gen. 16:15, 21:2.
[114] Gen. 25:21–28.
[115] Gen. 32:28.
[116] Gen. 49:1–28.
[117] Gen. 50:22; Ex. 1:1–6.
[118] Ex. 1:7–10.
[119] Ex. 1:11–14.
[120] Ex. 1:15–16.
[121] Ex. 2:1–2.
[122] Ex. 2:3–4.
[123] Ex. 2:5–9.
[124] Ex. 2:10.
[125] Ex. 2:11–12.
[126] Ex. 2:15–22.
[127] Ex. 2:23–25.

burning bush and revealed His name as "I AM THAT I AM" or just "I AM."[128] God commanded Moses to go to the Israelites and tell them how they would be delivered from bondage.[129]

After much struggling with Pharaoh, he finally let the Israelites go.[130] After the Israelites had left, Pharaoh had a change of heart and decided to pursue after them.[131] Moses, through the power of God, split the Red Sea and the Israelites passed through safely.[132] God then let the waters return and drowned the Egyptians.[133] Later in their journey, God gave the Israelites the famous Ten Commandments which are the following:

1. Thou shalt have no other gods before me. (Ex. 20:3)
2. Thou shalt not make unto thee any graven image. (Ex. 20:4)
3. Thou shalt not take the name of the Lord thy God in vain. (Ex. 20:7)
4. Remember the sabbath day, to keep it holy. (Ex. 20:8)
5. Honour thy father and thy mother. (Ex. 20:12)
6. Thou shalt not kill. (Ex. 20:13)
7. Thou shalt not commit adultery. (Ex. 20:14)
8. Thou shalt not steal. (Ex. 20:15)
9. Thou shalt not bear false witness against thy neighbor. (Ex. 20:16)
10. Thou shalt not covet. (Ex. 20:17)

Or,

1. Thou shalt have no other gods before me. (Ex. 20:3).
2. Thou shalt not take the name of the Lord thy God in vain. (Ex. 20:7).

---

[128] Ex. 3:1–14.
[129] Ex. 3:15–22.
[130] Ex. 13:17.
[131] Ex. 14:5–9.
[132] Ex. 14:21–22.
[133] Ex. 14:26–28.

3. Remember the sabbath day, to keep it holy. (Ex. 20:8).
4. Honour thy father and thy mother. (Ex. 20:12).
5. Thou shalt not kill. (Ex. 20:13).
6. Thou shalt not commit adultery. (Ex. 20:14).
7. Thou shalt not steal. (Ex. 20:15).
8. Thou shalt not bear false witness against thy neighbor. (Ex. 20:16).
9. Thou shalt not covet thy neighbor's wife (Ex. 20:17).
10. Thou shalt not covet thy neighbor's goods. (Ex. 20:17).

Regardless of which numbering method one subscribes to, these Ten Commandments are widely known and have affected the whole world since the day of their institution by God. Throughout the rest of Exodus and Leviticus, God lays out a multitude of laws and practices for the Israelites to follow and/or avoid. As the Israelites were preparing to enter the Promised Land, God told Moses to send spies into the land to assess the situation.[134] The spies came back saying,

> But the men that went up with him said, We be not able to go up against the people; for they are stronger than we. [32] And they brought up an evil report of the land which they had searched unto the children of Israel, saying, The land, through which we have gone to search it, is a land that eateth up the inhabitants thereof; and all the people that we saw in it are men of a great stature. [33] And there we saw the giants, the sons of Anak, which come of the giants: and we were in our own sight as grasshoppers, and so we were in their sight. (Num. 13:31–33)

The spies told the rest of the Israelites how much bigger and stronger the people of the land were and that they would not be able to defeat them. Because of this, the people refused to enter the

[134] Num. 13:1–2.

land.[135] Because of their lack of faith, God became angry and decided He would destroy all the Israelites except Moses and start over.[136] Moses then interceded for the people and God spared their lives.[137] Although He spared them, God still swore that this generation of Israelites would not enter the Promised Land.[138] This chapter says,

> After the number of the days in which ye searched the land, even forty days, each day for a year, shall ye bear your iniquities, even forty years, and ye shall know my breach of promise. [35] I the LORD have said, I will surely do it unto all this evil congregation, that are gathered together against me: in this wilderness they shall be consumed, and there they shall die. (Num. 14:34–35)

Instead of entering the Promised Land, this generation of Israelites would wander in the wilderness for forty years. The New Testament speaks about this, saying,

> For some, when they had heard, did provoke: howbeit not all that came out of Egypt by Moses. [17] But with whom was he grieved forty years? was it not with them that had sinned, whose carcases fell in the wilderness? [18] And to whom sware he that they should not enter into his rest, but to them that believed not? [19] So we see that they could not enter in because of unbelief. (Heb. 3:16–19)

---

[135] Num. 14:1–4.
[136] Num. 14:11–12.
[137] Num. 14:13–20.
[138] Num. 14:21–24.

First Corinthians says,

> Moreover, brethren, I would not that ye
> should be ignorant, how that all our fathers were
> under the cloud, and all passed through the sea;
> [2] And were all baptized unto Moses in the cloud
> and in the sea; [3] And did all eat the same spiri-
> tual meat; [4] And did all drink the same spiritual
> drink: for they drank of that spiritual Rock that
> followed them: and that Rock was Christ. [5] But
> with many of them God was not well pleased: for
> they were overthrown in the wilderness. [6] Now
> these things were our examples, to the intent
> we should not lust after evil things, as they also
> lusted. (1 Cor. 10:1–6)

Later, Moses disobeyed God thus prohibiting himself from
entering the Promised Land as well.[139] In the fortieth year, Moses
gave a speech to the Israelites to the new generation of Israelites to
prepare them to enter the Promised Land.[140] Moses reminded them
that God did not choose them because they were great or righteous,
but simply because of His love and covenant with Abraham, Isaac,
and Jacob.[141] He later warns them of the blessings they would receive
for obedience and curses for disobedience.[142] Since Moses would not
enter the Promised Land, he appointed Joshua to lead the Israelites
into the land.[143] God took Moses up to Mount Nebo to see the
Promised Land, but he still would not be allowed to enter because of
his disobedience.[144] Moses then died there and was buried.[145]

---

[139] Num. 20:12.
[140] Deut. 1–34.
[141] Deut. 7:7–9.
[142] Deut. 28.
[143] Deut. 31:7–8.
[144] Deut. 34:1–4.
[145] Deut. 34:5–6.

ENTERING THE PROMISED LAND

With Moses dead, Joshua led the people into battle. Joshua and the Israelites conquered the Hittites, the Amorites, the Canaanites, the Perizzites, the Hivites, and the Jebusites[146] and thirty-one kings in total.[147] Joshua then distributed the land to each tribe accordingly.[148] The Israelites had finally entered the Promised Land after all these years. By this time, Joshua was old.[149] He made a covenant with the people at Shechem and made one of the most widely known exhortations of all time:

> Now therefore fear the LORD, and serve him
> in sincerity and in truth: and put away the gods
> which your fathers served on the other side of
> the flood, and in Egypt; and serve ye the LORD.
> [15] And if it seems evil unto you to serve the LORD,
> choose you this day whom ye will serve; whether
> the gods which your fathers served that were on
> the other side of the flood, or the gods of the
> Amorites, in whose land ye dwell: but as for me
> and my house, we will serve the LORD. (Josh.
> 24:14–15).

Joshua died soon after.[150]

APOSTASY

With the absence of Joshua, Israel went into major apostasy. The Israelites went into a continuous cycle of disobedience, punishment, repentance, and deliverance. Those who delivered the Israelites were known as Judges. There were seven periods of apostasy and deliver-

---

[146] Josh. 12:8.
[147] Josh. 12:24.
[148] Josh. 13–22.
[149] Josh. 23:1.
[150] Josh. 24:29.

ance. The first period was the judge Othniel.[151] The second period were the judges Ehud and Shamgar.[152] The third period was the judge Deborah.[153] The fourth period was the judge Gideon.[154] The fifth period were the judges Tola and Jair.[155] The sixth period were the judges Jephthah, Ibzan, Elon, and Abdon.[156] The seventh period was the judge Samson.[157] Under the leadership of Moses and Joshua, the Israelites were under direct orders from God. But at this point in history, Israel had ultimately forsaken God. The only time they would return to Him was when they were in trouble. But their hearts were not right or in submission to God.

The book of Judges ends with a clear explanation of why so much wickedness was taking place, "In those days there was no king in Israel: every man did that which was right in his own eyes" (Judg. 21:25). Israel had slipped into moral relativism. Everybody did what they *felt* was right instead of what was actually right. The book of Judges goes to show exactly what happens to a society that forsakes God.

GIVE US A KING

As the Israelites witnessed their downfall, they desired to have a physical king to reign over them like the other nations.[158] God felt disrespected by their desire for a physical king, but He granted their wish anyway and gave them Saul as king[159] followed by the beloved king David.[160] As David advanced in age, his son Adonijah claimed succession.[161] But David had chosen his son Solomon to succeed

---

[151] Judg. 3:7–11.
[152] Judg. 3:12–31.
[153] Judg. 4:1–5:31.
[154] Judg. 6:1–8:32.
[155] Judg. 8:33–10:5.
[156] Judg. 10:6–12:15.
[157] Judg. 13:1–16:31.
[158] 1 Sam. 8:4–22.
[159] 1 Sam. 10:17–27.
[160] 2 Sam. 5:1–5.
[161] 1 Kings 1:5.

him.[162] Solomon was then crowned as the king.[163] With the passing of Solomon, his son Rehoboam came to the throne.[164] A man named Jeroboam and company came to Rehoboam saying, "Thy father made our yoke grievous: now therefore make thou the grievous service of thy father, and his heavy yoke which he put upon us, lighter, and we will serve thee" (1 Kings 12:4). Rehoboam took some time to think about their request. The elders told Rehoboam to grant their request.[165] Instead of heeding their counsel, Rehoboam went to his young friends for advice, and they told him not to grant the request of Jeroboam and company.[166] Rehoboam then told Jeroboam and company that he would not grant their request.[167] Because of this, Jeroboam and the rest of Israel rebelled against the House of David.[168] From that day forward, Israel split in two—Judah and Israel.[169] Eventually, both Israel and Judah went into captivity.[170] The Jews went from thriving under the rule of the God of the universe to being servants to foreign nations.

WHO WILL DELIVER ISRAEL?

While they were eventually allowed to return to their land,[171] the Israelites never returned to their glory. Malachi was the last prophet of the Israelites and he spoke around the fifth century BC.[172] Malachi said, "Behold, I will send my messenger, and he shall prepare the way before me: and the Lord, whom ye seek, shall suddenly come to his temple, even the messenger of the covenant, whom ye delight in: behold, he shall come, saith the LORD of hosts" (Mal. 3:1). Chapter

---

[162] 1 Kings 1:30.
[163] 1 Kings 1:38–40.
[164] 1 Kings 12:1.
[165] 1 Kings 12:7.
[166] 1 Kings 12:10–11.
[167] 1 Kings 12:12–14.
[168] 1 Kings 12:16–20.
[169] 1 Kings 12:20.
[170] 2 Kings 17–25.
[171] Ezra; Neh.; Hag.
[172] Mal. 1–4.

4 says, "Behold, I will send you Elijah the prophet before the coming of the great and dreadful day of the LORD: ⁶And he shall turn the heart of the fathers to the children, and the heart of the children to their fathers, lest I come and smite the earth with a curse" (Mal. 4:5–6). Malachi prophesied about a messenger that would come as Elijah and prepare the way for God.

After this final prophecy of Malachi, there is what is widely known as the four hundred silent years. In other words, for about four hundred years there were no prophets. The Israelites knew that a period like this with no communication from God was a sign of judgment. All throughout the history of Israel, the prophets spoke of a day in which somebody would come to deliver the Jews and restore their kingdom. This somebody is the messiah. The question is, who is the messiah?

HISTORICITY OF JESUS

Some Jews will take the skeptic stance that Jesus never existed. In this theory, Jesus was just a made-up legend that passed on. History and scholarship are not in favor of this theory. Since I am addressing Jews, I will quote from a Jewish source—Josephus. Josephus was a Jewish historian born within five years of Jesus's death. He wrote in *The Antiquities of the Jews* saying,

> Now, there was about this time Jesus, a wise man, if it be lawful to call him a man, for he was a doer of wonderful works—a teacher of such men as receive the truth with pleasure. He drew over to him both many of the Jews, and many of the Gentiles. He was [the] Christ; and when Pilate, at the suggestion of the principal men amongst us, had condemned him to the cross, those that loved him at the first did not forsake him, for he appeared to them alive again the third day, as the divine prophets had foretold these and ten thousand other wonderful things concerning him;

and the tribe of Christians, so named from him, are not extinct at this day.[173]

He mentioned Jesus again when speaking about His brother James:

> Festus was now dead, and Albinus was but upon the road; so he assembled the Sanhedrin of judges, and brought before them the brother of Jesus, who was called Christ, whose name was James, and some others, [or, some of his companions]; and when he had formed an accusation against them as breakers of the law, he delivered them to be stoned.[174]

It is clear that Jesus was not a created story or something of the sort, but rather He was a real person who lived and walked this Earth. After establishing His historicity, the question shifts to who He was. To see a full examination of the historical sources of Jesus, see the section titled "Extra-Biblical Historical Sources for the Resurrection of Jesus" in the "Atheism/Agnosticism" chapter.

PROPHECIES

One of the most compelling pieces of evidence for Jesus being the Messiah is all the Old Testament prophecies He fulfilled. Here is a list:

Gen. 3:15→Rom. 16:20; Gal. 4:4; Rev. 12:9, 17
Gen. 12:3→Acts 3:24–26
Gen. 22:1–18→John 3:16, Heb. 11:17–19

---

[173] Josephus, Flavius. Josephus: The Complete Works. Translated by Whiston William. Nashville, TN: Thomas Nelson Inc., 1998, 576.
[174] Josephus, 645.

Gen. 49:10➔Matt. 2:6, 11; Rom. 1:5, 15:18, 16:26; Heb. 7:14; Rev. 5:5

Ex. 12:1–51➔John 1:29, 36, 19:33, 36; 1 Cor. 5:7–8; 1 Pet. 1:19

Num. 21:6–9➔John 3:14–18

Num. 24:17➔Matt. 2:2, Rev. 22:16

Deut. 18:15–19➔Matt. 13:57, 21:46; Luke 24:19; John 1:21, 25, 6:14, 7:40; Acts 3:22, 7:37

Ruth 4:4–9➔Luke 1:50, 58, 68, 72, 78; 1 Pet. 1:18; Heb. 2:11

2 Sam. 7:12–16➔Matt. 1:1, Luke 1:32–33, Acts 15:15–16, Heb. 1:5

Ps. 2:1–12➔Mark 1:11; Luke 3:22; Acts 4:25–28, 13:33; Heb. 1:5, 5:5

Ps. 22:1–31➔Matt. 27:39, 43–44, 46; Mark 15:34; John 19:24; Heb. 2:12

Ps. 69➔Matt. 27:33–34; John 2:17, 15:25; Acts 1:20; Rom. 11:9–10, 15:1–3

Ps. 110:1–4➔Matt. 22:4–45; Mark 12:35–37; Luke 20:41–44; Acts 2:34–36; 1 Cor. 15:25–28; Heb. 1:3, 13, 4:14–5:10

Ps. 118:22–24➔Matt. 21:42, Mark 12:10–11, Luke 20:17–18, Acts 4:9–12, Eph. 2:20, 1 Pet. 2:6–8

Ps. 118:25–29➔Matt. 21:9, Mark 11:9–10, Luke 13:35, 19:38, John 12:13

Is. 7:14➔Matt. 1:22–23, Luke 1:31–35

Is. 9:1–2➔Matt. 4:13–16, Luke 1:76–79

Is. 9:6–7➔Luke 1:32–33, 79; John 6:51, 14:27; Acts 10:36; Rom. 9:5

Is. 11:1➔Matt. 2:23

Is. 35:5–6➔Matt. 11:4–6, Luke 7:20–23

Is. 40:3–5➔Matt. 3:1–3; Mark 1:1–3; Luke 1:76, 3:1–6, 7:27; John 1:22–23

Is. 42:1–7➔Matt. 12:15–18, Luke 2:27–32, John 8:12

Is. 52:13–53:12➔Matt. 8:16–17, 20:28, 26:28, 27:59–60; Mark 10:45, 14:24; Luke 22:20; John 12:37–

38; Acts 8:32–35; Rom. 10:16, Heb. 9:28; 1 Pet. 2:21–25

Is. 61:1–2➔Luke 4:17–21

Jer. 31:15➔Matt. 2:16–18

Dan. 7:13–14➔Matt. 9:6, 12:8, 13:41, 16:13, 27; Mark 8:31, Luke 6:22, 9:22; John 1:51, 3:13–14; Acts 7:56

Dan. 9:24–27➔Matt. 24:15–16, Mark 13:14–15, Gal. 4:4

Hos. 11:1➔Matt. 2:13–15

Mic. 5:2➔Matt. 2:1–6, John 7:40–43

Zech. 9:9➔Matt. 21:1–7

Zech. 11:12–13➔Matt. 26:14–15, 27:3, 9–10

Zech. 12:10➔Matt. 24:30, John 19:31–37, Rev. 1:7

Mal. 3:1➔Matt. 11:10, Mark 1:2, Luke 1:76

Mal. 4:5–6➔Matt. 11:14–15, 16:14, 17:9–13; Mark 6:14–16, 9:11–13; Luke 1:16–17; John 1:21

ISAIAH 53

Who hath believed our report? and to whom is the arm of the LORD revealed? ² For he shall grow up before him as a tender plant, and as a root out of a dry ground: he hath no form nor comeliness; and when we shall see him, there is no beauty that we should desire him. ³ He is despised and rejected of men; a man of sorrows, and acquainted with grief: and we hid as it were our faces from him; he was despised, and we esteemed him not. ⁴ Surely he hath borne our griefs, and carried our sorrows: yet we did esteem him stricken, smitten of God, and afflicted. ⁵ But he was wounded for our transgressions, he was bruised for our iniquities: the chastisement of our peace was upon him; and with his stripes we are healed. ⁶ All we like sheep have gone astray;

we have turned every one to his own way; and the LORD hath laid on him the iniquity of us all. [7] He was oppressed, and he was afflicted, yet he opened not his mouth: he is brought as a lamb to the slaughter, and as a sheep before her shearers is dumb, so he openeth not his mouth. [8] He was taken from prison and from judgment: and who shall declare his generation? for he was cut off out of the land of the living: for the transgression of my people was he stricken. [9] And he made his grave with the wicked, and with the rich in his death; because he had done no violence, neither was any deceit in his mouth. [10] Yet it pleased the LORD to bruise him; he hath put him to grief: when thou shalt make his soul an offering for sin, he shall see his seed, he shall prolong his days, and the pleasure of the LORD shall prosper in his hand. [11] He shall see of the travail of his soul, and shall be satisfied: by his knowledge shall my righteous servant justify many; for he shall bear their iniquities. [12] Therefore will I divide him a portion with the great, and he shall divide the spoil with the strong; because he hath poured out his soul unto death: and he was numbered with the transgressors; and he bare the sin of many, and made intercession for the transgressors. (Isa. 53:1–12)

The question comes down to who is this suffering servant in Isaiah 53? This chapter is clearly talking about Jesus.

Who hath believed our report? and to whom is the arm of the LORD revealed? [2] For he shall grow up before him as a tender plant, and as a root out of a dry ground: he hath no form nor comeliness; and when we shall see him, there is no beauty that we should desire him. [3] He is despised and rejected of men; a man of sorrows, and acquainted with grief: and we hid as it were our faces from him; he was despised, and we esteemed him not. [4] Surely he hath borne our griefs, and carried our sorrows: yet we did esteem him stricken, smitten of God, and afflicted. (Isa. 53:1–4)

This suffering servant was not believed. John chapter 1 says Jesus was rejected by His own people (John 1:10–11). Verse 1 was directly fulfilled in John 12:37–38. This passage also speaks of the appearance of Jesus. There was nothing special about His looks or His stature. This is reflected by the responses the people had to Jesus's words. For example,

And it came to pass, that when Jesus had finished these parables, he departed thence. [54] And when he was come into his own country, he taught them in their synagogue, insomuch that they were astonished, and said, Whence hath this man this wisdom, and these mighty works? [55] Is not this the carpenter's son? is not his mother called Mary? and his brethren, James, and Joses, and Simon, and Judas? [56] And his sisters, are they not all with us? Whence then hath this man all these things? [57] And they were offended in him. But Jesus said unto them, A prophet is not without honour, save in his own country, and in his own house. (Matt. 13:53–57)

The people saw Jesus as a nobody so when He began teaching, they were offended. It would be the equivalent to a peasant trying to teach a group of people. The people would not give him credibility nor the time of day. This passage also says that the servant was a "man of sorrows, and acquainted with grief." We see Jesus being sorrowful when He cried over Lazarus's death (John 11:35). We see this again when He was moved with compassion for the people (Matt. 14:14). Another example is prior to His death, "He went a little farther and fell on His face, and prayed, saying, "O My Father, if it is possible, let this cup pass from Me; nevertheless, not as I will, but as You will" (Matt. 26:39). Jesus was grieved over the death He would die, nonetheless He submitted to the Father's will.

> But he was wounded for our transgressions, he was bruised for our iniquities: the chastisement of our peace was upon him; and with his stripes we are healed. ⁶ All we like sheep have gone astray; we have turned every one to his own way; and the LORD hath laid on him the iniquity of us all… ⁸ He was taken from prison and from judgment: and who shall declare his generation? for he was cut off out of the land of the living: for the transgression of my people was he stricken. (Isa. 53:5–6, 8)

This passage says the servant was "bruised for our iniquities." When it says "our" it is speaking of God's people. Jesus is the servant discussed in this passage since we know that He died on the cross for the sins (iniquities) of the world (1 John 2:1–2). Verse 8 also speaks of an atonement. It says the servant was stricken for the transgressions of the people. Jesus was stricken for the transgressions of the world.

"He was oppressed, and he was afflicted, yet he opened not his mouth: he is brought as a lamb to the slaughter, and as a sheep before her shearers is dumb, so he openeth not his mouth" (Isa. 53:7).

This servant was oppressed and afflicted. While He was being oppressed, He did not open His mouth. While being led to death, He did not open His mouth. Jesus fulfilled this:

> Then Pilate therefore took Jesus, and scourged him. ² And the soldiers platted a crown of thorns, and put it on his head, and they put

on him a purple robe, ³And said, Hail, King of the Jews! and they smote him with their hands. ⁴Pilate therefore went forth again, and saith unto them, Behold, I bring him forth to you, that ye may know that I find no fault in him. ⁵Then came Jesus forth, wearing the crown of thorns, and the purple robe. And Pilate saith unto them, Behold the man! ⁶When the chief priests therefore and officers saw him, they cried out, saying, Crucify him, crucify him. Pilate saith unto them, Take ye him, and crucify him: for I find no fault in him. ⁷The Jews answered him, We have a law, and by our law he ought to die, because he made himself the Son of God. ⁸When Pilate therefore heard that saying, he was the more afraid; ⁹And went again into the judgment hall, and saith unto Jesus, Whence art thou? But Jesus gave him no answer. ¹⁰Then saith Pilate unto him, Speakest thou not unto me? knowest thou not that I have power to crucify thee, and have power to release thee? (John 19:1–10)

Jesus was being "oppressed" and "afflicted" when He was being scourged and stricken. He was being led to death because He was being led to His crucifixion. Jesus did not open His mouth at the end of the passage when Pilate was questioning Him. That is a direct fulfillment.

"And he made his grave with the wicked, and with the rich in his death; because he had done no violence, neither was any deceit in his mouth" (Isa. 53:9).

This servant's grave was with the wicked. We know Jesus was crucified next to two criminals—two of the wicked (Matt. 27:38). We know Jesus "had done no violence" and there was no "deceit in His mouth" because Pontius Pilate admitted it (Matt. 27:21–26).

Yet it pleased the LORD to bruise him; he hath put him to grief: when thou shalt make his soul an offering for sin, he shall see his seed, he shall prolong his days, and the pleasure of the LORD shall prosper in his hand. [11] He shall see of the travail of his soul, and shall be satisfied: by his knowledge shall my righteous servant justify many; for he shall bear their iniquities. [12] Therefore will I divide him a portion with the great, and he shall divide the spoil with the strong; because he hath poured out his soul unto death: and he was numbered with the transgressors; and he bare the sin of many, and made intercession for the transgressors. (Isa. 53:10–12)

Once again, this speaks of an atonement. This suffering servant "shall bear their iniquities." It also says that this servant is "an offering for sin." It is so clear that this describes the sacrifice and atonement of Jesus on the cross (Matt. 20:28). Some object that this cannot be Jesus because it speaks in the past tense saying, "He bore the sin of many." This is worded as something that has already happened and we know that Jesus was not born until hundreds of years after Isaiah was written. This must mean it cannot be speaking of Jesus, right? Wrong. One must remember that God is outside of time.

Everything that is future to us, has already occurred for Him. He foreknows all things. So even if it is in the future, it's as if it already happened for God. In fact, Revelation says Jesus was slain before the foundation of the world (Rev. 13:8). How could Jesus be slain if He had not even been incarnated yet? Like stated previously, future events are already complete in the mind of God. God is outside of time. This is the same thing we see in Isaiah 53.

THE ISSUE OF ATONEMENT

In the Old Testament, the Jews had to sacrifice animals to atone for their sins. God explained the reasoning for this saying, "For the life of the flesh is in the blood: and I have given it to you upon the altar to make an atonement for your souls: for it is the blood that maketh atonement for the soul" (Lev. 17:11). Blood atones for sin. There is one problem. The Jewish temple where the sacrifices took place was destroyed in AD 70. What does this mean? This means for the past about 1900 years, the Jews have had no atonement for their sins. This theological problem does not exist for the Christian because we believe Jesus is the once and for all, final sacrifice for sins. We are no longer required to sacrifice animals for our sins, because the lamb of God (Jesus) sacrificed Himself and atoned for our sins. Hebrews says,

> And almost all things are by the law purged with blood; and without shedding of blood is no remission. [23] It was therefore necessary that the patterns of things in the heavens should be purified with these; but the heavenly things themselves with better sacrifices than these. [24] For Christ is not entered into the holy places made with hands, which are the figures of the true; but into heaven itself, now to appear in the presence of God for us: [25] Nor yet that he should offer himself often, as the high priest entereth into the holy place every year with blood of others; [26] For then must he often have suffered since the foundation of the world: but now once in the end of the world hath he appeared to put away sin by the sacrifice of himself. [27] And as it is appointed unto men once to die, but after this the judgment: [28] So Christ was once offered to bear the sins of many; and unto them that look for him shall he appear the second time without sin unto salvation. (Heb. 9:22–28)

If there is no shedding of blood, there is no forgiveness of sins. That is what is said in the Old Testament as well (Lev. 17:11). The priests had to make offerings for sin multiple times, but Jesus offered Himself once and for all. That is why Jesus had to be offered and why the Jews would still have a theological problem even if they did still offer animal sacrifices:

> For the law having a shadow of good things to come, and not the very image of the things, can never with those sacrifices which they offered year by year continually make the comers thereunto perfect. ² For then would they not have ceased to be offered? Because that the worshippers once purged should have had no more conscience of sins. ³ But in those sacrifices there is a remembrance again made of sins every year. ⁴ For it is not possible that the blood of bulls and of goats should take away sins. (Heb. 10:1–4)

These animal sacrifices were just a shadow of things to come; a foreshadowing of the sacrifice of Jesus. The author of Hebrews makes a very simple argument. He explains that it is obvious animal sacrifices could never atone for sins because if they did, they would not need to be continuously offered. Animal sacrifices cannot take away sins.

> And every priest standeth daily ministering and offering oftentimes the same sacrifices, which can never take away sins: ¹² But this man, after he had offered one sacrifice for sins for ever, sat down on the right hand of God; ¹³ From henceforth expecting till his enemies be made his footstool. ¹⁴ For by one offering he hath perfected for ever them that are sanctified. ¹⁵ Whereof the Holy Ghost also is a witness to us: for after that he had said before, ¹⁶ This is the covenant that I will make with them after those days, saith the Lord, I will put my laws into their hearts, and in their minds will I write them; ¹⁷ And their sins and iniquities will I remember no more. ¹⁸ Now

where remission of these is, there is no more offering for sin. (Heb. 10:11–18).

The animal sacrifices were imperfect, evident by them having to be repeated. The sacrifice of Jesus can perfect sinners because He was perfect (1 John 3:5). The author of Hebrews then explains Jesus's sacrifice is the fulfillment of the promised new covenant:

> Behold, the days come, saith the LORD, that I will make a new covenant with the house of Israel, and with the house of Judah: ³² Not according to the covenant that I made with their fathers in the day that I took them by the hand to bring them out of the land of Egypt; which my covenant they brake, although I was an husband unto them, saith the LORD: ³³ But this shall be the covenant that I will make with the house of Israel; After those days, saith the LORD, I will put my law in their inward parts, and write it in their hearts; and will be their God, and they shall be my people. ³⁴ And they shall teach no more every man his neighbour, and every man his brother, saying, Know the LORD: for they shall all know me, from the least of them unto the greatest of them, saith the LORD: for I will forgive their iniquity, and I will remember their sin no more. (Jer. 31:31–34)

This prophecy has been fulfilled through Jesus. It says the law will be in the peoples' hearts. How does the Jew explain this? The Christian explains this through the Holy Spirit. The Spirit indwells each believer and leads them into all truth; He leads them in God's law (John 14:16–17, 26, 16:13).

THE PLURALITY OF GOD IN
THE OLD TESTAMENT

One of the biggest stumbling blocks for Jews (and other religions) regarding Christianity is the Trinity. The doctrine of the Trinity says there are three persons that make up one God. These three persons are the Father, the Son (Jesus), and the Holy Spirit. The word *trinity* is not found in the Bible, but it is a word used to describe the Godhead found in the Bible. The Trinity doctrine is a logical deduction from the truths of the Scripture. All you must do is put the pieces together to arrive at the doctrine of the Trinity. Here are the pieces:

1. The Father is God (Eph. 6:23).
2. The Son (Jesus) is God (Heb. 1:8–9).
3. The Holy Spirit is God (Acts 5:1–4).
4. There is only one God (Deut. 6:4).

Now we must put the pieces together. If there is only one God, yet three persons are identified as God, they must be one. Thus, we can conclude that God consists of three persons: Father, Son, and Holy Spirit. There is no way around the doctrine of the Trinity. Many try to reject it, but any true study of Scripture will lead you to the doctrine.

In the first verse of the whole Bible, Genesis 1:1, the Hebrew word *Elohim* is used for God. The interesting thing about the word "Elohim" is that it is plural. How can God be plural? The Jew will have problems answering this, but the Christian can explain this easily because we already believe in God as a plurality; it is called the Trinity. Later in the first chapter of Genesis, God speaks in the plural: "And God said, Let us make man in our image, after our likeness: and let them have dominion over the fish of the sea, and over the fowl of the air, and over the cattle, and over all the earth, and over every creeping thing that creepeth upon the earth" (Gen. 1:26).

God refers to Himself as "us." Who is "us"? Why is God speaking in the plural? Once again, the Christian can make sense of this.

This is the Trinity in action. The three persons of the Godhead communicate with each other. We see this in John, "But that the world may know that I love the Father; and as the Father gave me commandment, even so I do. Arise, let us go hence" (John 14:31). In this verse, we can see Jesus's relationship with His Father. This is shown again a little later in John during Jesus's prayer to His Father, "And now, O Father, glorify thou me with thine own self with the glory which I had with thee before the world was" (John 17:5). It is evident that the persons of the Godhead have a relationship with one another and always have. The Christian can easily explain why God refers to Himself as a plural. Continuing in Genesis,

> And the LORD appeared unto him in the plains of Mamre: and he sat in the tent door in the heat of the day; ² And he lift up his eyes and looked, and, lo, three men stood by him: and when he saw them, he ran to meet them from the tent door, and bowed himself toward the ground, ³ And said, My LORD, if now I have found favour in thy sight, pass not away, I pray thee, from thy servant:… ²²And the men turned their faces from thence, and went toward Sodom: but Abraham stood yet before the LORD. (Gen. 18:1–3, 22)

The very first sentence of this passage poses a major problem for the Jew. How can God appear to somebody if the Scripture says nobody can see God and live (Exod. 33:20)? The Christian can explain this easily. Jesus appeared to Abraham. The Bible says about Jesus, "Who is the image of the invisible God, the firstborn of every creature" (Col. 1:15). God is a Spirit (John 4:24), and Jesus makes God known (John 1:18). In the gospel of John, Philip wanted to know how he could see the Father. The passage says,

> Philip saith unto him, Lord, show us the Father, and it sufficeth us. ⁹ Jesus saith unto him, Have I been so long time with you, and yet hast

thou not known me, Philip? he that hath seen
me hath seen the Father; and how sayest thou
then, Show us the Father? [10] Believest thou not
that I am in the Father, and the Father in me?
the words that I speak unto you I speak not of
myself: but the Father that dwelleth in me, he
doeth the works. [11] Believe me that I am in the
Father, and the Father in me: or else believe me
for the very works' sake. (John 14:8–11)

When Philip asked to see the Father, Jesus said to see Him was
to see the Father. This explains the principle of Colossians 1:15.
Verse 22 of Genesis eighteen says two of the men that appeared to
Abraham went away, yet Abraham still stood before the LORD. This
means God was with Abraham in the form of a man. What religion
speaks of a God-Man? That would be Christianity and that God-
Man would be Jesus Christ. Jesus is God and He *became* flesh (John
1:1, 14). This explains how He is God and Man at the same time.
God appeared in the form of a man to Jacob as well:

And Jacob was left alone; and there wrestled a man with him until the breaking of the
day. [25] And when he saw that he prevailed not
against him, he touched the hollow of his thigh;
and the hollow of Jacob's thigh was out of joint,
as he wrestled with him. [26] And he said, Let me
go, for the day breaketh. And he said, I will not
let thee go, except thou bless me. [27] And he said
unto him, What is thy name? And he said, Jacob.
[28] And he said, Thy name shall be called no more
Jacob, but Israel: for as a prince hast thou power
with God and with men, and hast prevailed.
[29] And Jacob asked him, and said, Tell me, I pray
thee, thy name. And he said, Wherefore is it that
thou dost ask after my name? And he blessed him
there. [30] And Jacob called the name of the place

Peniel: for I have seen God face to face, and my
life is preserved. (Gen. 32:24–30)

In this passage, a Man wrestled with Jacob. After the struggle,
the Man renames Jacob to "Israel" and gives the reason that Jacob
struggled with God. What is interesting is that Jacob knew no man
could see God and live as echoed in Exodus 33:20. In fact, the last
verse of this passage reveals that Jacob was shocked to have survived
the encounter. This poses a question. How did Jacob see God and
live? It is simple for the Christian. Jacob saw Jesus, who is the image
of the invisible God. Many people saw Jesus all throughout His life.
Jesus can be looked upon, but the Father cannot. In the nineteenth
chapter of Genesis, it says, "Then the LORD rained upon Sodom
and upon Gomorrah brimstone and fire from the LORD out of
heaven" (Gen. 19:24). This verse says God rained fire and brimstone
"from the LORD out of heaven."

This fits perfectly with Christian theology since we believe God
the Father sits in the heavens and Jesus is the person of the Godhead
that appeared to people in time past. This passage clearly shows Jesus
raining fire and brimstone from the Father. The Jewish idea of the
Godhead cannot explain how there are two LORDs spoken of. This
is not the only passage that speaks of two LORDs. Psalm 110 says,
"The LORD said unto my Lord, Sit thou at my right hand, until I
make thine enemies thy footstool" (Ps. 110:1). How are there two
Lords? On the surface this might seem like polytheism—that is unless
you adopt the Christian concept of the Godhead called the Trinity.
Jesus explains this verse is speaking of Himself (Matt. 22:41–46).

Psalm 45 says, "Thy throne, O God, is for ever and ever: the
sceptre of thy kingdom is a right sceptre. Thou lovest righteousness,
and hatest wickedness: therefore God, thy God, hath anointed thee
with the oil of gladness above thy fellows" (Ps. 45:6–7). Once again,
the Hebrew Bible speaks of two different persons called God. How
does the Jew explain this? Who is the second person being called
God? For the Christian, this is obviously speaking of Jesus. The
author of Hebrews acknowledges that this second person called God
is Jesus as well (Heb. 1:1–9).

CONCLUSION

I love Jews. In fact, I love them so much that I worship one—Jesus Christ. The Jews were blessed with the covenants, the law, the adoption, etc. (Rom. 9:4). But because of their disobedience, the Gentiles have been grafted into the family of God (Rom. 11:32). The Jews are patiently waiting on their Messiah to come, but I am here to tell them, He has already come. His name is Jesus Christ. One must not think their ethnicity will save them from their sins. As the Scripture says,

> For circumcision verily profiteth, if thou keep the law: but if thou be a breaker of the law, thy circumcision is made uncircumcision. [26] Therefore if the uncircumcision keep the righteousness of the law, shall not his uncircumcision be counted for circumcision? [27] And shall not uncircumcision which is by nature, if it fulfil the law, judge thee, who by the letter and circumcision dost transgress the law? [28] For he is not a Jew, which is one outwardly; neither is that circumcision, which is outward in the flesh: [29] But he is a Jew, which is one inwardly; and circumcision is that of the heart, in the spirit, and not in the letter; whose praise is not of men, but of God. (Rom. 2:25–29)

A true Jew is one inwardly. A true Jew is one who follows the Jewish Messiah—Jesus. Being an ethnic Jew profits nothing if one lives wrong. Everybody, Jew or Gentile, needs the atonement of Jesus. That is why John the Baptist said to the Jews:

> Bring forth therefore fruits meet for repentance: [9] And think not to say within yourselves, We have Abraham to our father: for I say unto you, that God is able of these stones to raise up

children unto Abraham. [10] And now also the axe is laid unto the root of the trees: therefore every tree which bringeth not forth good fruit is hewn down, and cast into the fire. [11] I indeed baptize you with water unto repentance. but he that cometh after me is mightier than I, whose shoes I am not worthy to bear: he shall baptize you with the Holy Ghost, and with fire: [12] Whose fan is in his hand, and he will thoroughly purge his floor, and gather his wheat into the garner; but he will burn up the chaff with unquenchable fire. (Matt. 3:8–12)

John the Baptist told the Jews to bear fruits. It does not matter if a person is born a Jew or not. All people must repent and turn to Jesus. For everybody, Jew or Gentile, will be judged according to their works. For there is no partiality with God (Rom. 2:5–11). Jesus—God in the flesh—is the only way to heaven (John 14:6, Acts 4:12). Christianity is not a new religion. Christianity is New Covenant Judaism. Christianity is the *fulfillment* of Judaism. Christianity is the fulfillment of the promised new covenant in Jeremiah 31:31–34. The promises for Israel have been given to the true Israel of God—which is the Church (Gal. 6:16).

JUDAISM REFUTED

1. After the Jews' downfall, the prophets spoke of a redeemer to bring them back to glory (the Messiah). Jesus fits this description.
2. Jesus is historically attested by not only Christian and pagan sources, but also Jewish sources themselves (like Josephus).
3. Jesus fulfilled hundreds of prophecies from the Old Testament.
4. Jesus fits the description perfectly of the Suffering Servant in Isaiah 53.

5. Without the shedding of blood there is no atonement (Lev. 17:11). Without animal sacrifices in the temple, Jews have no atonement. This is because the once and for all sacrifice (shedding of blood) was Jesus on the cross (Heb. 10:10).
6. The Old Testament speaks of God in the plural (Gen. 1:26, Ps. 110:1, etc.) This can only be explained by the Christian doctrine of the Trinity.

CHAPTER 5

JOHN THE BAPTIST TO THE
FOUNDING OF ISLAM

THE BIRTH OF JOHN THE BAPTIST

A priest named Zacharias was married to a woman named Elizabeth who was barren.[175] One day, the angel Gabriel appeared to him and told him Elizabeth would bear a son named John.[176] The angel also said, "And he shall go before him in the spirit and power of Elias, to turn the hearts of the fathers to the children, and the disobedient to the wisdom of the just; to make ready a people prepared for the Lord" (Luke 1:17). Recall the last prophecies the Israelites had been given through the prophet Malachi, "Behold, I will send my messenger, and he shall prepare the way before me: and the Lord, whom ye seek, shall suddenly come to his temple, even the messenger of the covenant, whom ye delight in: behold, he shall come, saith the LORD of hosts" (Mal. 3:1).

Malachi also said, "Behold, I [God] will send you Elijah the prophet before the coming of the great and dreadful day of the LORD: 6 And he shall turn the heart of the fathers to the children, and the heart of the children to their fathers, lest I come and smite the earth

---

[175] Luke 1:5–7.
[176] Luke 1:11–13.

with a curse" (Mal. 4:5–6). This "messenger" is identified as John the Baptist in the New Testament.[177] After four hundred years of silence, the prophesied "Elijah" had finally come onto the scene. The conception of John the Baptist[178] declared that although God had been silent for a long time, He was not done with His people.

A man named Joseph of the house of David was betrothed to a woman named Mary.[179] The angel Gabriel appeared to Mary and told her that she would bare a Son from the Holy Spirit who would be called Jesus and be the Son of God.[180] Soon after, Elizabeth (Mary's cousin) gave birth to John the Baptist (Luke 1:57). Now after his birth, Zacharias (John the Baptist's father) prophesied about his son saying, "And thou, child, shalt be called the prophet of the Highest: for thou shalt go before the face of the Lord to prepare his ways" (Luke 1:76). This is a reference to Malachi's prophecy, "Behold, I will send my messenger, and he shall prepare the way before me: and the Lord, whom ye seek, shall suddenly come to his temple, even the messenger of the covenant, whom ye delight in: behold, he shall come, saith the LORD of hosts" (Mal. 3:1).

THE BIRTH OF JESUS AND HIS CHILDHOOD

Around 5 to 7 BC,[181] Joseph came to realize Mary was pregnant and decided to separate from her quietly to spare her life since the law of Moses commanded adulterers to be stoned.[182] Before Joseph could separate from Mary, an angel appeared to him and told him that the child was from God and His name would be JESUS and He would save His people from their sins.[183]

---

[177] Matt. 11:7–15.
[178] Luke 1:24.
[179] Luke 1:27.
[180] Luke 1:28–38.
[181] Eusebius. *The Church History*. Translated by Paul L. Maier. Grand Rapids, MI: Kregel Publications, 2007, 38.
[182] Lev. 20:10; Matt. 1:19.
[183] Matt. 1:20–21.

As Caesar Augustus decreed a census, Joseph and Mary went to Bethlehem to register.[184] As they were on their journey, Mary went into labor and gave birth to Jesus.[185] Mary wrapped Jesus in cloths and laid Him in a manger because there was no room for them in the inn.[186]

There was a group of shepherds in the fields when an angel appeared to them and told them of the birth of Jesus and how He was the Savior and Christ.[187] The angel told them that the sign to them would be a baby wrapped in cloth lying in a manger.[188] After this, the shepherds went to Bethlehem to see Jesus.[189] After they saw Jesus in the flesh, they went about spreading the news to everybody.[190]

On the eighth day after His birth, Jesus was circumcised and officially named "Jesus."[191] He was then brought to the temple in Jerusalem to present Him to the Lord and to offer a sacrifice according to the law of Moses.[192]

Now, some wise men came from the East looking for Jesus because they had seen His star in the sky.[193] The wise men came to baby Jesus in Bethlehem worshipping Him and giving gifts.[194] At this time, king Herod sought to kill Jesus, so an angel appeared to Joseph and told him to take his family to Egypt.[195] When Herod's plan of killing Jesus failed, he ordered the murder of every male child two years old and under[196] just like Pharaoh did in the time of Moses.[197]

---

[184] Luke 2:1–5.
[185] Luke 2:6–7.
[186] Luke 2:7.
[187] Luke 2:8–11.
[188] Luke 2:12.
[189] Luke 2:15–16.
[190] Luke 2:17–18.
[191] Luke 2:21.
[192] Luke 2:22–24.
[193] Matt. 2:1–2.
[194] Matt. 2:9–11.
[195] Matt. 2:13–15.
[196] Matt. 2:16–18.
[197] Ex. 1:15–16.

Around 4 BC[198] when Herod died, an angel appeared to Joseph again and told him to take his family to Israel and ended up resorting in the region of Galilee and the city of Nazareth.[199]

Years later, when Jesus was twelve years old, He and His parents went to the Feast of the Passover in Jerusalem.[200] His parents lost Him and sought Him.[201] After seeking Him, they found Him in the temple discussing with the teachers.[202] The teachers were amazed at Jesus's wisdom.[203] Luke records, "And Jesus increased in wisdom and stature, and in favour with God and man" (Luke 2:52).

THE PREACHING OF JOHN THE BAPTIST

Around AD 29[204] as John the Baptist became a man, he came preaching in the wilderness saying, "Repent ye: for the kingdom of heaven is at hand" (Matt. 3:1–2). John fulfilled another Old Testament prophecy that says, "The voice of him that crieth in the wilderness, Prepare ye the way of the LORD, make straight in the desert a highway for our God" (Isa. 40:3). John baptized many with a baptism of repentance.[205] John said, "I indeed baptize you with water unto repentance: but he that cometh after me is mightier than I, whose shoes I am not worthy to bear: he shall baptize you with the Holy Ghost, and with fire" (Matt. 3:11). By saying this, John spoke of Jesus who would baptize with the Holy Ghost. Jesus came to John

---

[198] Eusebius. *The Church History*. Translated by Paul L. Maier. Grand Rapids, MI: Kregel Publications, 2007, 40.

[199] Matt. 2:19–23.

[200] Luke 2:41–42.

[201] Luke 2:43–45.

[202] Luke 2:46.

[203] Luke 2:47.

[204] Eusebius. *The Church History*. Translated by Paul L. Maier. Grand Rapids, MI: Kregel Publications, 2007, 41.

[205] Matt. 3:5–6, 11.

at the Jordan River and John baptized Him.[206] The passage reads as follows:

> And Jesus, when he was baptized, went up straightway out of the water: and, lo, the heavens were opened unto him, and he saw the Spirit of God descending like a dove, and lighting upon him: [17] And lo a voice from heaven, saying, This is my beloved Son, in whom I am well pleased. (Matt. 3:16–17)

This is the first passage in the Bible where the Trinity is made very clear. Jesus (the Son) is being baptized while the Holy Spirit descends on Him and God the Father says He is "well pleased."

Jesus then went into the wilderness and fasted forty days and forty nights.[207] Satan tempted Him to disobey God three times and Jesus withstood all of them.[208] Hebrews says, "For we have not an high priest which cannot be touched with the feeling of our infirmities; but was in all points tempted like as we are, yet without sin" (Heb. 4:15). Jesus was tempted, yet never sinned.

THE MINISTRY OF JESUS AND DEATH OF JOHN THE BAPTIST

As time went on, Jesus chose twelve men to be apostles: Simon (Peter), Andrew, James, John, Philip, Bartholomew, Matthew, Thomas, James the son of Alphaeus, Simon the Zealot, Judas the son of James, and Judas Iscariot (the traitor).[209] Jesus and His apostles went out spreading the gospel under one main message, "I tell you, Nay: but, except ye repent, ye shall all likewise perish" (Luke 13:3). Jesus went through His ministry healing the sick, making the

---

[206] Matt. 3:13–15.
[207] Matt. 4:1–2.
[208] Matt. 4:3–11.
[209] Luke 6:12–16.

blind see, and even raising the dead.²¹⁰ Now it came to pass that king Herod was angry with John the Baptist because he rebuked him for taking his brother's wife.²¹¹ Herod wanted to put John to death but withheld for fear of the Jews.²¹² But it came to pass that at the birthday celebration of Herod, the daughter of Herodias danced for him and pleased him.²¹³

Because of this, he promised by oath to give her whatever she wanted.²¹⁴ The account says, "And she, being before instructed of her mother, said, Give me here John Baptist's head in a charger" (Matt. 14:8). Herod was sorry for making the oath but nonetheless kept it and ultimately had John beheaded.²¹⁵ The first century Jewish historian recorded this event in *The Antiquities of the Jews*:

> **Now, some of the Jews thought that the destruction of Herod's army came from God, and that very justly, as a punishment of what he did against John, that was called the Baptist; for Herod slew him, who was a good man**, and commanded the Jews to exercise virtue, both as to righteousness toward one another, and piety toward God, and so to come to baptism; for that the washing [with water] would be acceptable to him, if they made use of it, not in order to the putting away [or the remission] of some sins [only], but for the purification of the body; supposing still that the soul was thoroughly purified beforehand by righteousness. Now, when [many] others came in crowds about him, for they were greatly moved [or pleased] by hearing his words, Herod, who feared lest the great influence John

---

²¹⁰ John 11:1–44.
²¹¹ Matt. 14:3–4.
²¹² Matt. 14:5.
²¹³ Matt. 14:6.
²¹⁴ Matt. 14:7.
²¹⁵ Matt. 14:9–10.

had over the people might put it into his power and inclination to raise a rebellion (for they seemed ready to do anything he should advise), thought it best, by putting him to death, to prevent any mischief he might cause, and not bring himself into difficulties, by sparing a man who might make him repent of it when it should be too late. Accordingly, he was sent a prisoner, out of Herod's suspicious temper, to Macherus, the castle I before mentioned, and was there put to death. Now the Jews had an opinion that the destruction of this army was sent as a punishment upon Herod, and a mark of God's displeasure against him.[216]

With John out of the way, the Jewish leaders earnestly sought to get Jesus in trouble. Their main charge against Him was blasphemy:

> Your father Abraham rejoiced to see my day: and he saw it, and was glad. [57] Then said the Jews unto him, Thou art not yet fifty years old, and hast thou seen Abraham? [58] Jesus said unto them, Verily, verily, I say unto you, Before Abraham was, **I am.** [59] Then took they up stones to cast at him: but Jesus hid himself, and went out of the temple, going through the midst of them, and so passed by. (John 8:56–59)

After Jesus made this statement, the Jews sought to stone Him. But why? Why did they believe He deserved stoning for simply saying He was before Abraham? Recall the encounter Moses had with God in the burning bush, "And God said unto Moses, **I AM THAT I AM**: and he said, Thus shalt thou say unto the children of Israel, **I**

---

[216] Josephus, Flavius. Josephus: *The Complete Works*. Translated by Whiston William. Nashville, TN: Thomas Nelson Inc, 1998, 581.

AM hath sent me unto you" (Exod. 3:14). God's name is "I am." So when Jesus claimed to be the "I am," He was claiming to be God. Jesus went throughout the land performing miracles, giving amazing teachings, and claiming to be divine.

THE DEATH, BURIAL, AND RESURRECTION OF JESUS

On the night Jesus would be betrayed and delivered into the hands of the government officials, He instituted what is known as the Lord's Supper:

> And when the hour was come, he sat down, and the twelve apostles with him. [15] And he said unto them, With desire I have desired to eat this passover with you before I suffer: [16] For I say unto you, I will not any more eat thereof, until it be fulfilled in the kingdom of God. [17] And he took the cup, and gave thanks, and said, Take this, and divide it among yourselves: [18] For I say unto you, I will not drink of the fruit of the vine, until the kingdom of God shall come. [19] And he took bread, and gave thanks, and brake it, and gave unto them, saying, This is my body which is given for you: this do in remembrance of me. [20] Likewise also the cup after supper, saying, This cup is the new testament in my blood, which is shed for you. (Luke 22:14–20)

The bread was His body that He would give on the Cross and the wine was His blood that would be shed for the world. The passage goes on to say, "But, behold, the hand of him that betrayeth me is with me on the table. [22] And truly the Son of man goeth, as it was determined: but woe unto that man by whom he is betrayed! [23] And they began to enquire among themselves, which of them it was that should do this thing" (Luke 22:21–23).

One of Jesus's disciples, Judas Iscariot, would ultimately betray Him and have Him arrested.[217] Jesus is handed over to Pilate, the governor, to be questioned,[218] but Jesus did not answer[219] to fulfill the Scripture that says, "He was oppressed, and he was afflicted, yet he opened not his mouth: he is brought as a lamb to the slaughter, and as a sheep before her shearers is dumb, so he openeth not his mouth" (Isa. 53:7). Now it was tradition that at the feast, one prisoner was to be set free.[220] There was a prisoner called Barabbas and Pilate asked the people which one should be set free—Jesus or Barabbas.[221] The people said they wanted Barabbas to be set free and Jesus to be crucified.[222] Even Pilate knew Jesus was innocent saying, "Why, what evil hath he done?" (Matt. 27:23). But to please the crowd, he decided to grant their wish. The account says, "When Pilate saw that he could prevail nothing, but that rather a tumult was made, he took the water, and washed his hands before the multitude, saying, I am innocent of the blood of this just person: see ye to it" (Matt. 27:24). The soldiers then took Jesus, stripped Him, put a scarlet robe on Him, placed a crown of thorns on His head and a reed in His hand.[223] They then mocked Him, spat on Him, and beat Him.[224] They then took Him to a place called Golgotha, nailed Him to a cross, and raised it up.[225] From the sixth hour to the ninth hour there was darkness in the land.[226] In the ninth hour Jesus cried out "My God, my God, why hast thou forsaken me?" (Matt. 27:46). He felt the consequences of sin which includes alienation from God. Jesus finally gave up the spirit and died.[227] After this, the earth quaked, and the rocks split.[228]

---

[217] Luke 22:47–53.
[218] Matt. 27:11.
[219] Matt. 27:14.
[220] Matt. 27:15.
[221] Matt. 27:21.
[222] Matt. 27:21–22.
[223] Matt. 27:27–29.
[224] Matt. 27:29–31.
[225] Matt. 27:32–35.
[226] Matt. 27:45.
[227] Matt. 27:50.
[228] Matt. 27:51.

A man named Joseph (not Mary's husband) came to retrieve the body of Jesus.[229] He took the body, laid it in a tomb, and rolled a large stone against the door.[230] The chief priests and Pharisees then commanded guards to stand outside the tomb because they remembered that Jesus said He would rise after three days.[231] Now, on the first day of the week (Sunday), Mary Magdalene and another Mary came to the tomb and found the stone rolled away with an angel sitting on top of it.[232] The angel gave the good news that "he is risen."[233] Jesus rose from the dead! Hallelujah! The women then went to tell the disciples the news.[234] Jesus then appeared to the women and they worshipped Him.[235] After Jesus's tomb was found empty, the Jews decided to spread the rumor that "His disciples came by night, and stole him away while we slept" (Matt. 28:13). Prior to His ascension into heaven, Jesus said,

> Thus it is written, and thus it behooved Christ to suffer, and to rise from the dead the third day: [47] And that repentance and remission of sins should be preached in his name among all nations, beginning at Jerusalem. [48] And ye are witnesses of these things. [49] And, behold, I send the promise of my Father upon you: but tarry ye in the city of Jerusalem, until ye be endued with power from on high. (Luke 24:46–49)

Jesus told the disciples that repentance and remission of sins should be preached and that they should wait in Jerusalem for the "promise" which is the Holy Spirit. Jesus also gave His disciples what is known as the Great Commission: "Go ye therefore, and teach all

---

[229] Matt. 27:57–58.
[230] Matt. 27:59–60.
[231] Matt. 27:62–66.
[232] Matt. 28:1–2.
[233] Matt. 28:6.
[234] Matt. 28:8.
[235] Matt. 28:9–10.

nations, baptizing them in the name of the Father, and of the Son, and of the Holy Ghost: ²⁰ Teaching them to observe all things what-soever I have commanded you: and, lo, I am with you always, even unto the end of the world. Amen" (Matt. 28:19–20).

The disciples were commanded to go into the world and make disciples. After this Jesus ascended into heaven:

> And when he had spoken these things, while they beheld, he was taken up; and a cloud received him out of their sight. ¹⁰ And while they looked stedfastly toward heaven as he went up, behold, two men stood by them in white apparel; ¹¹ Which also said, Ye men of Galilee, why stand ye gazing up into heaven? this same Jesus, which is taken up from you into heaven, shall so come in like manner as ye have seen him go into heaven. (Acts 1:9–11)

And that is the life and ministry of Jesus. He performed many miracles and taught many things. He was killed, buried, and He rose again. And now He sits at the right hand of the Father.

THE ACTS OF THE APOSTLES

Jesus ascended into heaven around AD 33. At that time, the disciples were waiting in Jerusalem for the promise of the Holy Spirit.[236] They then chose a man named Matthias to take the place of Judas Iscariot (the traitor). Now on the Day of Pentecost,

> And suddenly there came a sound from heaven as of a rushing mighty wind, and it filled all the house where they were sitting. ³ And there appeared unto them cloven tongues like as of fire, and it sat upon each of them. ⁴ And they were all

---

[236] Acts 1:12–14.

filled with the Holy Ghost, and began to speak
with other tongues, as the Spirit gave them utterance. (Acts 2:2–4)

The promise of the Holy Spirit had finally come. The disciples
were filled with the Spirit and spoke in other tongues (languages).
Peter then gave a sermon in which he said, "Repent, and be baptized
every one of you in the name of Jesus Christ for the remission of sins,
and ye shall receive the gift of the Holy Ghost" (Acts 2:38). This was
the beginning of the Great Commission.[237] So, the disciples went
and preached the gospel, being told by the authorities not to preach.
But the disciples said, "We ought to obey God rather than men"
(Acts 5:29). One day, a Christian named Stephen was preaching and
rebuking the Jews.[238] The Jews became enraged: "And they stoned
Stephen, calling upon God, and saying, Lord Jesus, receive my spirit.
60 And he kneeled down, and cried with a loud voice, Lord, lay not
this sin to their charge. And when he had said this, he fell asleep"
(Acts 7:59–60).

Stephen was the first martyr of the church. Now at this time,
a devout Jew named Saul (commonly known as Paul) was making
havoc "of the church, entering into every house, and haling men and
women committed them to prison" (Acts 8:3). But soon everything
would change for Saul of Tarsus. One day while on the Damascus
road, a blinding, bright light shined from heaven.[239] Jesus began
speaking to him and said, "Saul, Saul, why persecutes thou me?"
(Acts 9:4). He then commanded Saul to go into the city.[240] Now
Jesus had chosen a man named Ananias to baptize Saul and allow
him to recover his sight.[241] Jesus said to Ananias, "Go thy way: for he
is a chosen vessel unto me, to bear my name before the Gentiles, and
kings, and the children of Israel" (Acts 9:15). Jesus chose Saul to go

---

[237] Matt. 28:19–20.
[238] Acts 7:1–53.
[239] Acts 9:3.
[240] Acts 9:6.
[241] Acts 9:10–12.

preach to the Gentiles. Now when Saul came to Ananias, he was baptized and received his sight back.[242] Following the conversion of Saul,

> And straightway he preached Christ in the synagogues, that he is the Son of God. [21] But all that heard him were amazed, and said; Is not this he that destroyed them which called on this name in Jerusalem, and came hither for that intent, that he might bring them bound unto the chief priests? [22] But Saul increased the more in strength, and confounded the Jews which dwelt at Damascus, proving that this is very Christ. (Acts 9:20–22)

Saul began preaching Christ after his conversion. He went from killing Christians to preaching Christ crucified. This is a powerful testimony. He even spoke of this in his first epistle to Timothy,

> And I thank Christ Jesus our Lord, who hath enabled me, for that he counted me faithful, putting me into the ministry; [13] Who was before a blasphemer, and a persecutor, and injurious: but I obtained mercy, because I did it ignorantly in unbelief. [14] And the grace of our Lord was exceeding abundant with faith and love which is in Christ Jesus. [15] This is a faithful saying, and worthy of all acceptation, that Christ Jesus came into the world to save sinners; of whom I am chief. (1 Tim. 1:12–15)

Saul testifies to the fact that he was a wicked sinner at this time, but God had mercy on him. After Saul was done preaching, the Jews sought to kill him, but the disciples helped him escape.[243] Many

---

[242] Acts 9:17–18.
[243] Acts 9:23–25.

wonder where the term "Christian" comes from. Jesus never used the term "Christian" and the disciples were originally identified as followers of "the Way"[244] because Jesus called Himself "the Way."[245] The term "Christian" was given to the followers of Jesus by others: "And the disciples were called Christians first in Antioch."[246] From there, followers of Jesus accepted the name and ran with it, as the Apostle Peter uses the word in his epistle.[247] Now sometime later, king Herod killed James the brother of John.[248] Through all these persecutions, the disciples continued fulfilling the Great Commission which was given to them by the Lord Jesus.

Because all the first Christians were Jews, they were confused as to whether Christians needed to be circumcised. This led to the first church council in church history known as "the Jerusalem Council." The council was led by James (not the one who Herod killed) and the church ultimately declared that Gentiles did not need to be circumcised, but rather just "abstain from meats offered to idols, and from blood, and from things strangled, and from fornication: from which if ye keep yourselves, ye shall do well" (Acts 15:29).

A while later, Paul was in the Temple when the Jews came making accusations against him.[249] Paul defended himself against the crowd.[250] He then gave a defense before the Sanhedrin.[251] He later defended himself before King Agrippa.[252] Paul was then sent to Rome.[253] The book of the Acts of the Apostles ends saying, "And Paul dwelt two whole years in his own hired house, and received all that came in unto him, 31 Preaching the kingdom of God, and teaching those things which concern the Lord Jesus Christ, with all confidence, no man forbidding him" (Acts 28:30–31).

---

[244] Acts 9:2.
[245] John 14:6.
[246] Acts 11:26.
[247] 1 Pet. 4:16.
[248] Acts 12:1–2.
[249] Acts 21:26–36.
[250] Acts 22:1–21.
[251] Acts 23:1–6.
[252] Acts 26:1–23.
[253] Acts 28:16.

PERSECUTION OF THE CHURCH

From the beginning, the church was persecuted. Suffering and persecution are part of the Christian life. Paul wrote in his second epistle to Timothy saying, "Yea, and all that will live godly in Christ Jesus shall suffer persecution" (2 Tim. 3:12). In AD 64, a fire broke out in Rome. Emperor Nero blamed the Christians for the fire and punished them. It was around this time that Peter and Paul both died in Rome. Clement of Rome writing in the late first century says,

> But not to dwell upon ancient examples, let us come to the most recent spiritual heroes. Let us take the noble examples furnished in our own generation. Through envy and jealousy, the greatest and most righteous pillars [of the Church] have been persecuted and put to death. Let us set before our eyes the illustrious apostles. **Peter**, through unrighteous envy, endured not one or two, but numerous labours; and when he had at length suffered martyrdom, departed to the place of glory due to him. Owing to envy, **Paul** also obtained the reward of patient endurance, after being seven times thrown into captivity, compelled to flee, and stoned. After preaching both in the east and west, he gained the illustrious reputation due to his faith, having taught righteousness to the whole world, and come to the extreme limit of the west, and suffered martyrdom under the prefects. Thus was he removed from the world, and went into the holy place, having proved himself a striking example of patience.[254]

---

[254] Clement of Rome. *The Ante-Nicene Fathers: The First Epistle of Clement.* Chapter V. Edited by Alexander Roberts, James Donaldson, and Arthur Cleveland Coxe. I. Vol. I. X vols. New York, NY: Cosimo Classics, 2007, 6.

Speaking of Emperor Nero, the fourth century church historian Eusebius writes, "So it happened that this man, the first to be announced publicly as a fighter against God, was led on to slaughter the apostles. It is related that in his reign Paul was beheaded in Rome itself and that Peter was also crucified, and the cemeteries there still called by the names of Peter and Paul confirm the record."[255]

The next Emperor who persecuted Christians was Domitian (AD 81–96). Following Domitian came Trajan (AD 98–117). Hadrian (AD 117–138) and Marchus Aurelius (AD 161–180) followed suit in persecuting the Christians solely for their name/title. Christians were not liked because of their exclusivity. Christians believed what Jesus taught in that He was the only way to be saved (John 14:6). This meant they would not do things like burn incense or call Caesar lord. They also had three main accusations against them: atheism, cannibalism, and incest.[256]

The accusation of atheism was given to anybody that didn't hold the normal religious views of the time. Since Christianity was a new faith (because it was the fulfillment of Judaism), they fit under this title of atheist. The accusation of cannibalism had to do with the language used in the Lord's supper about eating Jesus's flesh and drinking His blood. And finally, the charge of incest most likely had to do with Christians calling each other "brother" and "sister" and partaking in the "love feast."[257]

The Church soon entered a period of peace from AD 211 to AD 250. This peace was briefly interrupted in AD 235 by Maximinus. Christians especially flourished under Alexander Severus (AD 222–AD 235) and Philip the Arabian (AD 244–AD 249). This peace ended abruptly with the reign of Decius (AD 249–AD 251) and Valerian (AD 253–AD 260) who persecuted the Church. Christians once again returned to a period of peace from AD 260 to AD 303. What's known as the Great Persecution occurred in AD 303.

---

[255] Eusebius. *The Church History*. Translated by Paul L. Maier. Grand Rapids, MI: Kregel Publications, 2007, 75.

[256] Ferguson, Everett. *Church History, Volume One: From Christ to the Pre-Reformation*. Grand Rapids, MI: Zondervan Academic, 2013, 65.

[257] Ferguson, 66.

Christian buildings were destroyed, Bishops were arrested, Christians were forced to offer sacrifices to pagan gods, etc.[258]

In AD 312, Emperor Constantine was with his troops near the Tiber river when he had an experience that seemed to be a vision. In the vision, Constantine "was admonished to adopt the Chi Rho monogram (the first two letters of the word Christ in Greek) as the emblem for his troops."[259] Constantine then had his soldiers put the symbol on their weaponry. Constantine and his army ended up winning the battle of Milvian Bridge and he saw it as a sort of divine providence. In AD 313, he gave freedom of religion to Christians and all other religions as well in what is known as the "Edict of Milan." In AD 320, Licinius in the eastern part of the empire began persecuting Christians again. In AD 324, Constantine defeated Licinius and became the one and only ruler of the Roman empire. This leads right up to the infamous Council of Nicaea.

[258] Ferguson, 179.
[259] Ferguson, 182.

CHAPTER 6

PRIMITIVE CHRISTIANITY

Many Christians today are completely ignorant of the history of the church. For many Western Christians, church history started with Billy Graham and the sinner's prayer. This is the type of Christianity I was converted in—the skinny-jean-pastors, coffee-in-the-pew, strobe-light type of Christianity.

I am in no way bashing these megachurches as they do a lot of good and are where I first got interested in my faith, but this modernized version of Christianity is not *primitive* Christianity. For reference, the last book of the Bible, Revelation, was written around AD 96 by the Apostle John. This means the whole New Testament was completed by the close of the first century (AD 100).

Many of the early church writers were disciples of the disciples. For example, Ignatius and Polycarp were connected to the Apostle John. This means both of their writings are very trustworthy. The other church fathers connected to the apostles are Clement of Rome, who Paul referenced in Philippians 4:3, and Papias. Many of the other early church writers did not know the apostles personally, but they knew people who knew the apostles, and so they still had a connection to apostolic teaching.

For example, Irenaeus, who wrote around AD 180, did not know the apostles directly, but he knew Polycarp who knew the Apostle John, like Ignatius. The first ecumenical church council was the Council of Nicaea in AD 325, not including the Jerusalem Council in Acts 15.

The period of the early church prior to the Council of Nicaea (AD 325) is known as the Ante-Nicene Period. I stick mostly to quotations from the early church writers prior to the Council of Nicaea since many American Christians believe the church went "apostate" after this council. While I reject this historic revisionism, I will nonetheless provide quotes prior to the Council of Nicaea to refute the conspiracy theorists.

I ask the reader to examine this evidence with an open mind and heart. It may be shocking to many American Christians to recognize what the early church believed and how different it is from most modern churches. Once again, I ask the reader to examine the evidence with an open mind and heart. Let the reader know—history matters!

THE TRINITY

The major focus of the first four hundred years or so of the church was defining who Jesus was and expounding on the doctrine of God. Who is God? We know that the Jews followed the God of Abraham, Isaac, and Jacob—and Christianity is the *fulfillment* of Judaism. This means it must also be monotheistic. This was the clear teaching since Old Testament times when the Israelites would recite, "Hear, O Israel: The LORD our God is one LORD" (Deut. 6:4).

Clement of Rome affirmed this belief when he wrote to the church in Corinth very early in the first century saying, "That the name of the true and only God might be glorified; to whom be glory for ever and ever. Amen."[260] Clement made it clear that there is only one God. The Bible teaches that God the Father does not have a body. "God is a Spirit: and they that worship him must worship him in spirit and in truth" (John 4:24). Tatian wrote around AD

---

[260] Clement of Rome. *The Ante-Nicene Fathers: First Epistle of Clement.* Chapter XLIII. Edited by Alexander Roberts, James Donaldson, and Arthur Cleveland Coxe. I. Vol. I. X vols. New York, NY: Cosimo Classics, 2007, 16–17.

170 saying, "God is a Spirit, not pervading matter, but the Maker of material spirits, and of the forms that are in matter; He is invisible, impalpable, being Himself the Father of both sensible and invisible things."[261] While the Father cannot be seen (John 1:18, 4:24), Jesus can be because He is the "image of the invisible God" (Col. 1:15).

During His ministry, Jesus claimed to be God, calling Himself the "I AM" that appeared to Moses in the burning bush (Ex. 3:14; John 8:58). Ignatius, who was a disciple of the Apostle John, wrote to the Ephesians around AD 110, saying, "Elected through the true passion by the will of the Father, and Jesus Christ, our God." It is clear that there is only one God, yet Jesus and the Father are both called God. The Bible also calls the Holy Spirit God (Acts 5:1–4). It is evident in the early church that all three persons—the Father, the Son, and the Holy Spirit—are all God.

Theophilus wrote around AD 180, "The three days which were before the luminaries, are types of the Trinity, of God [the Father], and His Word [Jesus], and His wisdom [the Holy Spirit]."[262] Theophilus is the first record we have of the early church using the word *trinity*. The fact that he used the word so casually is good evidence that this term was already widely in use. Tertullian and Origen expounded on the Trinity soon after. Tertullian wrote around AD 218,

> We, however, as we indeed always have done (and more especially since we have been better instructed by the Paraclete, who leads men indeed into all truth), believe that there is one only God, but under the following dispensation...that this one only God has also a Son, His Word, who proceeded from Himself, by whom all things were made, and without whom nothing

[261] Tatian. *The Ante-Nicene Fathers: Address to the Greeks.* Chapter IV. Edited by Alexander Roberts, James Donaldson, and Arthur Cleveland Coxe. II. Vol. II. X vols. New York, NY: Cosimo Classics, 2007, 66.
[262] Theophilus. *The Ante-Nicene Fathers: To Autolycus.* Chapter XV. Edited by Alexander Roberts, James Donaldson, and Arthur Cleveland Coxe. II. Vol. II. X vols. New York, NY: Cosimo Classics, 2007, 100–101.

was made. Him we believe to have been sent by the Father into the Virgin, and to have been born of her—being both Man and God, the Son of Man and the Son of God, and to have been called by the name of Jesus Christ; we believe Him to have suffered, died, and been buried, according to the Scriptures, and, after He had been raised again by the Father and taken back to heaven, to be sitting at the right hand of the Father, and that He will come to judge the quick and the dead; who sent also from heaven from the Father, according to His own promise, the Holy Ghost, the Paraclete, the sanctifier of the faith of those who believe in the Father, and in the Son, and in the Holy Ghost. That this rule of faith has come down to us from the beginning of the gospel, even before any of the older heretics.[263]

Tertullian went on to say,

As if in this way also one were not All, in that All are of One, by unity (that is) of substance; while the mystery of the dispensation is still guarded, which distributes the Unity into a Trinity, placing in their order the three Persons— the Father, the Son, and the Holy Ghost: three, however, not in condition, but in degree, not in substance, but in form; not in power, but in aspect; yet of one substance, and of one condition, and of one power, inasmuch as He is one God, from whom these degrees and forms and

---

[263] Tertullian. *The Ante-Nicene Fathers: Against Praxeas*. Chapter II. Edited by Alexander Roberts, James Donaldson, and Arthur Cleveland Coxe. III. Vol. III. X vols. New York, NY: Cosimo Classics, 2007, 598.

aspects are reckoned, under the name of the
Father, and of the Son, and of the Holy Ghost.[264]

To sum it all up, "Thus the connection of the Father in the Son,
and of the Son in the Paraclete, produces three coherent Persons,
who are yet distinct One from Another. These Three are on essence,
not one Person, as it is said, 'I and my Father are One,' in respect of
unity of substance, not singularity of number."[265]

Tertullian makes it clear that the Father, the Son, and the Holy
Spirit are all three separate *persons* yet one *essence*. They are *distinct*
yet *one*. Origen wrote around AD 225 saying, "The statements made
regarding Father, Son, and Holy Spirit are to be understood as tran-
scending all time, all ages, and all eternity. For it is the Trinity alone
which exceeds the comprehension not only of temporal but even of
eternal intelligence; while other things which are not included in it
are to be measured by times and ages."[266]

Origen explains that all three persons are eternal. This means
they are all God, yet they are all one. The council of Nicaea convened
in May of AD 325. After much debate, the council came up with a
creed to affirm what they agreed the Scriptures taught.

We believe in one God the Father All-
sovereign, maker of all things visible and invisible; and in one Lord Jesus Christ, the Son of
God, begotten of the Father, only-begotten, that
is, of the substance of the Father, God of God,
Light of Light, **true God of true God, begotten**

[264] Tertullian. *The Ante-Nicene Fathers: Against Praxeas*. Chapter II. Edited by
Alexander Roberts, James Donaldson, and Arthur Cleveland Coxe. III. Vol. III.
X vols. New York, NY: Cosimo Classics, 2007, 598.

[265] Tertullian. *The Ante-Nicene Fathers: Against Praxeas*. Chapter XXV. Edited by
Alexander Roberts, James Donaldson, and Arthur Cleveland Coxe. III. Vol. III.
X vols. New York, NY: Cosimo Classics, 2007, 621.

[266] Origen. *The Ante-Nicene Fathers: De Principiis*. Section 28. Edited by Alexander
Roberts, James Donaldson, and Arthur Cleveland Coxe. IV. Vol. IV. X vols.
New York, NY: Cosimo Classics, 2007, 377.

not made, of one substance [homoousion] with the Father, through whom all things were made, things in heaven and things on the earth; who for us men and for our salvation came down and was made flesh, and became man, suffered, and rose on the third day, ascended into the heavens, is coming to judge the living and the dead; and in the Holy Spirit. And those who say "There was when he was not," and, "Before he was begotten he was not," and that, "He came into being from what-is-not," or those who allege that the Son of God is "of another substance or essence," or "created," or "changeable," or "alterable," these the Catholic and Apostolic Church anathematizes.[267]

The council agreed that the Scriptures taught Jesus to be God and not a created being (John 1:1–3; Col. 1:16–17). They also declared Arianism, the teaching that Jesus was created, to be a heresy. The deity of the Holy Spirit was expounded on soon after at the council of Constantinople (AD 381). And thus, from the evidence, it is clear that the early church believed in the doctrine of the Trinity. It is a confusing doctrine to comprehend with our finite minds, but it is true, nonetheless. As the Scripture says, "The grace of the Lord Jesus Christ, and the love of God, and the communion of the Holy Ghost, be with you all. Amen" (2 Cor. 13:14).

BAPTISM

Baptism is a sacrament of the church instituted by the Lord Jesus. Baptism is one of the most controversial topics in the faith. The first question that arises is how baptism should be performed. Many argue that baptism must be by immersion since the Greek word for baptism means "to immerse."

---

[267] Ferguson, 194.

While this is true, the Bible nowhere tells us the mode of baptism. The Bible is also a bit confusing in that Jesus commanded His disciples to baptize in the name of the Father, Son, and Holy Spirit (Matt. 28:19), while the book of Acts says people were baptized in the name of Jesus (Acts 2:38). This means we must look to outside sources to see what the early church believed about these passages. An early document called the *Didache* dates around AD 80–140, and it says, "But concerning baptism, thus baptize in the name of the Father, and of the Son, and of the Holy Spirit, in running water; but if thou hast not running water, baptize in some other water, and if thou canst not baptize in cold, in warm water; but if thou hast neither, pour water three times on the head, in the name of the Father, and of the Son, and of the Holy Spirit"[268] (Didache 7:1–3).

From this very early document, we can see that the church baptized in the name of the Trinity, not in the name of Jesus. From this document and the direct context in Acts, it is clear that being baptized "in the name of Jesus" means in the *authority* of Jesus; it is not a baptismal formula. Peter was speaking to Jews and told them to be baptized "in the name of Jesus" because they claimed to worship the Father but rejected the Son (Jesus).

The Bible says, "Whosoever denieth the Son, the same hath not the Father: (but) he that acknowledgeth the Son hath the Father also" (1 John 2:23). If one does not have the Son, they do not have the Father either! This is why Peter stressed to the Jews that they needed to be baptized "in the name of Jesus." He did not mean that was the baptismal formula. But rather, he was making the point that Jesus is who He claimed to be—the Son of God—and He has the authority to judge and forgive. As Jesus said, "All power is given unto me in heaven and in earth" (Matt 28:18), and "the Father judgeth no man, but hath committed all judgment unto the Son" (John 5:22). Cyprian, writing around AD 250, expounds on this same point.

> For whereas in the Gospels, and in the epis-
> tles of the apostles, the name of Christ is alleged

---

[268] *Didache: The Teaching of the Apostles.* Coppell, TX, 2020, 13.

for the remission of sins; it is not in such a way as that the Son alone, without the Father, or against the Father, can be of advantage to anybody; but that it might be shown to the Jews, who boasted as to their having the Father, that the Father would profit them nothing, unless they believed on the Son whom He had sent. For they who know God the Father the Creator, ought also to know Christ the Son, lest they should flatter and applaud themselves about the Father alone, without the acknowledgment of His Son, who also said, "No man cometh to the Father but by me.".... Peter makes mention of Jesus Christ, not as though the Father should be omitted, but that the Son also might be joined to the Father... Finally, when, after the resurrection, the apostles are sent by the Lord to the heathens, they are bidden to baptize the Gentiles "in the name of the Father, and of the Son, and of the Holy Ghost." How, then, do some say, that a Gentile baptized without, outside the Church, yea, and in opposition to the Church, so that it be only in the name of Jesus Christ, everywhere, and in whatever manner, can obtain remission of sin, when Christ Himself commands the heathen to be baptized in the full and united Trinity?[269]

Cyprian makes the same point that the Jews already believed in the Father but needed to know the Son, which is why they were commanded to be baptized "in the name of Jesus." He also makes the point that a baptism in the name of Jesus does not remit sins but only a baptism in the name of the Trinity. Being baptized "in the name

---

[269] Cyprian. *The Ante-Nicene Fathers: Letter LXXII.* Section 17–18. Edited by Alexander Roberts, James Donaldson, and Arthur Cleveland Coxe. V. Vol. V. X vols. New York, NY: Cosimo Classics, 2007, 383.

of the Father and of the Son and of the Holy Spirit" is the only valid baptismal formula. The other thing that is evident from the *Didache* passage is that while immersion seems to be the *preferred* method in the early church, other methods like sprinkling and pouring/affusion were also valid. Cyprian speaks of sprinkling and affusion as valid modes of baptism, saying,

> In the sacraments of salvation, when necessity compels, and God bestows His mercy, the divine methods confer the whole benefit on believers; nor ought it to trouble any one that sick people seem to be sprinkled or affused, when they obtain the Lord's grace, when Holy Scripture speaks by the mouth of the prophet Ezekiel, and says, "Then will I sprinkle clean water upon you, and ye shall be clean: from all your filthiness and from all your idols will I cleanse you. And I will give you a new heart, and a new spirit will I put within you.[270]

Cyprian explains that many people on their deathbeds are sprinkled or affused because they are not physically able to be immersed. He explains that this is a valid mode of baptism and appeals to the Old Testament prophecy of the new birth in which God says He will "sprinkle clean water" upon us and give us a "new heart" and a "new spirit." So it is evident that immersion, sprinkling, and affusion/pouring are all valid modes of baptism. The mode is not as important but rather what God does through it, which leads to the next question: what does baptism do?

Most Christians in America believe baptism is just a symbol. When I first converted to Christianity in 2018, I was told that baptism was a symbol. But even though I was told that, I still felt like

---

[270] Cyprian. *The Ante-Nicene Fathers: Letter LXXV*. Section 12. Edited by Alexander Roberts, James Donaldson, and Arthur Cleveland Coxe. V. Vol. V. X vols. New York, NY: Cosimo Classics, 2007, 401.

there was much more to it. When studying church history, my convictions were affirmed. Baptism is more than just a symbol. So what does baptism do? Peter said, "Repent, and be baptized every one of you in the name of Jesus Christ for the remission of sins, and ye shall receive the gift of the Holy Ghost" (Acts 2:38). In his first epistle, Peter also said, "Baptism doth also now save us" (1 Pet. 3:21). So baptism remits our sins, gives us the Holy Spirit, and saves us. That sounds like much more than a symbol!

The Bible speaks about baptism as regenerating us and joining us to Christ in many places (Rom. 6:3–4; 1 Cor. 12:13; Gal. 3:27; Tit. 3:4–5). The early church writer Ignatius wrote around AD 110 and said Jesus was baptized to "purify the water."[271] This seems to be an allusion to us being born again through the water, or else there would be no need for it to be "purified." How about John 3:3–5? "Jesus answered and said unto him, Verily, verily, I say unto thee, Except a man be born again, he cannot see the kingdom of God. ⁴Nicodemus saith unto him, How can a man be born when he is old? can he enter the second time into his mother's womb, and be born? ⁵Jesus answered, Verily, verily, I say unto thee, Except a man be born of water and of the Spirit, he cannot enter into the kingdom of God."

Jesus explained how one must be "born again" to see the kingdom of God. We all must be "born of water and of the Spirit." Most Christians in America think "born again" is some invisible, mystical experience. This false interpretation seemed to sprout up with the Anabaptists in the sixteenth century. Prior to the Anabaptists, being "born again" was always synonymous with being baptized because baptism is where we receive the Holy Spirit (Acts 2:38). Most American Christians will try to dance around John 3:3–5, saying the "water" is about physical birth from our mothers and the "Spirit" birth is the invisible one.

There are some major problems with that interpretation. First, in Greek, the term "of water and of the Spirit" refers to *one* event,

---

[271] Ignatius. *The Ante-Nicene Fathers: Epistle to the Ephesians.* Chapter XVIII. Edited by Alexander Roberts, James Donaldson, and Arthur Cleveland Coxe. I. Vol. I. X vols. New York, NY: Cosimo Classics, 2007, 57.

not *two* separate events. Second, Jesus is obviously referring to the same thing He spoke of in verse 3, which is being "born again." Once again, that is *one* event, not *two*. Thirdly, and probably the most compelling evidence, the unanimous interpretation of John 3:3–5 in the first 1,500 years of the church was a reference to baptism. Justin Martyr wrote around AD155, saying

> As many as are persuaded and believe that what we teach and say is true, and undertake to be able to live accordingly, are instructed to pray and to entreat God with fasting, for the remission of their sins that are past, we praying and fasting with them. Then they are brought by us where there is water, and are regenerated in the same manner in which we were ourselves regenerated. For, in the name of God, the Father and Lord of the universe, and of our Saviour Jesus Christ, and of the Holy Spirit, they then receive the washing with water. For Christ also said, "Except ye be born again, ye shall not enter into the kingdom of heaven."[272]

Irenaeus wrote around AD 180,

> "And dipped himself," says [the Scripture], "seven times in Jordan." It was not for nothing that Naaman of old, when suffering from leprosy, was purified upon his being baptized, but [it served] as an indication to us. For as we are lepers in sin, we are made clean, by means of the sacred water and the invocation of the Lord, from our old transgressions; being spiritually regenerated

---

[272] Justin Martyr. *The Ante-Nicene Fathers: The First Apology.* Chapter LXI. Edited by Alexander Roberts, James Donaldson, and Arthur Cleveland Coxe. I. Vol. I. X vols. New York, NY: Cosimo Classics, 2007, 183.

as new-born babes, even as the Lord has declared: "Except a man be born again through water and the Spirit, he shall not enter into the kingdom of heaven."[273]

Tertullian wrote around AD 203, "When, however, the prescript is laid down that 'without baptism, salvation is attainable by none' (chiefly on the ground of that declaration of the Lord, who says, "Unless one be born of water, he hath not life")."[274]
Hippolytus wrote around AD 217,

> The Father of immortality sent the immortal Son and Word into the world, who came to man in order to wash him with water and the Spirit; and He, begetting us again to incorruption of soul and body, breathed into us the breath (spirit) of life, and endued us with an incorruptible panoply. If, therefore, man has become immortal, he will also be [like] God. And if he is made [like] God by water and the Holy Spirit after the regeneration of the laver he is found to be also joint-heir with Christ after the resurrection from the dead. Wherefore I preach to this effect: Come, all ye kindreds of the nations, to the immortality of the baptism.[275]

---

[273] Irenaeus. *The Ante-Nicene Fathers: Fragments of Irenaeus.* Chapter XXXIV. Edited by Alexander Roberts, James Donaldson, and Arthur Cleveland Coxe. I. Vol. I. X vols. New York, NY: Cosimo Classics, 2007, 574.

[274] Tertullian. *The Ante-Nicene Fathers: On Baptism.* Chapter XII. Edited by Alexander Roberts, James Donaldson, and Arthur Cleveland Coxe. III. Vol. III. X vols. New York, NY: Cosimo Classics, 2007, 674–675.

[275] Hippolytus. *The Ante-Nicene Fathers: Discourse on the Holy Theophany.* Section 8. Edited by Alexander Roberts, James Donaldson, and Arthur Cleveland Coxe. V. Vol. V. X vols. New York, NY: Cosimo Classics, 2007, 237.

Cyprian wrote around AD 250, "For [once they have been baptized in the Church] then finally can they be fully sanctified, and be the sons of God, if they be born of each sacrament; since it is written, 'Except a man be born again of water, and of the Spirit, he cannot enter into the kingdom of God.'"[276]

I could quote many more that say this same thing, but it is clear that the early church believed being "born again" or being born "of the water and of the Spirit" referred to baptism. Baptism is not just a symbol. Rather, it is what makes us born again and joins us unto Christ's body.

Another major debate regarding baptism is *who* can be baptized. In the sixteenth century, a group called the "Anabaptists" spawned up and rejected infant baptism. The Reformers Martin Luther and John Calvin separated themselves from the Anabaptists because they both affirmed infant baptism and the rejection of infant baptism was totally foreign to the historic church. Most American Christians are part of churches that descend from the Anabaptist movement such as Baptists, churches of Christ, and other holiness movements. These groups argue that infants should not be baptized. But what did the early church believe? Let us recall what Peter said about baptism. "Then Peter said unto them, Repent, and be baptized every one of you in the name of Jesus Christ for the remission of sins, and ye shall receive the gift of the Holy Ghost. [39] For the promise is unto you, and to your children, and to all that are afar off, even as many as the Lord our God shall call" (Acts 2:38–39).

Most people stop at verse 38, but verse 39 explains that the promise of receiving remission of sins and the gift of the Holy Spirit through baptism is also for "children." Many Anabaptists argue that infants should not be baptized because there are no explicit examples of infant baptism in the Bible. There are a few main reasons why there are no explicit examples of infant baptism in the Bible.

---

[276] Cyprian. *The Ante-Nicene Fathers: Letter LXXI.* Section 1. Edited by Alexander Roberts, James Donaldson, and Arthur Cleveland Coxe. V. Vol. V. X vols. New York, NY: Cosimo Classics, 2007, 378.

First, the book of Acts is an account of the birth of the church. This was the time period when the church began its evangelism. This means, obviously, all the people first being baptized would be converts. There would be no second generation of Christians yet at this time. What I mean by that is that since Christianity was being preached for the first time, the people accepting the message would of course be adults. But this in no way discredits infant baptism.

Once second and third and so on generations of Christians emerged we see clear evidence of infant baptism—which makes sense logically. When the first Christians gave birth to children, these children would be baptized. But obviously, this would not be recorded in the book of Acts since it only deals with the very beginning of the church.

Second, the Bible is not a systematic theology textbook. The fact of the matter is, the Bible was never meant to tell us every single detail about the faith. The Apostle Paul said, "Therefore, brethren, stand fast, and hold the traditions which ye have been taught, whether by word, or our epistle" (2 Thess. 2:15). There are many doctrines of the faith that must be explained by the tradition of the church.

The Bible must be viewed through the lens of church history, or else one will make up their own interpretation of the Bible. Now while there are no *explicit* examples of infant baptism, there are *implicit* examples. The Bible speaks of whole "households" being baptized (Acts 16:15, 33, 18:8; 1 Cor. 1:16). In the Jewish context, it was normal for the whole family to follow suit if one parent converted.

The Bible cannot definitively prove or disprove infant baptism. It does not say for sure one way or the other. One must examine outside sources to determine if infant baptism was a practice of the early church or not. Another interesting thing is that Colossians says, "In whom also ye are circumcised with the circumcision made without hands, in putting off the body of the sins of the flesh by the circumcision of Christ: [12] Buried with him in baptism, wherein also ye are risen with him through the faith of the operation of God, who hath raised him from the dead" (Col. 2:11–12).

Baptism is compared to circumcision. Justin Martyr wrote around AD 155, making this same comparison saying, "And we, who have approached God through Him, have received not carnal, but spiritual circumcision, which Enoch and those like him observed. And we have received it through baptism, since we were sinners, by God's mercy; and all men may equally obtain it."[277] It is clear that the early church saw baptism as the new circumcision. This means to understand baptism, we should examine circumcision. In Genesis, God spoke to Abraham, saying,

> This is my covenant, which ye shall keep, between me and you and thy seed after thee; Every man child among you shall be circumcised. [11] And ye shall circumcise the flesh of your foreskin; and it shall be a token of the covenant betwixt me and you. [12] And he that is eight days old shall be circumcised among you, every man child in your generations, he that is born in the house, or bought with money of any stranger, which is not of thy seed. [13] He that is born in thy house, and he that is bought with thy money, must needs be circumcised: and my covenant shall be in your flesh for an everlasting covenant. (Gen. 17:10–13)

Circumcision was to be given to everybody in the house: infants, young adults, etc. In other words, there were household circumcisions; and likewise now, under the New Covenant, there are household baptisms. The early church made it clear that baptism was to be given to infants. In the martyrdom of Polycarp, dated to about AD 156, an account of Polycarp's words are recorded while standing before unbelieving authorities. "Eighty and six years have I served

---

[277] Justin Martyr. *The Ante-Nicene Fathers: Dialogue with Trypho*. Chapter XLIII. Edited by Alexander Roberts, James Donaldson, and Arthur Cleveland Coxe. I. Vol. I. X vols. New York, NY: Cosimo Classics, 2007, 216.

[Jesus], and He never did me any injury: how then can I blaspheme my King and my Saviour?"[278]

Polycarp was only eighty-six years old, and he claimed that He had served Jesus for eighty-six years. The question is, how can one serve Christ as an infant? The only way to be serving Christ is if one has the Holy Spirit. And the Holy Spirit is received through baptism. This seems to allude to the fact that Polycarp was baptized as an infant. Also, we should recall that Polycarp was a disciple of the Apostle John, which is good evidence that infant baptism is apostolic.

We have already seen that Irenaeus taught that baptism is what makes one born again of the water and of the Spirit.[279] He also wrote around AD 180 saying, "For [Jesus] came to save all through means of Himself—all, I say, who through Him are born again to God—infants, and children, and boys, and youths, and old men."[280]

Irenaeus says that infants can be "born again" to God. Once again, in the early church, the term "born again" was synonymous with baptism. Hippolytus wrote around AD 215, saying, "You are to baptize the little ones first. All those who are able to speak for themselves should speak. With regard to those who cannot speak for themselves, their parents, or somebody who belongs to their family, should speak."[281] Hippolytus explains that the "little ones" should be baptized first in the baptismal ceremony. If they "cannot speak for themselves," somebody will speak for them. This means although infants cannot speak, their parents or guardians will speak for them and have them baptized. Origen wrote around AD 249, saying, "Every soul that is born into flesh is soiled by the filth of wickedness

---

[278] *The Ante-Nicene Fathers: The Martyrdom of Polycarp.* Chapter XIV. Edited by Alexander Roberts, James Donaldson, and Arthur Cleveland Coxe. I. Vol. I. X vols. New York, NY: Cosimo Classics, 2007, 41.

[279] Irenaeus. *The Ante-Nicene Fathers: Fragments of Irenaeus.* Chapter XXXIV. Edited by Alexander Roberts, James Donaldson, and Arthur Cleveland Coxe. I. Vol. I. X vols. New York, NY: Cosimo Classics, 2007, 574.

[280] Irenaeus. *The Ante-Nicene Fathers: Against Heresies.* Book II. Chapter XXII. Section IV. Edited by Alexander Roberts, James Donaldson, and Arthur Cleveland Coxe. I. Vol. I. X vols. New York, NY: Cosimo Classics, 2007, 391.

[281] Hippolytus. *On the Apostolic Tradition.* Translated by Alistair C. Stewart. 2nd ed. Yonkers, NY: St Vladimir's Seminary Press, 2015, 133.

and sin... In the Church, baptism is given for the remission of sins, and, according to the usage of the Church, baptism is given even to infants. If there was nothing in infants that required the remission of sins and nothing in them pertinent to forgiveness, the grace of baptism would seem superfluous."[282]

Origen explains that baptism is given to infants since they are "born into flesh"—that is, "soiled by the filth of wickedness and sin." Origen also says, "The Church received from the apostles the tradition of baptizing infants too."[283] The practice of infant baptism comes directly from the apostles! Cyprian wrote around AD 250,

> But again, if even to the greatest sinners, and to those who had sinned much against God, when they subsequently believed, remission of sins is granted—and nobody is hindered from baptism and from grace—how much rather ought we to shrink from hindering an infant, who, being lately born, has not sinned, except in that, being born after the flesh according to Adam, he has contracted the contagion of the ancient death at its earliest birth, who approaches the more easily on this very account to the reception of the forgiveness of sins—that to him are remitted, not his own sins, but the sins of another.[284]

Cyprian makes it clear that infants must be baptized. To wrap it all up, Matthew gives us this account. "Then were there brought unto [Jesus] little children, that he should put his hands on them, and pray: and the disciples rebuked them. [14] But Jesus said, Suffer lit-

[282] Akin, Jimmy. *The Fathers Know Best*. El Cajon, CA: Catholic Answers Inc., 2010, 282.

[283] Jeremias, Joachim. *Infant Baptism in the First Four Centuries*. Eugene, OR: Wipf and Stock Publishers, 1960, 65.

[284] Cyprian. *The Ante-Nicene Fathers: Letter LVIII*. Section 5. Edited by Alexander Roberts, James Donaldson, and Arthur Cleveland Coxe. V. Vol. V. X vols. New York, NY: Cosimo Classics, 2007, 354.

tle children, and forbid them not, to come unto me: for of such is the kingdom of heaven. [15] And he laid his hands on them, and departed thence" (Matt. 19:13–15).

When little children were brought to Jesus, the disciples rebuked them, but Jesus said, "Forbid them not, to come unto me." So when Christian parents bring their children to Jesus's "purified"[285] font of baptism, we best not "forbid them" from coming to Him and receiving the promise (Acts 2:38–39; Eph. 1:13).

THE LORD'S SUPPER (THE EUCHARIST)

The Lord's supper is a sacrament of the church instituted by the Lord Jesus. Like baptism, it is widely debated as to what it is and does. Like baptism, most American Christians think the Lord's Supper is just a symbol.

This is what I was told when I came to Christ in 2018. In my study of church history, I have found that the Lord's Supper is much more than a symbol. The early church termed the Lord's supper "Eucharist," which means "thanksgiving." The Bible does not have a whole lot to say about the Eucharist.

In the account of the Last Supper, Jesus took the bread and said, "This is My body." And He took the wine and said, "This is my blood" (Matt. 26:26–28).

Martin Luther argued with Ulrich Zwingli in the sixteenth century over these words. Zwingli argued that Jesus meant they "signified" His body. Luther emphasized the literal meaning of the text. Besides the parallel passages in the synoptic gospels, there are only a few other descriptions we have of the Eucharist in the New Testament. One comes from the Apostle Paul, who says,

> For I have received of the Lord that which
> also I delivered unto you, that the Lord Jesus the

---

[285] Ignatius. *The Ante-Nicene Fathers: Epistle to the Ephesians.* Chapter XVIII. Edited by Alexander Roberts, James Donaldson, and Arthur Cleveland Coxe. I. Vol. I. X vols. New York, NY: Cosimo Classics, 2007, 57.

same night in which he was betrayed took bread: [24] And when he had given thanks, he brake it, and said, Take, eat: this is my body, which is broken for you: this do in remembrance of me. [25] After the same manner also he took the cup, when he had supped, saying, this cup is the new testament in my blood: this do ye, as oft as ye drink it, in remembrance of me. [26] For as often as ye eat this bread, and drink this cup, ye do shew the Lord's death till he come. (1 Cor. 11:23–26)

According to Paul, the Lord's Supper is to be done in remembrance of Jesus and His sacrifice. Partaking of the Lord's Supper is a proclamation of the Lord and His work on the Cross. Paul goes on to say,

Wherefore whosoever shall eat this bread, and drink this cup of the Lord, unworthily, shall be guilty of the body and blood of the Lord. [28] But let a man examine himself, and so let him eat of that bread, and drink of that cup. [29] For he that eateth and drinketh unworthily, eateth and drinketh damnation to himself, not discerning the Lord's body. [30] For this cause many are weak and sickly among you, and many sleep. [31] For if we would judge ourselves, we should not be judged. [32] But when we are judged, we are chastened of the Lord, that we should not be condemned with the world. [33] Wherefore, my brethren, when ye come together to eat, tarry one for another. [34] And if any man hunger, let him eat at home; that ye come not together unto condemnation. And the rest will I set in order when I come. (1 Cor. 11:27–34)

Paul explains that when people partake of the Lord's Supper in an unworthy manner, they will be judged accordingly. He goes on to say that the reason so many are sick among them is because they partook of the Supper unworthily and God judged them. In the previous chapter Paul explained that the cup of wine is "the communion of the blood of Christ" and the bread is "the communion of the body of Christ." (1 Cor. 10:16). Another important passage in the Bible regarding the Eucharist is in John chapter 6.

> "I am that bread of life. [49] Your fathers did
> eat manna in the wilderness, and are dead. [50] This
> is the bread which cometh down from heaven,
> that a man may eat thereof, and not die. [51] I am
> the living bread which came down from heaven:
> if any man eat of this bread, he shall live for ever:
> and the bread that I will give is my flesh, which
> I will give for the life of the world. [52] The Jews
> therefore strove among themselves, saying, How
> can this man give us his flesh to eat?" [53] Then Jesus
> said unto them, "Verily, verily, I say unto you,
> Except ye eat the flesh of the Son of man, and
> drink his blood, ye have no life in you. [54] Whoso
> eateth my flesh, and drinketh my blood, hath
> eternal life; and I will raise him up at the last
> day. [55] For my flesh is meat indeed, and my blood
> is drink indeed. [56] He that eateth my flesh, and
> drinketh my blood, dwelleth in me, and I in him.
> [57] As the living Father hath sent me, and I live by
> the Father: so he that eateth me, even he shall live
> by me. [58] This is that bread which came down
> from heaven: not as your fathers did eat manna,
> and are dead: he that eateth of this bread shall
> live for ever." (John 6:48–58)

Jesus says His flesh is meat indeed and His blood is drink indeed. This seems very literal. So literal that many left Jesus after this because it was a "hard saying" (John 6:60). Besides, this small amount of biblical data given to us, not much is said about the

Eucharist. To understand this sacrament fully, one must turn to the writings of the early church.

Ignatius was a disciple of the Apostle John. He held a very high view of the Eucharist. He wrote very early around AD 110, saying, "Let no man deceive himself: if any one be not within the altar, he is deprived of the bread of God."[286] Ignatius explains that those who do not come to the altar (the table) are deprived of the bread of the Lord. He also explains the Eucharist as "the medicine of immortality, and the antidote to prevent us from dying."[287] One of the most clear statements that Ignatius makes regarding the real presence of Christ in the Eucharist is in his letter to the Smyrneans. "[The Gnostics] abstain from the Eucharist and from prayer, because they confess not the Eucharist to be the flesh of our Saviour Jesus Christ, which suffered for our sins, and which the Father, of His goodness, raised up. Those, therefore, who speak against this gift of God, incur death in the midst of their disputes. But it were better for them to treat it with respect, that they also might rise again."[288]

Ignatius was refuting the Gnostics. These Gnostics rejected the idea that Jesus had a real physical body. They believed Jesus was just a spirit being without a physical body. The reason they believed this was because they believed that the material world was evil. This led them to the false teaching that Jesus did not have a physical (material) body. Because of their strange belief, they rejected the Eucharist. Why would they reject the Eucharist based on this belief?

They rejected the Eucharist because the church taught that it was truly a partaking of the body and blood of Jesus, and since the Gnostics rejected the fact that Jesus had a physical body, they also

---

[286] Ignatius. *The Ante-Nicene Fathers: Epistle to the Ephesians*. Chapter V. Edited by Alexander Roberts, James Donaldson, and Arthur Cleveland Coxe. I. Vol. I. X vols. New York, NY: Cosimo Classics, 2007, 51.

[287] Ignatius. *The Ante-Nicene Fathers: Epistle to the Ephesians*. Chapter XX. Edited by Alexander Roberts, James Donaldson, and Arthur Cleveland Coxe. I. Vol. I. X vols. New York, NY: Cosimo Classics, 2007, 58.

[288] Ignatius. *The Ante-Nicene Fathers: Epistle to the Smyrnaeans*. Chapter VII. Edited by Alexander Roberts, James Donaldson, and Arthur Cleveland Coxe. I. Vol. I. X vols. New York, NY: Cosimo Classics, 2007, 89.

rejected the fact that the Eucharist could be the body and blood of Jesus. So when certain Christian groups today reject the real presence of Christ in the Eucharist and say it is just a "symbol," they are actually siding with the Gnostics! Justin Martyr, writing around AD 155, said,

> And this food is called among us…[the Eucharist], of which no one is allowed to partake but the man who believes that the things which we teach are true, and who has been washed with the washing that is for the remission of sins, and unto regeneration, and who is so living as Christ has enjoined. For not as common bread and common drink do we receive these; but in like manner as Jesus Christ our Saviour, having been made flesh by the Word of God, had both flesh and blood for our salvation, so likewise have we been taught that the food which is blessed by the prayer of His word, and from which our blood and flesh by transmutation are nourished, is the flesh and blood of that Jesus who was made flesh.[289]

Justin explains that the Eucharist is not just "common bread and common drink," but rather, it is the "flesh and blood of that Jesus who was made flesh." Irenaeus wrote around AD 180,

> But our opinion is in accordance with the Eucharist, and the Eucharist in turn establishes our opinion. For we offer to [Jesus] His own, announcing consistently the fellowship and union of the flesh and Spirit. For as the bread,

---

[289] Justin Martyr. *The Ante-Nicene Fathers: The First Apology.* Chapter LXVI. Edited by Alexander Roberts, James Donaldson, and Arthur Cleveland Coxe. I. Vol. I. X vols. New York, NY: Cosimo Classics, 2007, 185.

which is produced from the earth, when it receives the invocation of God, is no longer common bread, but the Eucharist, consisting of two realities, earthly and heavenly; so also our bodies, when they receive the Eucharist, are no longer corruptible, having the hope of the resurrection to eternity.[290]

Irenaeus's quote is very insightful. Like Justin, he explains that the Eucharist is not "common bread," but rather, it consists of "two realities, earthly and heavenly." It looks, tastes, smells, and so forth like bread and wine (earthly reality), but it is truly the body and blood of the Lord Jesus (heavenly reality). Irenaeus also echoes Ignatius in describing the Eucharist in medicinal terms. He says it makes our bodies "no longer corruptible, having the hope of the resurrection to eternity." Both Ignatius and Irenaeus seem to link partaking of the Eucharist to the resurrection of our bodies at the second coming. Clement of Alexandria wrote around AD 197,

"Eat ye my flesh," [Jesus] says, "and drink my blood." Such is the suitable food which the Lord ministers, and He offers His flesh and pours forth His blood, and nothing is wanting for the children's growth. O amazing mystery! We are enjoined to cast off the old and carnal corruption, as also the old nutriment, receiving in exchange another new regimen, that of Christ, receiving Him if we can, to hide Him within; and that, enshrining the Saviour in our souls, we may correct the affections of our flesh."[291]

[290] Irenaeus. *The Ante-Nicene Fathers: Against Heresies.* Book IV. Chapter XVIII. Section 5. Edited by Alexander Roberts, James Donaldson, and Arthur Cleveland Coxe. I. Vol. I. X vols. New York, NY: Cosimo Classics, 2007, 486.
[291] Clement of Alexandria. *The Ante-Nicene Fathers: The Instructor.* Book I. Chapter VI. Edited by Alexander Roberts, James Donaldson, and Arthur Cleveland Coxe. II. Vol. II. X vols. New York, NY: Cosimo Classics, 2007, 220.

Clement refers to John 6 and, like Ignatius and Irenaeus, portrays the Eucharist in a nourishing/medicinal manner. Partaking of the Eucharist helps us to "correct the affections of our flesh." This shows how partaking of the Lord's body and blood helps us in our sanctification. Tertullian speaks of the Eucharist in a very similar manner around AD 210, saying, "[Our] flesh feeds on the body and blood of Christ, that the soul likewise may fatten on its God."[292] Once again, the Eucharist is described in a nourishing/medicinal way. This would make no sense if the Eucharist was just a symbol.

Hippolytus wrote around AD 217, saying, "And she hath furnished her table:" that denotes the promised knowledge of the Holy Trinity; it also refers to His [Jesus'] honoured and undefiled body and blood, which day by day are administered and offered sacrificially at the spiritual divine table, as a memorial of that first and ever-memorable table of the spiritual divine supper."[293]

Once again, the Eucharist is described in very literal terms. Origen wrote around AD 249, "Formerly there was baptism in an obscure way... Now, however, in full view, there is regeneration in water and in the Holy Spirit. Formerly, in an obscure way, there was manna for food; now, however, in full view, there is the true food, the flesh of the Word of God, as he himself says: 'My flesh is true food, and my blood is true drink' [Jn 6:56]."[294]

Origen explains that just as the Israelites ate manna from God, now we eat the Eucharist from God—which is the flesh and blood of Jesus. Cyprian wrote around AD 250,

> When, therefore, He says, that whoever
> shall eat of His bread shall live for ever; as it is

---

[292] Tertullian. *The Ante-Nicene Fathers: On the Resurrection of the Flesh*. Chapter VIII. Edited by Alexander Roberts, James Donaldson, and Arthur Cleveland Coxe. III. Vol. III. X vols. New York, NY: Cosimo Classics, 2007, 551.

[293] Hippolytus. *The Ante-Nicene Fathers: Fragment from Commentary on Proverbs*. Edited by Alexander Roberts, James Donaldson, and Arthur Cleveland Coxe. V. Vol. V. X vols. New York, NY: Cosimo Classics, 2007, 175.

[294] Akin, Jimmy. *The Fathers Know Best*. El Cajon, CA: Catholic Answers Inc., 2010, 295.

manifest that those who partake of His body and receive the Eucharist by the right of communion are living, so, on the other hand, we must fear and pray lest any one who, being withheld from communion, is separate from Christ's body should remain at a distance from salvation; as He Himself threatens, and says, "Unless ye eat the flesh of the Son of man, and drink His blood, ye shall have no life in you." And therefore we ask that our bread—that is, Christ—may be given to us daily, that we who abide and live in Christ may not depart from His sanctification and body.[295]

Cyprian appeals to John 6 and explains that the Eucharist is related to our salvation. This is why one is in danger when they go without the Eucharist. The Eucharist strengthens our faith and keeps us in communion with God, hence the name often ascribed to it—communion.

Besides the real presence of Christ in the Eucharist, it is also a spiritual sacrifice. In the early church, the Eucharist was described as the fulfillment of Malachi 1:11–14, which reads,

> For from the rising of the sun even unto the going down of the same my name shall be great among the Gentiles; and in every place incense shall be offered unto my name, and a pure offering: for my name shall be great among the heathen, saith the Lord of hosts. [12] But ye have profaned it, in that ye say, The table of the Lord is polluted; and the fruit thereof, even his meat, is contemptible. [13] Ye said also, Behold, what a weariness is it! and ye have snuffed at it, saith

---

[295] Cyprian. *The Ante-Nicene Fathers: On the Lord's Prayer*. Section 18. Edited by Alexander Roberts, James Donaldson, and Arthur Cleveland Coxe. V. Vol. V. X vols. New York, NY: Cosimo Classics, 2007, 452.

the Lord of hosts; and ye brought that which was torn, and the lame, and the sick; thus ye brought an offering: should I accept this of your hand? saith the Lord. ¹⁴ But cursed be the deceiver, which hath in his flock a male, and voweth, and sacrificeth unto the Lord a corrupt thing: for I am a great King, saith the Lord of hosts, and my name is dreadful among the heathen."

The *Didache*, which dates around AD 80–140, says that the Eucharist is "spiritual meat and drink"²⁹⁶ (Didache 10:3). It also says,

> But on the Lord's day, after that ye have assembled together, break bread and give thanks, having in addition confessed your sins, that your sacrifice may be pure. But let not any one who hath a quarrel with his companion join with you, until they be reconciled, that your sacrifice may not be polluted, for it is that which is spoken of by the Lord. In every place and time offer unto me a pure sacrifice, for I am a great King, saith the Lord, and my name is wonderful among the Gentiles.²⁹⁷ (Didache 14:1–3)

The *Didache* says one must confess their sins before partaking of the Eucharist that their sacrifice "may not be polluted." This seems to be an allusion to when Paul warned the church in Corinth to "examine" themselves before partaking of the Eucharist lest they eat and drink "damnation" to themselves (1 Cor. 11:28–29). Justin Martyr also spoke of the Eucharist being a sacrifice around AD 155, saying,

> Hence God speaks by the mouth of Malachi, one of the twelve [prophets], as I said before,

²⁹⁶ *Didache: The Teaching of the Apostles*. Coppell, TX, 2020, 16.
²⁹⁷ *Didache: The Teaching of the Apostles*. Coppell, TX, 2020, 22.

about the sacrifices at that time presented by you: 'I have no pleasure in you, saith the Lord; and I will not accept your sacrifices at your hands: for, from the rising of the sun unto the going down of the same, My name has been glorified among the Gentiles, and in every place incense is offered to My name, and a pure offering: for My name is great among the Gentiles, saith the Lord: but ye profane it.' [So] He then speaks of those Gentiles, namely us, who in every place offer sacrifices to Him, i.e., the bread of the Eucharist, and also the cup of the Eucharist, affirming both that we glorify His name, and that you profane [it].[298]

Justin appeals to the same Scripture as the *Didache* (Mal. 1:11–14). He argues that the Eucharistic sacrifice is the fulfillment of that prophecy. Irenaeus wrote around AD 180 and, like the *Didache* and Justin Martyr, related the Eucharist to the prophecy in Malachi 1.[299]

The Eucharist is a very deep and profound doctrine to expound. So let us be thankful for the sacrament of the body and blood of the Lord. Let us come to His body and blood with repentant hearts. And most importantly, let us not end up like the unbelieving disciples who turned away from Jesus because His teaching on the real presence of Himself in the Eucharist was too "hard" of a saying to understand (John 6:60–61). The Eucharist is indeed a mystery, but those who partake of it do really partake of the body and blood of the Lord. How that can be possible, I do not know. But I do know that "without faith it is impossible to please [God]" (Heb. 11:6). Knowing all that, I choose to have childlike faith and believe Jesus when He says that the Eucharist really is His body and blood. Because we all must

---

[298] Justin Martyr. *The Ante-Nicene Fathers: Dialogue with Trypho.* Chapter XLI. Edited by Alexander Roberts, James Donaldson, and Arthur Cleveland Coxe. I. Vol. I. X vols. New York, NY: Cosimo Classics, 2007, 215.

[299] Irenaeus. *The Ante-Nicene Fathers: Against Heresies.* Book IV. Chapter XVII. Section 5. Edited by Alexander Roberts, James Donaldson, and Arthur Cleveland Coxe. I. Vol. I. X vols. New York, NY: Cosimo Classics, 2007, 484.

become like little children to enter the kingdom of heaven (Matt 18:3). Thank the Lord Jesus for this beautiful sacrament given to the church!

ETERNAL HELL

There are some groups such as the Seventh-day Adventists who teach a doctrine known as annihilationism, which teaches that when the wicked are judged, they will be destroyed or annihilated from existence rather than being tormented for all eternity. This is contradictory to the teachings of Christianity since Jesus Himself described hell as "everlasting fire" (Matt. 25:41) and a place where "their worm dieth not, and the fire is not quenched" (Mark 9:48). Worms will not die in hell because nothing is "annihilated" there. While the picture of worms being in hell may just be figurative speech, the point Jesus makes is clear—everybody and everything in hell will be eternal, which means their suffering will also be eternal. Speaking of those who take the mark of the beast in the end times, Revelation says,

> And the third angel followed them, saying with a loud voice, If any man worship the beast and his image, and receive his mark in his forehead, or in his hand, [10] The same shall drink of the wine of the wrath of God, which is poured out without mixture into the cup of his indignation; and he shall be tormented with fire and brimstone in the presence of the holy angels, and in the presence of the Lamb: [11] And the smoke of their torment ascendeth up for ever and ever: and they have no rest day nor night, who worship the beast and his image, and whosoever receiveth the mark of his name. (Rev. 14:9–11)

Revelation also describes the lake of fire as a place where people "shall be tormented day and night for ever and ever" (Rev. 20:10). Not only is the Bible clear about hell being eternal, but the early church writers were as well. Justin Martyr wrote around AD 155 explaining how when Jesus returns He "shall send those of the wicked, endued with eternal sensibility, into everlasting fire with the wicked devils."[300] Justin makes it clear that in hell, people will have "eternal sensibility," meaning they will experience torment physically, mentally, and spiritually.

This is the doctrine often called "eternal conscious torment." Athenagoras wrote around AD 175, saying, "God has not made us as sheep or beasts of burden, a mere by-work, and that we should perish and be annihilated. On these grounds it is not likely that we should wish to do evil, or deliver ourselves over to the great Judge to be punished."[301]

Athenagoras clearly refutes the false doctrine of annihilationism, explaining how we are different from animals in that we will *not* be "annihilated." Humans have souls and will live forever. We will live forever either in the presence of the Lord or in torment. Tertullian wrote around AD 197 explaining how "the wicked" will suffer "the doom of fire at once without ending and without break."[302] Hippolytus wrote around AD 215 describing the judgment as such

> And being present at His [Jesus'] judicial decision, all, both men and angels and demons, shall utter one voice, saying, "Righteous is Thy judgment." Of which voice the justification will be seen in the awarding to each that which is just; since to those who have done well shall be assigned righteously eternal bliss, and to the lov-

---

[300] Justin Martyr. *The Ante-Nicene Fathers: The First Apology*. Chapter LII. Edited by Alexander Roberts, James Donaldson, and Arthur Cleveland Coxe. I. Vol. I. X vols. New York, NY: Cosimo Classics, 2007, 180.

[301] Athenagoras. *The Ante-Nicene Fathers: A Plea for the Christians*. Chapter XXXI. Edited by Alexander Roberts, James Donaldson, and Arthur Cleveland Coxe. II. Vol. II. X vols. New York, NY: Cosimo Classics, 2007, 146.

[302] Tertullian. *The Ante-Nicene Fathers: Apology*. Chapter XVIII. Edited by Alexander Roberts, James Donaldson, and Arthur Cleveland Coxe. III. Vol. III. X vols. New York, NY: Cosimo Classics, 2007, 32.

ers of iniquity shall be given eternal punishment. And the fire which is unquenchable and without end awaits these latter, and a certain fiery worm which dieth not, and which does not waste the body, but continues bursting forth from the body with unending pain. No sleep will give them rest; no night will soothe them; no death will deliver them from punishment; no voice of interceding friends will profit them.[303]

Hippolytus describes hell as "eternal punishment" and a place of "unquenchable" fire. This fire will "not waste the body, but continues bursting forth from the body with unending pain." This means those in hell will suffer torment from the fire, yet their body will not be destroyed or annihilated. The torment will last forever. Nothing will end these sufferings: not sleep, not night, not death, and not friendly intercessions. Nothing will end the torment of hell. This is the true Christian doctrine of hell. Our finite minds cannot fully comprehend what it would be like, and none of us want to find out. Praise the Lord Jesus for saving us.

THE SABBATH AND THE LORD'S DAY

In the Old Covenant, God gave the Israelites the command to keep the Sabbath day—which is Saturday (Ex. 20:8–11). Some groups today, like the Seventh-day Adventists, argue that Christians must keep the Saturday Sabbath under the New Covenant as well. This false teaching is a form of Judaizing. When Jesus worked and healed on the Sabbath day, the Pharisees accused Him saying, "Is it lawful to heal on the sabbath days?" (Matt. 12:10).

Jesus pointed out their hypocrisy saying, "And he [Jesus] said unto them, What man shall there be among you, that shall have

[303] Hippolytus. *The Ante-Nicene Fathers: Against Plato, On the Cause of the Universe.* Section 3. Edited by Alexander Roberts, James Donaldson, and Arthur Cleveland Coxe. V. Vol. V. X vols. New York, NY: Cosimo Classics, 2007, 222–223.

one sheep, and if it fall into a pit on the sabbath day, will he not lay hold on it, and lift it out? [12] How much then is a man better than a sheep? Wherefore it is lawful to do well on the sabbath days" (Matt. 12:11–12).

Jesus pointed out how they too do certain work on the Sabbath day, which makes them hypocrites. Jesus says it is lawful to do well on the Sabbath. Previously in the same chapter, He explained "the Son of man is Lord even of the sabbath day" (Matt. 12:8). Jesus created the Sabbath day, which means His teaching about the Sabbath and its meaning is true.

In the parallel account in Mark, Jesus said, "The sabbath was made for man, and not man for the sabbath" (Mark 2:27). The Sabbath was made to help man relieve his burdens for one day out of the week. It was so people could have rest. But the Pharisees, and modern groups like the Seventh-day Adventists, had turned it into a legalistic thing. Once again, the whole point of the Sabbath was to give people rest, and it was only "a shadow of things to come" (Col. 2:16–17). The rest of the Sabbath was only a "shadow" of the true rest that is found in Christ as He said, "Come unto me, all ye that labour and are heavy laden, and I will give you rest. [29] Take my yoke upon you, and learn of me; for I am meek and lowly in heart: and ye shall find rest unto your souls. [30] For my yoke is easy, and my burden is light" (Matt. 11:28–30).

Justin Martyr wrote to Trypho the Jew around AD 155, explaining why God gave the Israelites certain laws like circumcision, keeping the Sabbath, etc. He said,

The Lawgiver is present, yet you do not see Him; to the poor the Gospel is preached, the blind see, yet you do not understand. You have now need of a second circumcision, though you glory greatly in the flesh. The new law requires you to keep perpetual sabbath, and you, because you are idle for one day, suppose you are pious, not discerning why this has been commanded you: and if you eat unleavened bread, you say

the will of God has been fulfilled. The Lord our
God does not take pleasure in such observances:
if there is any perjured person or a thief among
you, let him cease to be so; if any adulterer, let
him repent; then he has kept the sweet and true
sabbaths of God. If any one has impure hands, let
him was and be pure… For we too would observe
the fleshly circumcision, and the Sabbaths, and
in short all the feasts, if we did not know for what
reason they were enjoined you,—namely, on
account of your transgressions and the hardness
of your hearts…" Moreover, that God enjoined
you to keep the Sabbath, and impose on you
other precepts for a sign, as I have already said,
on account of your unrighteousness, and that of
your fathers."[304]

Justin explains to Trypho that the Jews were given these laws
because of their "transgressions" and the "hardness" of their hearts.
He explains that God does not take pleasure in us going through the
motions of days and rituals but rather that we be holy in our conduct
by ceasing to be a "thief," an "adulterer," etc. That is what God truly
takes delight in—holiness. Tertullian wrote around AD 203, discussing the Sabbath.

In fine, let him who contends that the
Sabbath is still to be observed as a balm of salvation, and circumcision on the eighth day because
of the threat of death, teach us that, for the time
past, righteous men kept the Sabbath, or practised
circumcision, and were thus rendered "friends of
God." For if circumcision purges a man since

[304] Justin Martyr. *The Ante-Nicene Fathers: Dialogue with Trypho.* Chapter XII,
XVIII, XXI. Edited by Alexander Roberts, James Donaldson, and Arthur
Cleveland Coxe. I. Vol. I. X vols. New York, NY: Cosimo Classics, 2007, 200,
203–204.

God made Adam uncircumcised, why did He not circumcise him, even after his sinning, if circumcision purges? At all events, in settling him in paradise, He appointed one uncircumcised as colonist of paradise. Therefore, since God originated Adam uncircumcised, inobservant of the Sabbath, consequently his offspring also, Abel, offering Him sacrifices, uncircumcised and inobservant of the Sabbath, was by Him commended; while He accepted what he was offering in simplicity of heart, and reprobated the sacrifice of his brother Cain, who was not rightly dividing what he was offering. Noah also, uncircumcised—yes, and inobservant of the Sabbath— God freed from the deluge. For Enoch, too, most righteous man, uncircumcised and inobservant of the Sabbath, He translated from this world; who did not first taste death, in order that, being a candidate for eternal life, he might by this time show us that we also may, without the burden of the law of Moses, please God. Melchizedek also, "the priest of the most high God," uncircumcised and inobservant of the Sabbath, was chosen to the priesthood of God. Lot, withal, the brother of Abraham, proves that it was for the merits of righteousness, without observance of the law, that he was freed from the conflagration of the Sodomites. But Abraham, (you say,) was circumcised. Yes, but he pleased God before his circumcision; nor yet did he observe the Sabbath... And through this arises the question for us, what sabbath God willed us to keep? For the Scriptures point to a sabbath eternal and a sabbath temporal. For Isaiah the prophet says, "Your sabbaths my soul hateth;" and in another place he says, "My sabbaths ye have profaned." Whence we discern that the temporal sabbath is human, and the eternal sabbath is accounted divine; concerning which He predicts through Isaiah: "And there shall be," He says, "month after month, and day after day, and sabbath after sabbath; and all flesh shall come to adore in Jerusalem, saith the Lord;" which we understand to have been fulfilled in the times of Christ, when "all flesh"—that is, every nation—"came to adore in Jerusalem" God the Father, through Jesus Christ His Son, as was predicted through Jesus Christ His Son, as was predicted through the prophet: "Behold, proselytes through me shall go unto Thee." Thus, therefore, before this temporal sabbath, there was withal an eternal sabbath foreshown and foretold; just as before the carnal circumcision there was withal a spiritual circumcision foreshown.[305]

Tertullian makes the point that God created Adam uncircumcised and inobservant of the Sabbath. If God made the first man like this, it is obvious that He does not care about circumcision or Sabbath keeping. He also makes the point that men like Abel, Noah, Enoch, and Lot all pleased God while being uncircumcised and without keeping the Sabbath.

This is proof that the purpose of the Sabbath and circumcision was not for salvation. But because of the hardness of the Jews' hearts, it was given to them. This is the true meaning of the Sabbath Day, and it was only for Jews living under God's theocracy. Christians are under the New Covenant, which means we are not required to keep the Sabbath as the Jews did. Historically, Christians always met and worshipped on Sunday because that is the day Jesus rose from

---

[305] Tertullian. *The Ante-Nicene Fathers: Answer to the Jews*. Chapter 2–4. Edited by Alexander Roberts, James Donaldson, and Arthur Cleveland Coxe. III. Vol. III. X vols. New York, NY: Cosimo Classics, 2007, 153, 155.

the dead and they wanted to separate themselves from the Jews who worshipped on Saturday (the Sabbath).

The book of Acts says the Christians came together to break bread on "the first day of the week [Sunday]" (Acts 20:7). Ignatius wrote around AD 110, saying, "No longer observing the Sabbath, but living in the observance of the Lord's Day [Sunday], on which also our life has sprung up again by Him and by His death."[306] Ignatius explains that Christians worship on Sunday, not Saturday, because it is the day on which Jesus rose again and gave us new life. Justin Martyr wrote around AD 155, explaining how Christians meet on Sunday.

> And on the day called Sunday, all who live in cities or in the country gather together to one place, and the memoirs of the apostles or the writings of the prophets are read, as long as time permits... But Sunday is the day on which we all hold our common assembly, because it is the first day on which God, having wrought a change in the darkness and matter, made the world; and Jesus Christ our Saviour on the same day rose from the dead. For He was crucified on the day before that of Saturn (Saturday); and on the day after that of Saturn, which is the day of the Sun, having appeared to His apostles and disciples, He taught them these things, which we have submitted to you also for your consideration.[307]

Just like Ignatius, Justin's reasoning for Christians meeting on Sunday is because it is the day of the resurrection. In sum, Christians

---

[306] Ignatius. *The Ante-Nicene Fathers*: *Epistle to the Magnesians*. Chapter IX. Edited by Alexander Roberts, James Donaldson, and Arthur Cleveland Coxe. I. Vol. I. X vols. New York, NY: Cosimo Classics, 2007, 62.

[307] Justin Martyr. *The Ante-Nicene Fathers*: *The First Apology*. Chapter LXVII. Edited by Alexander Roberts, James Donaldson, and Arthur Cleveland Coxe. I. Vol. I. X vols. New York, NY: Cosimo Classics, 2007, 186.

are not required to keep the Sabbath like in the Old Covenant. We keep the Sabbath in our own way. We do this, not only by meeting to worship on Sunday (the Lord's Day) but also by our holy conduct at all times.

CONCLUSION

1. God is a Trinity. The Father, the Son, and the Holy Spirit are all distinct *persons* that make up one *being*.
2. The baptismal formula is in the name of the Trinity. Immersion is the preferred method of baptism, but sprinkling and pouring/affusion are valid modes of baptism as well. Baptism washes away sins and gives the gift of the Holy Spirit, making one born again. Baptism is for believers *and* children of believers.
3. The Eucharist is not just a symbol, but rather, it is truly the body and blood of Jesus. The Eucharist helps Christians in their sanctification, strengthening their faith, holiness, and relationship with God. The Eucharist is also a spiritual sacrifice.
4. Hell is eternal conscious torment. When the wicked go to their place of suffering, they will be there for all eternity. Annihilationism is false.
5. The Sabbath was a shadow of things to come, and Christians are not obligated to keep it in the manner of the Old Covenant. Christians keep the Sabbath by meeting together to worship on Sunday, living holy, and resting in the finished work of Christ.

These are the beliefs that marked the early church. This is not meant to be an in-depth analysis of the early church but rather a brief overview. To go into more detail on the early church would require a full book in and of itself. But this short overview suffices for the present.

CHAPTER 7

ISLAM

INTRODUCTION

From AD 33 to AD 610, the doctrine of the Trinity was the belief concerning Jesus and the Godhead. In AD 610, a man named Muhammad was in a cave worshipping when he was (supposedly) visited by the angel Gabriel. There is something very interesting about this claim since the Apostle Paul wrote around AD 55, saying,

> I marvel that ye are so soon removed from him that called you into the grace of Christ unto another gospel: [7] Which is not another; but there be some that trouble you, and would pervert the gospel of Christ. [8] But though we, or an angel from heaven, preach any other gospel unto you than that which we have preached unto you, let him be accursed. [9] As we said before, so say I now again, if any man preach any other gospel unto you than that ye have received, let him be accursed. (Gal. 1:6–9)

Around 550 years before Muhammad claimed to be visited by an angel, the Apostle Paul warned about people perverting the Gospel. The ironic part is that he warned specifically about angels.

He explained that even if somebody claims to have been visited by an angel (like Muhammed) and preaches a different religion, they are accursed. This alone proves Islam to be false. Muhammed was at first confused about the encounter, but his wife convinced him he was a prophet of God. He began spreading his newly founded religion. Muhammed died in AD 632. One important thing to note is that Muhammed did not write anything down. Soon after he died, his followers began writing down his teachings from memory and formed the book we know as the Quran. Muslims claim the Quran is the final revelation from God. The Quran says,

> Say, 'He who is an enemy to Gabriel, because it is he who has brought down this (Qur'an) on your heart by the command of Allah, and which confirms (the Scriptures) which preceded it, and is a guidance and good tidings to the believers, '(Let him bear in mind that) whoever is an enemy to Allah and His angels and His Messengers and Gabriel and Michael, then, of course, Allah (Himself) is an enemy to such disbelievers.'[308] (Quran 2:97–98)

The *sunnah* and *hadith* are also writings that Muslims subscribe to which consist of sayings and practices of Muhammad, but they do not claim them to be divinely inspired.

THE PERSON OF JESUS AND THE GODHEAD

Like proven previously, leading up to the founding of Islam, the accepted belief about Jesus was that He was God and the second

---

[308] 'Omar, Amatul Rahman, and 'Abdul Mannan 'Omar, trans. *The Holy Qur'ān: Arabic Text—English Translation*. Hockessin, DE: Noor Foundation International Inc., 2010, 15. (All Quran quotations taken from here).

person of the Trinity. Muslims came five hundred years later and rejected this belief. The Quran says,

> O people of the Scripture! Do not go beyond the limits (of propriety) in the matter of your religion, nor say anything regarding Allah except that which is perfectly true. The Messiah, Jesus, son of Mary was only a Messenger of Allah, and (a fulfillment of) His word which He communicated to Mary, and a mercy from Him. Believe, therefore, in Allah and in all His Messengers, and do not say, '(There are) three (Gods).' Refrain (from following this doctrine) it will be better for you. Verily, Allah is the One and only worthy of worship. He is Holy. Far above having a son. To Him belongs whatever is in the heavens and whatever is in the earth. And Allah suffices as a Disposer of affairs. (Quran 4:171)

After centuries of believing Jesus to be God, Muhammed came and claimed Jesus was just a messenger of God and not God Himself. What is interesting is that "Allah" refers to Christians as "people of the Scripture." This shows a major internal contradiction in Islam. They claim that the Christians have the Scripture from God, yet they do not believe what those Scriptures say. I will address this point more in depth later. In this passage, Allah misrepresents the beliefs of Christians. Allah claims that Christians believe in multiple gods, which is neither historically nor biblically accurate. As demonstrated previously, Christians always held to three divine persons in one God.

This leaves us with one of two options regarding Allah. Either Allah really does not know that Christians believe in one God, which would mean he's not omniscience and thus proving that he's not God or Allah lied about what Christians believe, making him a liar and thus once again proving that he is not God because God does not lie (Num. 23:19, Tit. 1:2, Heb. 6:18). In fact, the father of lies is Satan according to the Scripture (John 8:44). Satan is also called a deceiver

(Rev. 12:9). In this Quranic verse, Allah is being deceitful by lying about Christians. The Quran also says this regarding Allah, "And they (the persecutors of Jesus) planned (to crucify him) and Allah planned (to save him) and Allah is the best of the planners" (Quran 3:54). Allah is the "best of planners." Some translations render it "best of schemers." Scheming is deception and deception is a Satanic quality, not a Godly one. So far, Allah has resembled Satan more than God. This same point can be made for Quran 5:73.

Returning to the deity of Jesus, the Quran says, "Say, '(The fact is) He is Allah, the One and Alone in His Being. 'Allah is that Supreme Being Who is the, Independent and Besought of all and Unique in all His attributes. 'He begets none and is begotten by no one. 'And there is none His equal'" (Quran 112:1–4).

This passage in the Quran says God does not beget nor is He begotten, obviously attacking the Trinity. The Bible says, "For God so loved the world that He gave His only begotten Son, that whoever believes in Him should not perish but have everlasting life" (John 3:16). So the Quran says God does not beget, yet the New Testament says He did beget a Son. Which source should I believe? I think I will stick with the source that came five hundred years prior to the other. The prophet Isaiah, writing around the eighth century BC said, "For unto us a child is born, unto us a son is given: and the government shall be upon his shoulder: and his name shall be called Wonderful, Counsellor, the mighty God, the everlasting Father, the Prince of Peace" (Isa. 9:6).

Isaiah prophesied of a Child/Son being born that was God. If that's not enough, the second Psalm was written around the eleventh century BC and says, "I will declare the decree: the LORD hath said unto me, Thou art my Son; this day have I begotten thee" (Ps. 2:7). This verse speaks of a Son being begotten. Granted, many will claim this is speaking about David, but this was understood by the early church to be speaking of Jesus (Heb. 1:5). The Quran also says, "(Recall the time) when the angels said, 'O Mary! Allah gives you good tidings through a (prophetic) **word from [Allah]** (about the birth of a son) whose name is the Messiah, Jesus, son of Mary, (he shall be) worthy of regard in this world and in the Hereafter and one of the nearest ones (to Him)" (Quran 3:45).

This verse calls Jesus the word of Allah [God]. John chapter 1 says, "In the beginning was the Word, and the Word was with God, and the Word was God" (John 1:1). The Quran calls Jesus the word of Allah in Surah 4:171 as well. Jesus is the Word of God in both the Gospels and the Quran. The Gospel says the Word of God was God. The Quran says to believe the Gospels (Quran 5:68). This means the Quran indirectly calls Jesus God.

INTERNAL CONTRADICTIONS

If you speak with a Muslim today, they most likely will not accept anything in the New Testament as inspired. This presents an internal contradiction since the Quran says,

> (Believers!) observe all the propriety when you argue with the people of the Scripture; but those who are bent upon behaving unjustly among them do not agree to these principles (so deal with them accordingly). And say (to them), 'We believe in all that is revealed to us and in that which has been revealed to you, and our God and your God is One, and to Him we stand resigned.' (Quran 29:46)

This verse claims that Muslims believe in all that was revealed to the Christians. That means they claim to believe in the Gospels. The Gospel of Matthew says,

> When Jesus came into the coasts of Caesarea Philippi, he asked his disciples, saying, Whom do men say that I the Son of man am? [14] And they said, Some say that thou art John the Baptist: some, Elias; and others, Jeremias, or one of the prophets. [15] He saith unto them, But whom say

ye that I am? [16] And Simon Peter answered and said, Thou art the Christ, the Son of the living God. (Matt. 16:13–16)

So let me get this straight. Muslims claim to believe in the Gospels. The Gospels say Jesus is the Son of God. Yet the Quran says God (Allah) has no son (Quran 112:1–4). So the Quran teaches that Jesus is the Son of God (by saying they believe the Gospels) whilst simultaneously teaching that God has no son and that Jesus is just a messenger (Quran 4:171, 112:1–4). So here we see an internal contradiction in the Quran thus proving it is not from God. Let us examine another logical contradiction. The Quran says,

(Recall the time) when the angels said, 'O Mary! Allah gives you good tidings through a (prophetic) word from Him (about the birth of a son) whose name is the Messiah, Jesus, son of Mary, (he shall be) worthy of regard in this world and in the Hereafter and one of the nearest ones (to Him), 'And he will speak to the people when in the cradle (as a child) and when of old age, and shall be of the righteous.' She said, 'My Lord! How can I and whence shall I have a child while no man has yet touched me (in conjugal relationship)?' (The Lord) said, 'Such are the ways of Allah, He creates what He will. When He decrees a thing He simply commands it, "Be" and it comes to be.' (Quran 3:45–47)

This passage in the Quran says that Jesus was born of a virgin (Mary). Now I have one question for the Muslim. If Mary was a virgin, who is Jesus's Father? As a Christian I can answer this easily. Jesus's Father is God (Matt. 3:17). Muslims cannot explain who Jesus's Father is if He was born from a virgin. The only explanation is that His Father is God! Not to mention, taking into consideration the previous examined passage (Quran 29:46), the Muslim should believe Matthew 3:17 since they claim to believe all the Scriptures the Christians have. Here is another contradiction:

> (Believers!) observe all the propriety when you argue with the people of the Scripture; but those who are bent upon behaving unjustly among them do not agree to these principles (so deal with them accordingly). And say (to them), 'We believe in all that is revealed to us and in that which has been revealed to you, **and our God and your God is One**, and to Him we stand resigned.' (Quran 29:46)

This verse says that Muslims and Christians have the same God. Yet Quran 3:85 says anybody who is not a Muslim goes to hell. If Christians worship the same God, how would they go to hell? That makes no sense. Not to mention, if Christians and Muslims have the same God, why does the God of the Bible have a Son (Matt. 3:17) while Allah does not (Quran 112:1–4)? If a guy named Terry has a child and another guy named Terry doesn't, are they the same Terry? Obviously not. So once again, the Quran makes a logical contradiction. Usually, the claim Muslims will make to avoid accepting these internal contradictions is that the Gospels were corrupted. I just have one question—when? When were the Gospels corrupted? Let me show how this makes no sense.

The Quran was formulated around the mid-seventh century AD. The Gospels of Matthew, Mark, and Luke were all completed by about AD 67 and the Gospel of John around AD 90. The Muslim claim is that these Gospels were corrupted. I must ask, why did Allah say Muslims believe in the same Scriptures as the Christians (Quran 29:46) if they were corrupt? In fact, there are zero verses in the Quran that claim the Gospels or the Torah have been corrupted. The answer can be one of two options. Either Allah did not know they were corrupt which would mean he is not omniscient and thus not God or he did know but purposely told his followers to refer to corrupt books which would mean he was a deceiver, thus proving once again that he's not God. So either way, Allah is not God.

One of the most famous stories in the Bible is in Genesis about Abraham offering his son Isaac as a sacrifice at the command of God:

> And it came to pass after these things, that God did tempt Abraham, and said unto him, Abraham: and he said, Behold, here I am. ² And he said, Take now thy son, **thine only son Isaac**, whom thou lovest, and get thee into the land of Moriah; and **offer him there for a burnt offering** upon one of the mountains which I will tell thee of. ³ And Abraham rose up early in the morning, and saddled his ass, and took two of his young men with him, and Isaac his son, and clave the wood for the burnt offering, and rose up, and went unto the place of which God had told him. ⁴ Then on the third day Abraham lifted up his eyes, and saw the place afar off. ⁵ And Abraham said unto his young men, Abide ye here with the ass; and I and the lad will go yonder and worship, and come again to you. ⁶ And Abraham took the wood of the burnt offering, and laid it upon Isaac his son; and he took the fire in his hand, and a knife; and they went both of them together. ⁷ And Isaac spake unto Abraham his father, and said, My father: and he said, Here am I, my son. And he said, Behold the fire and the wood: but where is the lamb for a burnt offering? ⁸ And Abraham said, My son, God will provide himself a lamb for a burnt offering: so they went both of them together. ⁹ And they came to the place which God had told him of; and Abraham built an altar there, and laid the wood in order, and bound Isaac his son, and laid him on the altar upon the wood. ¹⁰ And Abraham stretched forth his hand, and took the knife to slay his son. ¹¹ And the angel of the LORD called unto him out

of heaven, and said, Abraham, Abraham: and he said, Here am I. [12] And he said, Lay not thine hand upon the lad, neither do thou any thing unto him: for now I know that thou fearest God, seeing thou hast not withheld thy son, thine only son from me. (Gen. 22:1–12)

This story in Genesis makes it clear that Abraham offered his son Isaac on the altar. Now look what the Quran says,

Now, when that (son, Ismail) was (old enough) to work along with him, (his father, Abraham) said, 'My dear son! I have seen in a dream that I sacrifice you. So consider (it and tell me) what you think (of it).' (The son) said, 'My dear father! Do as you are commanded. If Allah will you will find me of the calm and steadfast.' Now, (it so happened) when both of them submitted themselves (to the will of God) and he (Abraham) had laid him (Ismail) down on his forehead, We called out to him (saying), 'O Abraham! 'You have already fulfilled the vision.' That is how We reward those who perform excellent deeds. That was obviously a disciplinary test (crowned with a mighty reward,) And a great sacrifice was the ransom with which We redeemed him (Ismail). (Quran 37:102–107)**

In the Quranic account of the story, Abraham offers Ishmael! So which one is it? Did Abraham offer Isaac or Ishmael on the altar? The Bible, which was written thousands of years prior to the Quran, says Abraham offered Isaac, while the Quran that was written thousands of years later says Abraham offered Ishmael. This presents a serious problem for Islam. Either Allah got it wrong, and Isaac really was the one Abraham sacrificed—meaning Allah is not omniscient and thus not God. Or the Quran has been tampered with and we do not have the original manuscripts. Either way, Islam falls flat on its face. The Quran says,

> And We sent Jesus, son of Mary, in the footsteps of these (Prophets), fulfilling that which was (revealed) before him, of the Torah, and We gave him the Evangel which contained guidance and light, fulfilling that which was (revealed) before it, of the Torah, and was a (means of) guidance and an exhortation for those who guard against evil. And let the followers of the Evangel judge according to what Allah has revealed therein. And indeed those who do not judge according to what Allah has revealed it is these who are the real disobedient. (Quran 5:46–47)

Allah tells Christians to judge according to what is in the Evangel (the Gospels) and the Torah (Old Testament). Now following this command from Allah, I can go to Isaiah in the Old Testament, which says, "For unto us a child is born, unto us a son is given: and the government shall be upon his shoulder: and his name shall be called Wonderful, Counsellor, The mighty God, The everlasting Father, The Prince of Peace" (Isa. 9:6). Isaiah spoke of a child that would be born and be called God! Who is both a man and God? Jesus! He is the only one who fits this description. Now if I take Allah's advice again and this time refer to the Gospels, it says,

> When Jesus came into the coasts of Caesarea Philippi, he asked his disciples, saying, Whom do men say that I the Son of man am? [14] And they said, Some say that thou art John the Baptist: some, Elias; and others, Jeremias, or one of the prophets. [15] He saith unto them, But whom say ye that I am? [16] And Simon Peter answered and said, Thou art the Christ, the Son of the living God. (Matt. 16:13–16)

Once again, the Gospel tells us that Jesus is the Son of God. So the Quran tells us to refer to the Old Testament and the Gospels. The Old Testament and the Gospels tell us that Jesus is the Son of God and God in the flesh. This means the Quran admits Jesus is God without even realizing it. Jesus wins. The Quran is full of self-contradictions, proving that it is not from God. If the Quran is inspired by God, Christianity is true. And if the Quran is false, Christianity is still true. Either way, Christianity is true.

One final point that needs to be addressed regarding Islam and the Quran is its reliance on the Bible. That is right. Without the Bible, Islam has no ground to stand on. For example, the Quran talks about Abraham, Isaac, Jacob, Jesus, Mary, and all the rest, but it never explains who they are. It mentions their names and parts of their stories, but never fully explains who they are and how they are relevant. This is because the Quran was written with the *assumption* that the reader has already read or at least been familiar with the Bible! The Quran talks a lot about Jesus but does not explain much about Him! Because the Quran *assumes* the reader has read the Gospels which talk about Jesus! So the Quran relies on the Bible for its foundation, yet if you speak with a Muslim today, they will say the Bible is corrupt! Logically speaking there is no way the Quran is inspired by God!

SWOON THEORY

Muslims hold to the swoon theory. This theory says that Jesus did not really die on the cross. The Quran says, "And they (the persecutors of Jesus) planned (to crucify him) and Allah planned (to save him) and Allah is the best of the planners" (Quran 3:54). According to this verse, Jesus did not really die on the cross, but rather Allah saved Him. This passage makes it clearer:

> And because of their (falsely) claiming, 'We did kill the Messiah, Jesus, son of Mary, the (false) Messenger of Allah,' whereas they killed him not, nor did they cause his death by crucifixion, but

he was made to them to resemble (one crucified to death). Verily, those who differ therein are certainly in (a state of) confusion about it. They have no definite knowledge of the matter but are only following a conjecture. They did not kill him, this much is certain (and thus could not prove the Christ as accursed). Rather Allah exalted him with all honour to His presence. And Allah is All-Mighty, All-Wise. And there is none from among the people of the Scripture (the Jews and the Christians) but most certainly will believe in this (incident, that Jesus died on the cross) before his death, (while as a matter of fact they have no sure knowledge about Jesus dying on the cross). And on the Day of Resurrection he (Jesus) will be a witness against them. (Quran 4:157–159)

According to this passage, Jesus did not actually die on the cross, but rather Allah made it look like He did. First, if this is true, that means Allah is a deceiver. The whole faith of Christianity is based on the crucifixion and resurrection of Jesus (1 Cor. 15:17). This means that if Allah truly did deceive everybody and make it look like Jesus died on the cross, he deceived many people into a false belief (in this situation, Christianity) which would lead them to hell (Quran 3:85). Second, this theory is historically inaccurate. The Apostle Paul wrote in his first epistle to the Corinthians, saying, "For I delivered unto you first of all that which I also received, how that Christ died for our sins according to the scriptures; ⁴And that he was buried, and that he rose again the third day according to the scriptures: ⁵And that he was seen of Cephas, then of the twelve" (1 Cor. 15:3–5).

Now Muslims don't accept Paul's writings as Scripture, but that's only because of their theological bias. Because even unbelieving agnostic/atheist scholars accept this as an authentic early church creed. Gary Habermas says, "One of the earliest and most important is quoted in Paul's first letter to the Corinthian church... Several factors mark this as an ancient creed that was part of the earliest traditions of the Christian Church and that predate the writings of Paul."[309]

So even if a Muslim rejects Paul as authoritative, this passage is accepted even by unbelieving scholars as an early church creed that *predates* Paul. This is one of the earliest pieces of evidence we have for the crucifixion of Jesus written around AD 55. **Ignatius of Antioch** wrote to the Trallians around AD 110 prior to being martyred saying, "But if, as some that are without God, that is, the unbelieving, say, that [Jesus] only seemed to suffer (they themselves only seeming to exist), then why am I in bonds? Why do I long to be exposed to the wild beasts? Do I therefore die in vain? Am I not then guilty of falsehood against [the cross of] the Lord?"[310]

He also wrote to the Smyrneans saying, "Now, [Jesus] suffered all these things for our sakes, that we might be saved. And He suffered truly, even as also He truly raised up Himself, not, as certain unbelievers maintain, that He only seemed to suffer, as they themselves only seem to be [Christians]."[311]

Ignatius makes it clear that Jesus truly did die on the cross and rose again. There are also sources from unbelievers attesting to this same thing. See the section titled, "Extra-Biblical Historical Sources for the Resurrection of Jesus" in the "Atheism/Agnosticism" chapter.

CHARACTER OF ALLAH AND ATONEMENT

There is a major holiness flaw in the attributes of Allah. Allah is an unjust judge, and I will demonstrate how. He can either be merciful or just, but not at the same time. This issue comes down to how sinners are forgiven in the theology of Islam. A Muslim must believe

[309] Habermas, 52.
[310] Ignatius. *The Ante-Nicene Fathers: Epistle to the Trallians.* Chapter X. Edited by Alexander Roberts, James Donaldson, and Arthur Cleveland Coxe. I. Vol. I. X vols. New York, NY: Cosimo Classics, 2007, 70.
[311] Ignatius. *The Ante-Nicene Fathers: Epistle to the Smyrneans.* Chapter II. Edited by Alexander Roberts, James Donaldson, and Arthur Cleveland Coxe. I. Vol. I. X vols. New York, NY: Cosimo Classics, 2007, 87.

in Allah and do more good works/deeds than bad works/deeds to enter Paradise. Regarding salvation, the Quran says,

> On [Judgment] day the weighing (the judging of deeds) will be just and true, then he whose scales (of good deeds) are heavy, it is these only who shall attain their goal. And those whose scales are light (and their deeds of little account), it is they who have made their souls suffer losses because they have been unjust with regard to Our Messages. (Quran 7:8–9)

This passage explains that on the day of judgment, Muslims will be judged by their good deeds. Their deeds will be put on "scales." If their good deeds outweigh their bad deeds, they can enter Paradise. If their bad deeds outweigh their good deeds, they will go to hell. Here is a similar passage: "(As for) those who believe and do deeds of righteousness—We charge no soul except according to its capacity. It is these who are the rightful owners of Paradise where they shall abide forever" (Quran 7:42).

So to be saved in Islam, one must have faith in Allah and their good works/deeds must outnumber their bad works/deeds. Christians will not have their works measured on a scale for salvation because of the sacrifice of Jesus (the atonement). A major problem arises for the Muslim—there is no sacrifice in Islam. Christians have the sacrifice of Christ to atone for sins. Islam has no such thing. This is where the character of Allah is revealed.

Imagine a judge in a courtroom. The criminal stands before the judge while he reads off what he did. The criminal murdered somebody and was about to be sentenced to life in prison. Right before the verdict, the criminal interjects, "Wait! I gave money to charity! I also helped old ladies cross the street! You cannot send me to prison! I'm a good person!" The criminal thinks that his good deeds can atone for his sin. Now how would a good judge respond to this? Imagine if the judge said, "You know what, you're right. You've done a lot of good deeds, so I'll let you go free." That would not be a good judge!

By letting the man go free for his crimes, he forsakes justice! By allowing the criminal to walk, the judge endangers the community! Imagine if the president gave a pardon to all the murderers and rapists in prison. Would that be loving? No! That would be unloving because the innocent people would be put in danger from all the criminals walking around. Despite the unloving aspect of it, the main problem is justice. If a judge lets a criminal walk with no punishment, he is merciful, but not just.

On the other hand, if a judge does punish the criminal, he's just, but not merciful. So in the theology of Islam, Allah cannot be both merciful and just. He can only be one or the other. If Allah sends all sinners to hell, he would be just, but not merciful. On the other hand, if Allah lets sinners into Paradise just because they did good deeds, he would be merciful, but not just. It does not matter how many good things I have done in my life if I am a criminal. My good deeds in life do not cancel out my crimes. Just because the murderer gave to charity and helped old ladies cross the street, does not mean he will not be punished for his crime. Good deeds cannot atone for sins. But what can? Allow me to present a story.

Long ago, there was a king. This king was highly respected. He upheld justice in his kingdom. The citizens knew that he would not back down from showing justice. He had a duty to keep order in the kingdom. One of the laws was concerning adultery. To minimize adultery in the kingdom, the punishment was severe. If a person were caught committing adultery, they would have both of their eyes poked out with a hot poker so they could never lust again.

One day, a man was brought before the king. He had been caught in the act of adultery. The guards uncovered his head and the king saw who it was. The man that was caught in adultery was the king's very own son. The king was broken. What should the king do? If the king lets his son go free, he would be merciful, but not just. If he punished his son, he would be just, but not merciful. How could the king be both merciful and just at the same time?

Later, the king appeared before the people wearing an eyepatch. His son was wearing an eyepatch as well. Instead of poking out both of his son's eyes or completely letting him go free, the king poked out one of his son's eyes and one of his own eyes. The law called for two eyes to be poked out. By doing this, the king was just because he fulfilled the law, but also merciful because he allowed his son to keep one eye. This is how a judge can be both merciful and just—it is called sacrifice.

And likewise, the reason Christians can be forgiven is because of the sacrifice of Christ. The God of the Bible is both merciful and just. He is merciful because He allows sinners to enter the kingdom of God, but He is also just because He took care of sin on the cross. God bore the consequence we deserve. And by doing this, He fulfilled His justice (the law) while also fulfilling His mercy.

ALLAH IS NOT SELF-SUFFICIENT

We previously looked at the flaws in the character of Allah. Now I will address a major flaw in the nature of Allah—namely that he is not self-sufficient. The crux of this argument is regarding the doctrine of the Trinity. As discussed previously, Muslims reject the Trinity (Quran 4:171, 5:73). Because of this, a problem arises for Allah. In Christian theology, there are three persons in one God— Father, Son, and Holy Spirit. These three persons have a relationship with each other. We see this throughout the Bible. Matthew says, "And Jesus, when he was baptized, went up straightway out of the water: and, lo, the heavens were opened unto him, and he saw the Spirit of God descending like a dove, and lighting upon him: [17] And lo a voice from heaven, saying, This is my beloved Son, in whom I am well pleased" (Matt. 3:16–17).

At Jesus's baptism, all three persons of the Trinity interacted with each other. They have a relationship. This relationship can be seen again at the Transfiguration, "While [Peter] yet spake, behold, a bright cloud overshadowed them: and behold a voice out of the cloud, which said, This is my beloved Son, in whom I am well pleased; hear ye him. [6] And when the disciples heard it, they fell on their face, and were sore afraid" (Matt. 17:5–6).

Once again, distinct persons of the Godhead (in this case the Father and Son) have a relationship with each other. Jesus said, "And now, O Father, glorify thou me with thine own self with the glory which I had with thee before the world was" (John 17:5).

This verse is particularly important in this discussion because it shows how the persons of the Trinity had a relationship even before the world was created. See, God is eternal. So I have a question for the Muslim. How did Allah have relationships before the world was created? Once Allah created angels and humans, he could have a relationship with them. But before Allah created them, how did he have relationships? He could not. If Allah is a Unity and not a Trinity, he could not have had any relationships before the creation of angels and humans. Why is this problematic?

Well, because if Allah has no relationships, that means he is not self-sufficient. Because Allah is a Unity and not a Trinity, he *relies* on angels and human beings for relationships. Allah *needs* angels and human beings to have relationships. When there were no angels or human beings, Allah had no relationships. Relationships are required for love.

Thus, instead of being self-sufficient (a necessary attribute of God), Allah is reliant on angels and human beings to complete his attribute of love. Speaking of Allah, the Quran says, "And He is the Protector, the Most Loving" (Quran 85:14). The Bible says, "He that loveth not knoweth not God; for God is love" (1 John 4:8). Notice a big difference between Allah and the God of the Bible. Allah *has* love and *shows* love. But the God of the Bible literally *is* love; love is His being. This may seem like a small difference, but it is huge.

As stated previously, love requires relationships. And as previously demonstrated, because of the Unity of Allah, he had no relationships before the creation of angels and humans. Therefore, Allah cannot *be* love because he cannot have relationships amongst himself like the Trinitarian God of the Bible can. Allah *needs* human beings and/or angels to have relationships. On the other hand, the God of the Bible does not just *show* love, but rather He *is* love because in eternity past, before any humans or angels were created, He was able to have loving relationships amongst the three persons of the Godhead—Father, Son, and Holy Spirit.

Because the God of the Bible is a Trinity and has always had relationships, even before the creation of angels and humans, His whole being is love and He is thus self-sufficient. Tertullian writing in the early third century speaks on this a bit saying, "I may therefore without rashness first lay this down (as a fixed principle) that even then before the creation of the universe God was not alone, since He had within Himself both Reason, and, inherent in Reason, His Word, which He made second to Himself by agitating it within Himself."[312]

In this same work, Tertullian defines God's Reason and Word as Jesus. So in this quote Tertullian is explaining that God has never been alone because the Father has always had the Son. He does not elaborate on the Holy Spirit in this specific place, but the concept is the same for the Spirit. The Spirit has always been there with the Father and Son and thus the Triune God of the Bible is self-sufficient. The persons of the Trinity have always had a relationship with each other. Allah, being a Unity, did not have relationships before the creation of angels and human beings. So not only is Allah not self-sufficient, but he also cannot *be* love. He might be able to *show* love. But he cannot *be* love like the God of the Bible is. The Trinity is a necessary doctrine for God to be God. It is the only way for God to be self-sufficient and love from all eternity.

CONCLUSION OF ISLAM

Islam is one of the largest religions next to Christianity and is growing very rapidly. I have much respect for Muslims in that they seem to be very modest and devoted to their religion. But devotion means little if the beliefs are false. When examining the Quran, it is evident that there are massive amounts of contradictions and inconsistencies. Not only are the claims of Islam rejected by the Bible, but they are also rejected by history. Jesus was surely crucified, He surely

---

[312] Tertullian. *The Ante-Nicene Fathers: Against Praxeas*. Chapter V. Edited by Alexander Roberts, James Donaldson, and Arthur Cleveland Coxe. III. Vol. III. X vols. New York, NY: Cosimo Classics, 2007, 601.

resurrected, and He is surely God. He is not just a messenger or a prophet. He is God in the flesh as the Bible, history, and, ironically, the Quran (Quran 3:45, 4:171→ John 1:1) all demonstrate.

ISLAM REFUTED

1. The Quran says Allah does not have a son (Quran 112:1–4), but the Bible says God does have a Son (Matt. 3:16–17, John 3:16). The Bible came hundreds of years before the Quran.
2. The Quran says Christians and Muslims have the same God (Quran 29:46), yet it says Allah does not have a son (Quran 112:1–4), while the Bible says God does (Matt. 3:16–17, John 3:16).
3. The Quran teaches that Jesus did not die on the cross (Quran 4:157–159), while the Bible says He did (Matt. 27:50; 1 Cor. 15:3–5) and outside sources attest to His death on the cross as well (Ignatius's letter to the Trallians—AD 110).
4. Allah cannot be both loving and merciful because there is no sacrifice in Islam. Allah can be merciful by letting everybody go to heaven or he can be just by sending everybody to hell, but without a sacrifice (like that of Jesus in Christianity), Allah cannot be both merciful and just. Only the God of the Bible can be both merciful and just due to the sacrifice of Christ. In Christianity, the law was fulfilled while also showing mercy to the law breakers.
5. Because Allah is a Unity and not a Trinity like the God of the Bible, Allah relies on humans and angels for relationships. In other words, Allah needs humans and angels for relationships. The God of the Bible is a Trinity and does not need anybody for relationships because the three persons of the Trinity (Father, Son, and Holy Spirit) have always had relationships with each other from all eternity. Thus, the God of the Bible is self-sufficient, but Allah is not.

CHAPTER 8

FOUNDING OF ISLAM TO THE
FOUNDING OF MORMONISM

THE GREAT SCHISM

While Islam was spreading, the Church was doing its own thing. After the founding of Islam, these councils followed: The Third Council of Constantinople (681), the Second Council of Nicaea (787), and the Fourth Council of Constantinople (869). By the time of the eleventh century, the eastern (modern Eastern Orthodox) and western (modern Roman Catholic) churches had already been slowly growing apart, but now it was reaching a tipping point.

Everett Ferguson says, "The Eastern church drew its self-understanding more from the local assembly united in eucharistic fellowship, from the sacraments, and from the ecumenical creeds. In contrast, the Western church was coming to define itself more in terms of canon law and hierarchical submission to a monarchic head."[313]

Timothy Ware says,

> The Byzantines did not mind if the western
> Church was centralized, so long as the Papacy
> did not interfere in the east. The Pope, however,

---

[313] Ferguson, 400.

believed his immediate power of jurisdiction to extend to the east as well as to the west; and as soon as he tried to enforce this claim within the eastern Patriarchates, trouble was bound to arise. The Greeks assigned to the Pope a primacy of honour, but not the universal supremacy which he regarded as his due. The Pope viewed infallibility as his own prerogative; the Greeks held that in matters of the faith the final decision rested not with the Pope alone, but with a Council representing *all* the bishops of the Church. Here we have two different conceptions of the visible organization of the Church.[314]

The western church was more focused on their primacy and authority over all of Christendom through their claimed ruling power of the pope while the eastern church was more focused on the unified authority of the churches and ecumenical councils. The Eastern Church gave Rome *primacy* because it is the place the Apostles Peter and Paul died, but they did not give Rome *supremacy*. The East gave Rome a special position but not in the way the Western Church saw it. The East generally viewed Rome as the *first among equals*, but Rome seemed to view themselves as *first among inferiors*. This was only part of the issue. They also disputed over issues of the eucharist, celibate clergy, eating strangled meat, etc.[315]

These issues were put forth by Michael Cerularius, the Patriarch of Constantinople in the East (1043–1058 AD). Another one of the disputes was regarding something called the "filioque." Filioque means "and from the Son" in Latin. The Western church said the Holy Spirit proceeded from the Father "and from the Son" while the Eastern Church said the Holy Spirit proceeded from the Father period. This is based on a passage in the gospel of John where Jesus

---

[314] Ware, Timothy. *The Orthodox Church: An Introduction to Eastern Christianity.* New ed. Penguin Books, 1963, 47.
[315] Ferguson, 400.

says, "But when the [Holy Spirit] is come whom I will send unto you from the Father, even **the Spirit of truth, which proceedeth from the Father,** he shall testify of me" (John 15:26).

The West would argue that while the Spirit proceeds from the Father "and from the Son," He does not proceed from the Son in the same way as He does the Father. The East would generally agree that the Spirit proceeds from the Father *through* the Son, but not *from* the Son. Many Christians argue that the two views are really the same view articulated differently while others see it as a vast difference. To the average person, this probably just seems like semantics, but to the East it threatened the doctrines of Christ and God. The Eastern churches claimed that this phrase was added to the Nicaeno-Constantinopolian Creed. The Western churches claimed it was the orthodox belief. This issue created great tension between the east and west. The East still rejects the filioque to this day.

Pope Leo IX of the western church disagreed with many of the practices of the eastern church like married clergy, rebaptizing Latins that came to the eastern church, waiting until the eighth day to baptize infants, and probably most importantly (like discussed previously) the western church pushed a belief in their primacy and authority over the whole church.[316] Pope Leo IX of the west claimed Rome had primacy over all of Christendom and that all churches separate from Rome were "synagogues of Satan."[317] These arguments and accusations caused much tension between the eastern and western churches. It is hard to pinpoint an exact date of the Great Schism between the East and West because the split was gradual over the centuries through cultural, political, and other contributing factors. A common date usually given is 1054. One very important event happened this year which is described by Timothy Ware:

One summer afternoon in the year of 1054,
as a service was about to begin in the Church of
the Holy Wisdom at Constantinople, Cardinal

---

[316] Ferguson, 400–401.
[317] Ferguson, 401.

Humbert and two other legates of the Pope entered the building and made their way up to the sanctuary. They had not come to pray. They placed a Bull of Excommunication upon the altar and marched out once more. As he passed through the western door, the Cardinal shook the dust from his feet with the words: 'Let God look and judge.' A deacon ran out after him in great distress and begged him to take back the Bull. Humbert refused; and it was dropped in the street.[318]

Like stated previously, the schism between the East and West was gradual rather than pertaining to a specific date, but this event in history marks a major point of what is known in history as the "Great Schism." The East and West are still split to this day. The Eastern Church is what is known today as the "Eastern Orthodox Church" and the Western Church is what is known today as the "Roman Catholic Church." The Eastern Orthodox Church is rather unknown in the United States. For the most part, America only thinks of Roman Catholicism and Protestantism.

THE CRUSADES

The primitive Christians very much resembled pacifists. An argument can be made biblically for self-defense, but that is beyond the scope of this work. Jesus said to love your enemies (Matt. 5:44). Consider this passage from the Gospel of Luke:

> And it came to pass, when the time was come that he should be received up, he sted-fastly set his face to go to Jerusalem, [52] And sent messengers before his face: and they went, and entered into a village of the Samaritans, to make

---

[318] Ware, 41.

ready for him. [53] And they did not receive him, because his face was as though he would go to Jerusalem. [54] And when his disciples James and John saw this, they said, Lord, wilt thou that we command fire to come down from heaven, and consume them, even as Elias did? [55] **But he turned, and rebuked them, and said, Ye know not what manner of spirit ye are of.** [56] **For the Son of man is not come to destroy men's lives, but to save them.** And they went to another village. (Luke 9:51–56)

James and John wanted to kill the Samaritans because they rejected Jesus. Jesus rebuked them and explained that He wanted to save lives, not destroy them. It is our job as Christians to spread the gospel, not threaten people who reject it. Peter writing under the persecution of Nero in Rome said, "Yet if any man suffer as a Christian, let him not be ashamed; but let him glorify God on this behalf" (1 Pet. 4:16). The church never advocated fighting against the government or killing in any way. Justin Martyr said,

For from Jerusalem there went out into the world, men, twelve in number, and these illiterate, of no ability in speaking: but by the power of God they proclaimed to every race of men that they were sent by Christ to teach to all the word of God; and **we who formerly used to murder one another do not only now refrain from making war upon our enemies, but also, that we may not lie nor deceive our examiners, willingly die confessing Christ.**[319]

---

[319] Martyr, Justin. *The Ante-Nicene Fathers: The First Apology.* Chapter XXXIX. Edited by Alexander Roberts, James Donaldson, and Arthur Cleveland Coxe. I. Vol. I. X vols. New York, NY: Cosimo Classics, 2007, 175–176.

Athenagoras wrote in *A Plea for the Christians* saying, "**For we have learned, not only not to return blow for blow**, nor to go to law with those who plunder and rob us, but to those who smite us on one side of the face to offer the other side also, and to those who take away our coat to give likewise our cloak."[320]

There are many more quotations like this, but these should suffice to show the early church's view on killing. Augustine (AD 354–AD 430) advocated for "just war," but even he believed anyone involved in the war needed to do penance to be forgiven of their war sins.[321] Returning to the eleventh century, the church began to adopt the theory of "just war" (which is biblical if and only if it is properly defined). Many will argue that the crusades were a result of the Church being bloodthirsty, while many others would argue they were defensive in nature. The Crusades were as such: first (1096–1099), second (1147–1149), third (AD 1187–AD 1192), fourth (AD 1208–AD 1271), fifth (AD 1217–AD 1221), sixth (1228–1229), seventh (AD 1248–AD 1254), and eighth (AD 1270–AD 1271).

THE INQUISITION

It should be known that there was a reformation before the sixteenth century reformation. Centuries before Martin Luther, there were already objections to the Roman Catholic Church and their teachings. In the twelfth century, Henry the Monk objected to the sacrifice of the Mass, confession to priests, prayers for the dead, original sin, infant baptism, and the necessity of church buildings.[322] Another man in the twelfth century named Peter de Bruys objected to many of these same things.[323]

---

[320] Athenagoras. *The Ante-Nicene Fathers: A Plea for the Christians*. Chapter I. Edited by Alexander Roberts, James Donaldson, and Arthur Cleveland Coxe. II. Vol. II. X vols. New York, NY: Cosimo Classics, 2007, 129.
[321] Ferguson, 415.
[322] Ferguson, 506.
[323] Ferguson, 506.

One group that formed was the Cathari. They believed the flesh was evil and rejected doctrines like hell and purgatory.[324] In 1209, Pope Innocent III approved a crusade against the Cathari.[325] Heresy had already been decreed to be equal with treason.[326] In 1231, Pope Gregory IX approved the burning of heretics.[327] In 1252, Pope Innocent IV's papal bull made torture an acceptable tool for the Roman Catholic Church to use against heretics.[328] The Inquisition resembled that of the witch hunts of the seventeenth century.

One of the most interesting heretical groups is known by the name of the Waldenses AKA the Vaudois. The name "Vaudois" comes from the Latin word "Vallis," which in English is valley.[329] This name was based off the location where the Vaudois lived. They were also known as "Waldenses." A man named Peter Waldo was a rich merchant from Lyons.[330] In 1173, he began a simple, poverty stricken preaching life.[331]

Now, Waldo did not start the group because this group dates long before him, although he did seem to make it known. Stephen G. Beus says, "At least one historian contends that Waldo's role was not as an originator, but rather to gather together the dispersed remnants of these dissident groups into one body of worship which took the name of Vaudois either because their principal place of refuge was in the Alpine valleys or because of their organizer's name."[332]

---

[324] Ferguson, 510.
[325] Ferguson, 510.
[326] Ferguson, 511.
[327] Ferguson, 511.
[328] Beus, Stephen G. *The Vaudois: Last Faith Standing*. Pittsburgh, PA: Harmony Street Publishers, 2018, 126.
[329] Beus, 19.
[330] Ferguson, 508.
[331] Ferguson, 508.
[332] Beus, 58.

It is difficult to know exactly what this group believed since there are very few writings available about them and most are from their opposition. Stephen G. Beus quotes Alexis Muston who says,

> The Vaudois of the Alps, are, in our view, primitive Christians, or inheritors of the primitive Church, who have been preserved in these valleys from the alterations successively introduced by the church of Rome into the evangelical worship. It is not they who separated from Catholicism, but Catholicism which separated from them, in modifying the primitive worship. Hence the impossibility of assigning a precise date to the origin. The church of Rome, which in its commencement also formed part of the primitive church, did not modify itself all at once, but as it became powerful, it assumed, together with the scepter of rule, the display, the pride, and the spirit of domination which ordinarily accompany power; whilst amid the Vaudois valleys, the primitive church, existing in comparative obscurity, remained in isolation, free, and without tendency to abandon the simplicity of its infancy.[333]

According to Muston, while the church at Rome was growing in power and losing the simple faith of the Apostles, this group in the Alps was preserving the primitive faith. J. A. Wylie writes,

> When their co-religionists on the plains entered within the pale of the Roman jurisdiction, they retired within the mountains, and, spurning alike the tyrannical yoke and the corrupt tenets of the Church of the Seven Hills [the Roman Catholic Church], they preserved in its

---

[333] Beus, 18.

purity and simplicity the faith their fathers had
handed down to them. Rome manifestly was the
schismatic, she it was that had abandoned what
was once the common faith of Christendom,
leaving by that step to all who remained on the
old ground the indisputably valid title of the True
Church.[334]

According to Wylie, it was the Waldenses who held onto the
primitive faith of the Apostles. Do I agree with Wylie's assessment?
No, I do not, but it is interesting to hear his take nonetheless—especially since the Waldenses were so persecuted. As to the antiquity of
the Waldenses, Beus quotes Maclaine who claimed, "the Leonists as
being synonymous with the Waldenses as a sect that had flourished
for above 500 years [that is, from before AD 750]."[335] J. A. Wylie
quotes Rorenco of Turin who spoke of the Waldenses saying, "they
were not a new sect in the ninth and tenth centuries, and that Claude
of Turin must have detached them from the Church in the ninth
century."[336] These early dates should be taken with a grain of salt. C.
H. Pappas makes a comment regarding the fall of Rome:

The Homoousians [Trinitarians], the true
saints, suffered immensely after the fall of the
Roman Empire. No less than five thousand bishops, priests, and deacons perished. Also, many
saints who were true to the faith were maimed
and left to wander from place to place in search
for food and shelter. Yet, there remained a faithful
witness of Waldensians who dwelt in the rugged

---

[334] Wylie, J.A. *The History of the Waldenses*. Coppell, TX: Cassell and Company,
1860, 8.
[335] Beus, 37.
[336] Wylie, 9.

mountains of the Alps. They had the Scriptures
and evangelized Europe.[337]

According to this argument, as the Church fell more and more,
the Waldenses seemed to preserve a simple faith in the Alps. Once
again, I do not adhere to this theory of a hidden church throughout
history, but as an unbiased historian, I will provide these perspec-
tives for the reader. The basic beliefs of the Waldenses were the New
Testament as the sole basis for faith, a simple life of poverty, only two
sacraments in Baptism and the Lord's Supper, no images or relics,
and no papal authority.[338] Speaking of their doctrine, J. A. Wylie says,

> The atoning death and justifying righ-
> teousness of Christ was its cardinal truth. This,
> the Nobla Leycon and other ancient documents
> abundantly testify. The Nobla Leycon sets forth
> with tolerable clearness the doctrine of the
> Trinity, the fall of man, the incarnation of the
> Son, the perpetual authority of the Decalogue as
> given by God, the need of Divine grace in order
> to [do] good works, the necessity of holiness, the
> institution of the ministry, the resurrection of the
> body, and the eternal bliss of heaven.[339]

Evidently, the doctrine of the Waldenses was similar to that of
the sixteenth century reformers.

The Catholic Church of this time was without a doubt over-
stepping their bounds and abusing their power—but the sins of certain men cannot be placed on the people as a whole. With all these
things building up, it was only a matter of time before reform took
place.

---

[337] Pappas, C.H. *In Defense of the Authenticity of 1 John 5:7 Second Edition.*
Bloomington, IN: WestBow Press, 2016, 112.
[338] Beus, 25.
[339] Wylie, 13.

THE REFORMATION

In 1513, Pope Leo X wanted to build St. Peter's Basilica. A project as large as this required a fund to match it. Pope Leo X approved the sale of indulgences which had been previously permitted by Pope Julius II in 1507 AD.[340] Regarding indulgences, the *Catechism of the Catholic Church* states,

> An indulgence is a remission before God of the temporal punishment due to sins whose guilt has already been forgiven, which the faithful Christian who is duly disposed gains under certain prescribed conditions through the action of the Church which, as the minister of redemption, dispenses and applies with authority the treasury of the satisfactions of Christ and the saints." "An indulgence is partial or plenary according as it removes either part or all of the temporal punishment due to sin." The faithful can gain indulgences for themselves or apply them to the dead.[341] (CCC 1471)

In short, an indulgence is a way to remove temporal punishment of sin in Roman Catholic theology. Johann Tetzel was a German Dominican known for selling indulgences. He would go into towns and try to convince people to buy indulgences just like a salesman. His famous saying was, "Once a coin into the coffer clings, a soul from purgatory springs."[342] In other words, Tetzel told the people that as soon as the money they dropped in the collection basket hit the bottom, a soul made it out of purgatory and into heaven. Regarding purgatory, the Catechism of the Catholic Church says, "All who die in God's grace and friendship, but still imperfectly puri-

---

[340] Woodbridge, 112.
[341] *Catechism of the Catholic Church*. Citta del Vaticano: Libreria Editrice Vaticana, 1994, 411.
[342] Woodbridge, 112.

fied, are indeed assured of their eternal salvation; but after death they undergo purification, so as to achieve the holiness necessary to enter the joy of heaven"[343] (CCC 1030).

In lay terms, purgatory is a place of final purification before a Christian can enter heaven. The people that go to purgatory are all guaranteed heaven, but they do not know how long they will have to be "purified" in purgatory. The Catholic Church makes it clear that it is not the same type of pain as hell and does not define how long this purification process takes. Because of this doctrine of purgatory, many citizens began buying indulgences. Out of concern for their deceased loved ones, they began giving the money they had to the Church. Once again, the Catholic Church had definitely taken advantage of its people. These are sad points in history for the Church.

Martin Luther was a German monk of the Roman Catholic Church and was ordained to the priesthood in 1507 AD. When he saw Johann Tetzel and the abuse of indulgences, it provoked him to act. He wrote a work known as the "Ninety-five Theses" which listed ninety-five points as to why selling indulgences was wrong. Luther wrote,

> 50. Christians should be taught that, if the Pope were acquainted with the exactions of the preachers of pardons, he would prefer that the Basilica of St. Peter should be burnt to ashes, than that it should be built up with the skin, flesh and bones of his sheep. 51. **Christians should be taught that, as it would be the duty, so it would be the wish of the Pope, even to sell, if necessary, the Basilica of St. Peter, and to give of his own money to very many of those from whom the preachers of pardons extract money.** 52. Vain is the hope of salvation through letters of pardon, even if a commissary—nay, the Pope

---

[343] Catechism of the Catholic Church, 291.

himself—were to pledge his own soul for them. 53. They are enemies of Christ and of the Pope who, **in order that Pardons may be preached, condemn the word of God to utter silence in other churches. 54. Wrong is done to the word of God when, in the same sermon, an equal or longer time is spent on pardons than on it.**[344]

Luther pointed out that Christians should realize that the pope should be willing to sell the Basilica of St. Peter if it meant not swindling money out of the pockets of citizens. Not only that, but the preaching of indulgences in the church was focused on more than the word of God! Luther's attack on indulgences was viewed by many as an attack on Papal authority. With Luther's ninety-five theses in October of 1517 AD, the beginning of what is known as the Protestant Reformation had begun.

Luther was full of anxiety and did not have much peace with God. One day while studying, he had what many Protestants would call a "revelation." He stumbled upon this passage, "For therein is the righteousness of God revealed from faith to faith: as it is written, The just shall live by faith" (Rom. 1:17). It was at this moment that Martin Luther began to believe the Catholic teaching of justification was wrong. The Bible says, "Therefore we conclude that a man is justified by faith without the deeds of the law" (Rom. 3:28).

Because this passage says, "without the deeds of the law," Luther concluded this meant *all works* that one can do. This led Luther to believe that one is justified by *faith alone* and changed this verse in his German translation to read, "Therefore we conclude that a man is justified by faith *alone* without the deeds of the law" (Rom. 3:28). Protestants believe Luther's conclusion, but Roman Catholics, Eastern Orthodox, and a few other sects of Christians argue (correctly) that "works of the law" or "deeds of the law" only refer to Jewish laws like circumcision. This is based on Paul's attack on Judaizers in the

---

[344] Luther, Martin. *The Ninety-Five Theses*. Eastford, CT: Martino Fine Books, 2018, 15.

early church and certain historical documents such as 4QMMT in the dead sea scrolls which talks about these "deeds of the law" or "observances of the law" as Jewish rituals/laws like keeping things clean and not moral laws like adultery, murder, etc.[345] Justification by faith alone versus the traditional understanding of justification is still widely disputed today amongst Christians. Luther's conclusion that faith is the only thing that justifies was based on his own sensitive conscience and a misreading of Paul. The Bible says, "Ye see then how that by works a man is justified, and **not by faith only**" (Jas. 2:24; emphasis added). Justification by faith alone is a false teaching created by Luther, which many Christians blindly follow to this day.

ANABAPTISTS AND BAPTISTS

When examining Church history, many people only think of Roman Catholicism/Eastern Orthodoxy and Protestantism. This is a false dichotomy. There is one more stream of Christians, which for the sake of simplicity I will label Anabaptists. Ulrich Zwingli (1484–1531) was a priest over a parish in the Swiss town of Glarus. Zwingli was somewhat of a hypocrite to some reformers. Zwingli's motto was, "I came at length to trust in no words so much as those which proceeded from the Bible. If I saw a teaching could bear the test, I accepted it; if not, I rejected it."[346]

He claimed to only believe what was in the Bible, yet he still held to infant baptism—which many argued is nowhere in the Scriptures. While the Bible nowhere explicitly states infants are baptized, it is clear that the Bible often speaks of whole "households" being baptized as well as comparing baptism to circumcision—and babies were circumcised. Not to mention, according to the historical evidence, infant baptism was without a doubt a practice in the primitive Church (see the chapter "Primitive Christianity"—Baptism).

---

[345] Vermes, Geza, trans. *The Complete Dead Sea Scrolls in English*. Penguin Books, n.d., 222–229.
[346] Woodbridge, 154.

Continuing on, Conrad Grebel (1448–1526) was a friend of Zwingli and he rejected infant baptism based on not seeing it in Scripture.[347] Grebel's followers ended up calling themselves the Swiss Brethren. On January 21, 1525, Grebel baptized a man by the name of Georg Blaurock in the house of Felix Manz, which is a vital event in the origins of Anabaptism.[348] Anabaptism simple means "re-baptism." Those who rejected infant baptism were labeled "re-baptizers" because they baptized people who had already been baptized as babies.

While it is true that many Anabaptists were radical, they were quite misrepresented. The label "Anabaptist" was pretty much given to anybody that rejected infant baptism. This word was almost seen as a boogeyman. The problem is that Anabaptism was not a monolith. There were some crazy groups of Anabaptists that advocated violence and thought they were modern-day prophets sent from God.[349] Other groups of Anabaptists were pacifists, advocating for no violence at all—which was much more passive than the violence used historically by the Roman Catholic Church in their burning/torture of heretics and even some Protestants.[350]

All groups of Christians have had their shameful moments in history. This goes to show that imperfect human beings can never perfectly represent a perfect God! Now, there are three main groups of Anabaptists that can be identified. The first is the mainstream group who held many shared beliefs with the reformers and for the most part were identified as the "Swiss Brethren." Speaking of this main group, William R. Estep says,

> For the Swiss and south German Anabaptists, the final authority for the Christian life and the faith and order of the church was the New Testament, in particular the life and teachings of Christ. While they tended to inter-

[347] Woodbridge, 154.
[348] Woodbridge, 154.
[349] Woodbridge, 187–188.
[350] Woodbridge, 188.

pret the Scriptures in a literal sense, they were Christocentric. It was Christ who in the actual formulation of the faith became the ultimate authority to which they appealed. Although they did not reject the Old Testament in a Marcionite fashion, it was never allowed to take precedence over the New Testament or to become normative for the Christian faith. Theirs was a New Testament hermeneutic that assumed a progression in the biblical revelation that culminated in the Christevent. Therefore the Old Testament, although useful and often quoted, could never stand alone, unqualified by the New Testament.[351]

The second group focused on 'experience' and they can be identified as the "Spiritualists." Because they focused on experience and feelings, many of these Spiritualists were violent. The third group focused on their intellect rather than faith and can be identified as the "Rationalists." Many of these Rationalists rejected the Trinity. The main four beliefs of the Anabaptists which are very common to this day in the twenty-first century is justification by faith alone, Sola Scriptura (meaning the Bible is the sole infallible rule of faith), believer's baptism, and a memorialist view of the Lord's Supper—in other words, the Lord's Supper is something done to remember the Lord Jesus and His sacrifice, not His literal body and blood like the Roman Catholic Church, Eastern Orthodox Church, Luther, and the early church fathers all taught and still teach.[352]

Like the Waldenses, the Anabaptists were widely persecuted. From the period of 1525 to 1625 between one and five thousand "radical" Anabaptists were executed.[353] Michael Sattler was an

[351] Estep, William R. *The Anabaptist Story: An Introduction to Sixteenth-Century Anabaptism*. Grand Rapids, MI: Wm. B. Eerdmans Publishing Co., 1996, 22.
[352] Estep 191–192, 196–197, 203; Woodridge, 188.
[353] Woodbridge, 155.

Anabaptist who was put to a brutal death in May of 1527 AD. His sentence said,

> Michael Sattler shall be committed to the executioner. The latter shall take him to the square and there first cut out his tongue, and then forge him fast to a wagon and there with glowing iron tongs twice tear pieces from his body, then on the way to the site of execution five times more as above and then burn his body to powder as an arch-heretic.[354]

William Estep quotes the *Martyrs' Mirror*, which describes another murder of Anabaptists, saying,

> In this year 1538, in the month of August, ten, or seventeen persons, male and female, were apprehended in the town, who were accused of rebaptism. These were principally of the poorer class, except one, a goldsmith, called Paul von Drusnen, of whom it is reported that he was their teacher. Paul, and three others, were put to death at Vucht, in the theatre, then afterwards burnt on the 9th of September.[355]

These murders occurred time and time again for the Anabaptists. Dr. Balthasar Hubmaier was a prominent leader in the Anabaptist movement. Regarding the Roman Catholic Church and the Inquisition he said, "the inquisitors are the biggest heretics of all since against the teaching and example of Christ they have condemned heretics to the flames and before the time of the harvest root up the wheat together with the tares."[356] In another place he said,

---

[354] Estep, 57.
[355] Estep, 73.
[356] Estep, 85.

"Now it is apparent to everyone, even the blind, that the law which demands the burning of heretics is an invention of the Devil."[357]

On March 10, 1528 AD, Hubmaier was burned at the stake. Menno Simons was a Roman Catholic priest who converted to Anabaptism. He's one of the more famous names of the Anabaptist movement and is where the group known as the "Mennonites" get their name. Once again, persecutions came. On January 21, 1539, an edict was set forth forcing all Anabaptists out of Groningen. A few years later in 1541, Charles V put forth an edict against Menno with a reward for his murder. Menno survived through that but died of an illness on January 31, 1561. Just like the Waldenses and Vaudois centuries before, the Anabaptists were persecuted by the Roman Catholic Church and even by some Protestants.

While Baptists share much of their beliefs with the Anabaptists, they are not the exact same. In the latter part of the sixteenth century, a group known as the "Puritans" spawned who sought to worship according to what was strictly in the Bible and not by what they called traditions. At the end of the sixteenth century, many groups began to separate from the Church of England and became known as the "Separatists."

One of the most influential people in Baptist history is John Smyth, a leader of a separatist congregation in the early seventeenth century. Smyth and his congregation were harassed by the Protestant state and forced to leave England.

In 1609, Smyth rejected infant baptism and accepted believer's baptism as he believed the Scriptures taught. Soon after, he rejected Calvinism and accepted Arminianism—namely he began to believe each person had the free will to accept or reject Christ. Those who agreed with Smyth became known as General Baptists—meaning they believed Jesus died for everybody (general atonement). Particular Baptists (Calvinists) are those who believe Jesus only died for a certain elect people (particular atonement). The first Baptists that arrived in America in New England were persecuted once again.

---

[357] Estep, 86.

Baptists in Massachusetts were forbidden from gathering to worship.[358] Even in the new world Baptists were persecuted.

The Roman Catholic and Protestant Churches of that time both believed strongly that religion should control the government. Baptists did not share this belief. Baptists believe strongly in separation of church and state as well as freedom of religion. Roger Williams became a Puritan (Particular Baptist) after his collegiate studies. He was one of the first advocates of freedom of religion. He published *The Bloudy Tenent of Persecution, for Cause of Conscience* (1644), which was a work on freedom of religion.[359] William's friend Oliver Cromwell once said, "with much Christian zeal and affection...that he had rather that Mahumetanism [Islam] were permitted amongst us, than that one of God's children should be persecuted."[360]

When Roger Williams served as governor of modern-day Rhode Island, he allowed Jews and Quakers to live amongst them.[361] This revealed his strong belief in freedom of religion. More persecution followed the Baptists. The book *The Baptist Story: From English Sect to Global Movement* says,

> Between 1660 and 1688, the various Puritan communities—collectively known to history as Nonconformists or Dissenters—were persecuted fiercely. In the words of Gerald R. Cragg, "They were harried in their homes and in their meeting houses; they were arrested, tried and imprisoned. A few were transported [to the Caribbean in exile]; many died.[362]

---

[358] Chute, Anthony L., Nathan A. Finn, and Michael A.G. Haykin. *The Baptist Story: From English Sect to Global Movement*. Nashville, TN: B&H Publishing Group, 2015, 28.
[359] Chute, 30.
[360] Chute, 30.
[361] Chute, 30.
[362] Chute, 42.

Just like the Waldenses and the Anabaptists, the Baptists of the seventeenth century were persecuted. In 1689, William III passed the Act of Toleration which gave Baptists religious freedom. Baptists have a long and complex history, but this brief elaboration should suffice.

RESULTS OF THE REFORMATION

The reformation spawned many beliefs and denominations. As you can see, one man (Luther) changed Christianity forever. As discussed previously, there are three main streams of Christianity. The first would be the Catholic and Orthodox churches (these two do have major differences but I have grouped them together for the sake of simplicity). The second would be the Protestant churches like Lutheran, Anglican, Presbyterian, and Reformed/Calvinist churches. The last stream consists of all the denominations that submit to believer's baptism, reject infant baptism, and are much less liturgical—which for the sake of simplicity, I have put under the umbrella of Anabaptist. Reformed Baptists are the exception since they hold to both believer's baptism and Calvinist theology, which allows them to fall under both the second and third streams of Christianity. Ever since the Reformation, Christians have been extremely divided. I find myself praying the same prayer that Jesus prayed before His crucifixion:

> Neither pray I for these alone, but for them also which shall believe on me through their word; **21 That they all may be one**; as thou, Father, art in me, and I in thee, that they also may be one in us: that the world may believe that thou hast sent me. **22** And the glory which thou gavest me I have given them; that **they may be one, even as we are one**: **23** I in them, and thou in me, that they may be made perfect in one; and that the world may know that thou hast sent me, and hast loved them, as thou hast loved me. (John 17:20–23)

Jesus prayed that the Church would be one. And I too keep hope that somehow, some way, all Christians will be one again. May God bless all Christians and bring us back together! The nineteenth century would bring multiple lies claiming to be the true religion of Jesus—as I will soon demonstrate.

CHAPTER 9

MORMONISM

INTRODUCTION

In 1823, a man named Joseph Smith claimed that an angel named Moroni visited him in a vision while in New York. This sounds remarkably similar to what Muhammad claimed. Muhammad claimed to be visited by the angel Gabriel (Quran 2:97–98). Remember what the Apostle Paul said about people claiming angel visitations:

> I marvel that ye are so soon removed from him that called you into the grace of Christ unto another gospel: [7] Which is not another; but there be some that trouble you, and would pervert the gospel of Christ. [8] But though we, or an angel from heaven, preach any other gospel unto you than that which we have preached unto you, let him be accursed. [9] As we said before, so say I now again, if any man preach any other gospel unto you than that ye have received, let him be accursed. (Gal. 1:6–9)

There were people in Galatia being led astray by false teachers. Paul said not to listen to anybody preaching a different gospel, even if they claimed to be visited by an angel! How ironic that two of the largest religions after Christianity both started how the Apostle Paul predicted false religions would. Supposedly the Angel Moroni told Joseph Smith of some golden plates that had contained the story of a group of Israelites that lived in America long ago. After Smith translated these plates into English, he published the Book of Mormon and started the Church of Jesus Christ of Latter-day Saints—in other words "Mormons." Thus, the official founding of Mormonism is 1830.

Mormons also read *Doctrine and Covenants*, *The Pearl of Great Price*, teachings of LDS prophets, *Ensign Magazine*, and *Liahona Magazine* alongside the *Book of Mormon* and the Bible (although they believe the Book of Mormon must correct the Bible). Brigham Young was Joseph Smith's successor, and he took over after Smith's death in 1844. One of the most controversial practices of the Mormons was polygamy. They church did not abolish polygamy until 1890, although Mormons still believe the practice of polygamy will be restored in the Millennial Kingdom of Christ.[363]

WHO IS GOD?

The monotheistic beliefs about God up to this point in history, whether it be Judaism, Christianity, or Islam, have always been that God is eternal and uncreated. If He was created, then He is not God. This belief was challenged by Joseph Smith when he said, "**I am going to tell you how God came to be God**. We have imagined and supposed that God was God from all eternity. I will refute that idea, and take away the veil, so that you may see… It is the first principle of the Gospel to know for a certainty the character of God and to know…that **he was once a man like us**."[364]

Joseph Smith claimed that God used to be a man. The ironic part is that he admits that the orthodox belief about God has always

[363] Carden, Paul, ed. *World Religions Made Easy*. Peabody, MA: Rose Publishing, 2018, 18.
[364] Smith Jr., Joseph. The Church of Jesus Christ of Latter-Day Saints: The King Follett Sermon. Accessed February 24, 2021. https://www.churchofjesuschrist.org/study/ensign/1971/04/the-king-follett-sermon?lang=eng.

been that He is God "from all eternity." But instead of accepting this orthodox teaching of the faith, he says he will "refute that idea." In other words, Joseph Smith "refuted" Christianity—yet still claims to be Christ's church. It does not seem to make much sense. Joseph Smith says God used to be a man, but what does the Bible say, "Before the mountains were brought forth, or ever thou hadst formed the earth and the world, even from everlasting to everlasting, thou art God" (Ps. 90:2).

God is from "everlasting to everlasting." He has always been God. Yet Joseph Smith says God used to be a man and became God. So it is clear already that Mormonism is not Christianity. Isaiah says, "Ye are my witnesses, saith the LORD, and my servant whom I have chosen: that ye may know and believe me, and understand that I am he: before me there was no God formed, neither shall there be after me" (Isa. 43:10).

The Bible says there was no God formed before God, yet Joseph Smith said God used to be a man. If that is true, who was God before the current God? And if there are multiple gods, is that not polytheism? This verse also says that there will be no God formed after the LORD. Yet Joseph Smith said, "Here, then is eternal life-to know the only wise and true God; and **you have got to learn how to be Gods yourselves**, and to be kings and priests to God, the same as all Gods have done before you."[365]

God says there will be no more gods...yet Joseph Smith says humans must become gods. I think we should side with God rather than Joseph Smith. Speaking of God, the question of the person of Jesus arrives. Who is Jesus? The Muslims say He is just a prophet. Who do the Mormons say He is? Mormons believe He is more than a prophet but reject Him being God, which leaves them with some serious problems. John says, "In the beginning was the Word, and the Word was with God, and the Word was God. ² The same was in

[365] Smith Jr., Joseph. The Church of Jesus Christ of Latter-Day Saints: The King Follett Sermon. Accessed February 24, 2021. https://www.churchofjesuschrist.org/study/ensign/1971/04/the-king-follett-sermon?lang=eng.

the beginning with God. ³ All things were made by him; and without him was not any thing made that was made" (John 1:1–3).

This passage says Jesus was *with* God in the beginning and *is* God at the same time. This makes perfect sense for the Christian since we believe in the doctrine of the Trinity. Jesus was with the Father in the beginning, so they are distinct yet both part of the Godhead along with the Holy Spirit. Mormons reject the Trinity which means they have multiple gods, making them polytheistic once again. Now, Exodus is the first time God's name is revealed. It says, "And God said unto Moses, **I AM THAT I AM**: and he said, Thus shalt thou say unto the children of Israel, **I AM** hath sent me unto you" (Exod. 3:14).

God revealed His name as "I AM." From this point forward, the Jews always knew God's name to be "I AM." These were sacred words, and nobody dared to blaspheme. That is why the people were stirred up in the Gospel of John, "Jesus said unto them, Verily, verily, I say unto you, Before Abraham was, **I am**. ⁵⁹ Then took they up stones to cast at him: but Jesus hid himself, and went out of the temple, going through the midst of them, and so passed by" (John 8:58–59).

If you were a Jew in the first century and you heard somebody refer to themselves as "I AM," you would know what they were claiming. This was a claim to be God and not just any God, but the God of Abraham, Isaac, and Jacob. Some object that Jesus was just saying He existed before Abraham but was not claiming to be God. To start, no first century Jew would have understood the statement like this. Second, the Jews' response in verse 59 to stone Him reveal how serious of a claim He made. He was not just claiming some sort of generic deity. He was claiming to be the God who spoke to Moses in the burning bush. Jesus claimed to be God. Isaiah says,

> Ye are my witnesses, saith the LORD, and
> my servant whom I have chosen: that ye may
> know and believe me, and understand that **I am**
> **he**: before me there was no God formed, neither
> shall there be after me. (Isa. 43:10)

Another way God referred to Himself was the phrase/title "I am He." In the same chapter of John, Jesus said, "I said therefore unto you, that ye shall die in your sins: for if ye believe not that **I am he**, ye shall die in your sins." (John 8:24)

In this same passage as the last, Jesus makes another claim to be God. In this instance, He specifically says that if you do not believe He is the God that spoke to Moses and the God that spoke in Isaiah, you will die in your sins! This presents another problem the Mormon must answer; why are multiple persons called God in the Old Testament? To examine Christ and the Trinity in the Old Testament, see the section titled "The Plurality of God in the Old Testament" in the Judaism chapter. The next problem is regarding the worship of God. Here is the Great Commission passage:

Then the eleven disciples went away into Galilee, into a mountain where Jesus had appointed them. [17] And when they saw him, **they worshipped him**: but some doubted. [18] And Jesus came and spake unto them, saying, All power is given unto me in heaven and in earth. [19] Go ye therefore, and teach all nations, baptizing them in the name of the Father, and of the Son, and of the Holy Ghost: [20] Teaching them to observe all things whatsoever I have commanded you: and, lo, I am with you always, even unto the end of the world. Amen. (Matt. 28:16–20)

Before ascending into heaven, Jesus stood before His disciples. They began to worship Him. Jesus could have easily rebuked them for worshipping somebody other than God, but He did not. Why is that? Acts says, "And as Peter was coming in, Cornelius met him, and fell down at his feet, and worshipped him. [26] But Peter took him up, saying, **Stand up; I myself also am a man**" (Acts 10:25–26).

Cornelius began worshipping Peter and Peter rebuked him. Why did Jesus not rebuke His disciples for worshipping Him? Revelation says,

> And [the angel] saith unto me, Write, Blessed are they which are called unto the marriage supper of the Lamb. And he saith unto me, These are the true sayings of God. [10] And I fell at his feet to worship him. And he said unto me, See thou do it not: I am thy fellowservant, and of thy brethren that have the testimony of Jesus: worship God: for the testimony of Jesus is the spirit of prophecy. (Rev. 19:9–10)

When John fell down to worship the angel, the angel rebuked him and said he was a fellow servant. Why did Jesus not tell His disciples that He was just a "fellow servant"? Jesus did not rebuke His disciples for worshipping Him because He is God. Now, the Mormon has two options. They can say they do not worship Jesus, which would mean they do not follow the religion of the Apostles. Or they can say they do worship Jesus; but Mormons do not believe Jesus is God. So if they worship Jesus *and* God (according to their Christology), that means they are polytheistic. Either way, they prove to not be Christians. To see what the early sources said about the deity of Jesus, see the section titled "The Trinity" in the chapter titled "Primitive Christianity." The Apostle Paul said,

> But I fear, lest by any means, as the serpent beguiled Eve through his subtilty, so your minds should be corrupted from the simplicity that is in Christ. [4] For if he that cometh preacheth **another Jesus**, whom we have not preached, or if ye receive another spirit, which ye have not received, or another gospel, which ye have not accepted, ye might well bear with him." (2 Cor. 11:3–4)

Paul was worried that the Corinthians were being led astray to "another Jesus" and a "another gospel." As previously demonstrated, the Bible and history both teach that Jesus is God. Therefore, since Mormons do not believe Jesus is God, they have another Jesus. Their Jesus is not the real Jesus. Their Jesus is made up, just like the Muslim Jesus. And a fake Jesus cannot save a person. Unless you believe that Jesus is the I AM, you will die in your sins (John 8:24, 58). Another point to address is regarding the Trinity. Mormons reject the Trinity.

For a fuller understanding of the Trinity, see the section titled "The Plurality of God in the Old Testament" in the Judaism chapter as well as the section titled "The Trinity" in the chapter titled "Primitive Christianity." The Bible says the Father is God (Eph. 6:23, 2 John 1:3, Gal. 1:3). The Bible says Jesus is God (Isa. 43:10→John 8:24, Ex. 3:14→John 8:58, John 20:28). The Bible says the Holy Spirit is God (Acts 5:1–4). The Bible also shows distinctions between these three persons (Matt. 3:16–17, John 1:1, 14:26, 17:1–5). Mormons would agree that all three persons—Father, Son, and Holy Spirit—are distinct.

The official Mormon website states, "[**The Father, Son, and Holy Spirit**] **are distinct beings**, but they are one in purpose and effort. They are united as one in bringing to pass the grand, divine plan for the salvation and exaltation of the children of God."[366]

Notice the difference between the Mormon teaching on the Godhead and the orthodox Christian understanding. Christians say the three are distinct persons, but one being. Mormons say they are three distinct beings. Now, we must put the pieces together. Since all three *persons* are proven to be God in the Scriptures, and the Mormons believe they are all distinct *beings*, this means Mormons believe in three gods. Thus, Mormons are polytheists; and not only because of their belief about three distinct beings, but also because they believe they will become gods when they die. Recall, "Here, then is eternal life-to know the only wise and true God; and **you**

---

[366] Hinckley, Gordon B. The Church of Jesus Christ of Latter-Day Saints: The Father, Son, and Holy Ghost. Accessed February 24, 2021. https://www.churchjesuschrist.org/study/ensign/1986/11/the-father-son-and-holy-ghost?lang=eng. Brackets mine.

have got to learn how to be Gods yourselves, and to be kings and priests to God, the same as all Gods have done before you."[367]

Mormons believe in three gods—Father, Son, and Holy Spirit—plus all themselves who they believe will become gods when they die. That means they believe in thousands of gods. Examine the creation account from the Mormon *Book of Abraham*:

> And then the Lord said: Let us go down. And they went down at the beginning, and they, that is **the Gods**, organized and formed the heavens and the earth. And the earth, after it was formed, was empty and desolate, because they had not formed anything but the earth; and darkness reigned upon the face of the deep, and **the Spirit of the Gods** was brooding upon the face of the waters.[368] (Abraham 4:1–2)

Now compare this to the biblical creation account: "In the beginning **God** created the heaven and the earth. ²And the earth was without form, and void; and darkness was upon the face of the deep. And **the Spirit of God** moved upon the face of the waters" (Gen. 1:1–2).

Mormonism portrays multiple gods in creation while the Bible makes it clear that there is only one God. Mormonism cannot make sense of the use of "Us" in Genesis because they reject the Trinity. This forces them to say there are multiple "gods" in creation. For more on this, see the section titled "The Plurality of God in the Old Testament" in the Judaism chapter. Mormonism has forsaken monotheism and has entered polytheism.

---

[367] Smith Jr., Joseph. The Church of Jesus Christ of Latter-Day Saints: The King Follett Sermon. Accessed February 24, 2021. https://www.churchofjesuschrist. org/study/ensign/1971/04/the-king-follett-sermon?lang=eng.

[368] *Book of Mormon; Doctrine and Covenants; Pearl of Great Price*. Salt Lake City, UT: The Church of Jesus Christ of Latter-day Saints, 1981. (All Book of Mormon/D&C/PoGP quotations taken from here).

INTERNAL CONTRADICTIONS
AND FALSE TEACHINGS

We have seen in a previous section that Joseph Smith taught God used to be a man, but "became" God. In *The Book of Moses*, which is found in another Mormon writing called *The Pearl of Great Price*, it says, "And God spake unto Moses, saying: Behold, I am the Lord God Almighty, and Endless is my name; for I am without beginning of days or end of years; and is not this endless?" (POGP 1:3).

This says that God has no beginning, yet Joseph Smith said God did have a beginning. Which one is it? Here is another interesting passage from the same writing:

> And every plant of the field before it was in the earth, and every herb of the field before it grew. For I, the Lord God, created all things, of which I have spoken, spiritually, before they were naturally upon the face of the earth. For I, the Lord God, had not caused it to rain upon the face of the earth. And I, the Lord God, had created all the children of men; and not yet a man to till the ground; for in heaven created I them; and there was not yet flesh upon the earth, neither in the water, neither in the air. (Moses 3:5)

According to this passage, God created everything and everybody spiritually before creating them physically. This sounds like the heresy of Origenism, which was condemned by the Church in the sixth century. Nothing like this is found in the Genesis account. This book goes on to say,

> And in that day Adam blessed God and was filled, and began to prophesy concerning all the families of the earth, saying: Blessed be the name of God, for because of my transgression my eyes

are opened and in this life I shall have joy, and again in the flesh I shall see God. And Eve, his wife, heard all these things and was glad, saying: Were it not for our transgression we never should have had seed, and never should have known good and evil, and the joy of our redemption, and the eternal life which God giveth unto all the obedient. (Moses 5:10–11)

This passage makes it sound as if Adam and Eve were happy that they sinned. This is simply not true. Adam and Eve were both ashamed of their sin and tried to blame it on another (Gen. 3:9–19). Here is another quote:

And God cursed the earth with a sore curse, and was angry with the wicked, with all the sons of men whom he had made; For they would not hearken unto his voice, nor believe on his Only Begotten Son, even in him whom he declared should come in the meridian of time, who was prepared from the foundation of the world. (Moses 5:56–57)

This passage says that in the times of Genesis, God cursed the earth because men would not believe on Jesus. There is one major problem. Jesus was not revealed yet. There is nothing in Genesis about Jesus being preached. Continuing, "And thus [Adam] was baptized, and the Spirit of God descended upon him, and thus he was born of the Spirit, and became quickened in the inner man" (Moses 6:65).

This teaches that Adam was baptized. The problem is that Christian baptism was not introduced until the New Testament times. The Book of Moses also says, "And thou art after the order of him who was without beginning of days or end of years, **from all eternity to all eternity**" (Moses 6:67).

Now compare this quote to what Joseph Smith said,

> For I am going to tell you how God came to be God. **We have imagined and supposed that God was God from all eternity. I will refute that idea**, and take away the veil, so that you may see… He was once a man like us; yea, that God himself, the Father of us all, dwelt on an earth, the same as Jesus Christ Himself did.[369]

The Mormon document titled *The Book of Moses* says that God has been God from all eternity. The founder of Mormonism, Joseph Smith, said he refutes that idea. So Mormonism literally refutes itself. Another Mormon writing is called *The Book of Abraham*. Here is a quotation from it: "And [God's] voice was unto me: Abraham, Abraham, behold, my name is Jehovah, and I have heard thee, and have come down to deliver thee, and to take thee away from thy father's house, and from all thy kinsfolk, into a strange land which thou knowest not of" (Abraham 1:16).

Mormonism's account of Genesis 12:1–3 says God revealed his name to Abraham. This is not found in the Bible. In the Scriptures, God's name is not revealed until Exodus 3:14 in the time of Moses. The Book of Abraham also says,

> And I, Abraham, had the Urim and Thummim, which the Lord my God had given unto me, in Ur of the Chaldees; And I saw the stars, that they were very great, and that one of them was nearest unto the throne of God; and there were many great ones which were near unto it; And the Lord said unto me: These are the governing ones; and the name of **the great**

---

[369] Smith Jr., Joseph. The Church of Jesus Christ of Latter-Day Saints: The King Follett Sermon. Accessed February 24, 2021. https://www.churchofjesuschrist.org/study/ensign/1971/04/the-king-follett-sermon?lang=eng.

one is Kolob, because it is near unto me, for I am
the Lord thy God: I have set this one to govern
all those which belong to the same order as that
upon which thou standest… And thus there shall
be the reckoning of the time of one planet above
another, until thou come nigh unto **Kolob**,
which **Kolob** is after the reckoning of the Lord's
time; which **Kolob** is set nigh unto the throne of
God, to govern all those planets which belong to
the same order as that upon which thou standest.
(Abraham 3:1–3, 9)

This is one of the strangest beliefs that Mormons hold. They
believe in a star called "Kolob" that governs all other stars. You will
not find anything like this in the Bible. And modern science has not
found such a planet/star. It is a very strange teaching. Now examine
this writing from Joseph Smith:

But, exerting all my powers to call upon
God to deliver me out of the power of this enemy
which had seized upon me, and at the very
moment when I was ready to sink into despair
and abandon myself to destruction—not to an
imaginary ruin, but to the power of some actual
being from the unseen world, who had such
marvelous power as I had never before felt in any
being—just at this moment of great alarm, I saw
a pillar of light exactly over my head, above the
brightness of the sun, which descended gradually
until it fell upon me. It no sooner appeared than
I found myself delivered from the enemy which
held me bound. When the light rested upon me
I saw two Personages, whose brightness and
glory defy all description, standing above me in
the air. One of them spake unto me, calling me
by name and said, pointing to the other—This

is My Beloved Son. Hear Him! (Joseph Smith,
History 1:16–17)

According to Joseph Smith, He saw the Father and Jesus. There is
one main problem. Nobody can see the Father and live (Exod. 33:20).
Anytime a person saw God in the Bible, they saw Jesus, because He
is the image of the invisible God (Col. 1:15). For more on this, see
the section titled "The Plurality of God in the Old Testament" in
the Judaism chapter. Joseph Smith says he saw the Father. The Bible
not only says that the Father is invisible (Col. 1:15), but it also says,
"God is Spirit, and those who worship Him must worship in spirit
and truth" (John 4:24). How can you see somebody that is invisible?
How can you see a spirit?

Another strange teaching in Mormonism is regarding the family and the afterlife. Consider this quote from the *Doctrines and
Covenants*:

> And again, verily I say unto you, **if a man
> marry a wife by my word**, which is my law, and
> by the new and **everlasting covenant**, and it is
> sealed unto them by the Holy Spirit of promise, by him who is anointed, unto whom I have
> appointed this power and the keys of this priesthood; and it shall be said unto them—Ye shall
> come forth in the first resurrection; and if it be
> after the first resurrection, in the next resurrection; and shall inherit thrones, kingdoms, principalities, and powers, dominions, all heights and
> depths—then shall it be written in the Lamb's
> Book of Life, that he shall commit no murder
> whereby to shed innocent blood, and if ye abide
> in my covenant, and commit no murder whereby
> to shed innocent blood, it shall be done unto
> them in all things whatsoever my servant hath
> put upon them, in time, and **through all eternity**; and shall be of full force when they are out

of the world; and they shall pass by the angels, and the gods, which are set there, to their exaltation and glory in all things, as hath been sealed upon their heads, which glory shall be a fulness and continuation of the **seeds forever and ever.** [20] **Then shall they be gods, because they have no end; therefore shall they be from everlasting to everlasting**, because they continue; then shall they above all, because all things are subject unto them. Then shall they be gods, because they have all power, and the angels are subject unto them. (D&C 132:19–20)

Mormons believe they will be married in heaven and have heavenly sex, creating spiritual children. They believe they will be "gods" on their own planets. Compare this to the encounter between Jesus and the Sadducees:

The same day came to him the Sadducees, which say that there is no resurrection, and asked him, [24] Saying, Master, Moses said, If a man die, having no children, his brother shall marry his wife, and raise up seed unto his brother. [25] Now there were with us seven brethren: and the first, when he had married a wife, deceased, and, having no issue, left his wife unto his brother: [26] Likewise the second also, and the third, unto the seventh. [27] And last of all the woman died also. [28] Therefore in the resurrection whose wife shall she be of the seven? for they all had her. [29] Jesus answered and said unto them, Ye do err, not knowing the scriptures, nor the power of God. [30] **For in the resurrection they neither marry, nor are given in marriage, but are as the angels of God in heaven.** [31] But as touching the resurrection of the dead, have ye not read that which was spoken unto you by God, saying, [32] I am the God of Abraham, and the God of Isaac, and the God of Jacob? God is not the God of the dead, but of the living. [33] And when the multitude heard this, they were astonished at his doctrine. (Matt. 22:23–33)

Mormons try to get around this passage by saying that only those who enter marriages that are not blessed by God will be like the angels in heaven in the afterlife like Jesus said while those who were in a marriage blessed by God will remain married. There is one major problem. Jesus never made a distinction between those whose marriage is blessed by God and those whose marriage is not. Jesus made it clear: in the afterlife nobody will be married. We will all be like the angels in heaven. God is not the author of confusion (1 Cor. 14:33). It cannot get any clearer than this. Nobody will be married in heaven. Mormonism teaches that a person will be married in heaven and have spiritual sex to create spiritual children. Jesus rebuked the Sadducees for "not knowing the Scriptures nor the power of God" when they assumed there would be marriage in heaven. Thus, it is accurate to say, Mormons do err not knowing the Scriptures nor the power of God.

CONCLUSION

I have to say that I have a lot of respect for Mormons. They seem to genuinely care for others. I always see them walking around spreading their message. If Christians had that same zeal, the world would be a lot better. Just like the Apostle Paul said about the Jews, Mormons "have a zeal of God, but not according to knowledge" (Rom. 10:2). Mormons do have a zeal for God, but they do not follow the true God of the Bible. I pray they turn to Jesus!

MORMONISM REFUTED

1. The founder of Mormonism, Joseph Smith, taught that God used to be a man but became God. On the other hand, the Bible says God has always been God (Ps. 90:2).
2. Mormons reject that Jesus is God, but both the Bible and history say that He is (John 1:1, 8:24, 58).
3. Mormons teach that you will be married in heaven, but Jesus said you will not (Matt. 22:23–33).
4. Mormons teach that Joseph Smith saw the Father but the Bible says the Father is a spirit (John 4:24).

CHAPTER 10

JEHOVAH'S WITNESSES

INTRODUCTION

Around the same time Mormonism was founded, there were many sects trying to predict the Second Coming of Christ. Like many, they predicted wrong. A man named Charles Taze Russell became relevant around 1870 with his predictions of the Second Coming. Russell formed the International Bible Students Association and the Watch Tower Bible and Tract Society in 1884. The group name was changed in 1931 to "Jehovah's Witnesses" by Russell's succeeding President, Joseph Franklin Rutherford. After Rutherford, a man named Nathan Homer Knorr became president and had the New World Translation of the Bible written.

This is the official Bible used by Jehovah's Witnesses. When engaging with them, they will most likely only accept verses quoted from the King James Version of the Bible, although they will "correct" it when need be according to their *New World Translation* (just like the Mormons "correct" the Bible according to their Book of Mormon). They also produce their own literature known as the *Watchtower Magazine, Awake! Magazine, What Can the Bible Teach Us?*, and *How to Remain in God's Love.*

WHO IS GOD?

Like the Mormons, Jehovah's Witnesses reject the Trinity. They believe God is a Unity and they insist on calling Him Jehovah. They believe Jesus is a created being (like the old arian heresy discussed in an earlier section). To JWs, Jesus is not God, but a lesser god below the Father. They believe Jesus was Michael the Archangel until He came to earth and at that point was just a perfect human, but when He went back to heaven, He was Michael the Archangel again.[370] Knowing that consider this passage in Hebrews:

> God, who at sundry times and in divers manners spake in time past unto the fathers by the prophets, ² Hath in these last days spoken unto us by his Son, whom he hath appointed heir of all things, by whom also he made the worlds; ³ Who being the brightness of his glory, and the express image of his person, and upholding all things by the word of his power, when he had by himself purged our sins, sat down on the right hand of the Majesty on high: ⁴ **Being made so much better than the angels, as he hath by inheritance obtained a more excellent name than they. ⁵ For unto which of the angels said he at any time, Thou art my Son, this day have I begotten thee? And again, I will be to him a Father, and he shall be to me a Son? ⁶ And again, when he bringeth in the firstbegotten into the world, he saith, And let all the angels of God worship him.** ⁷ And of the angels he saith, Who maketh his angels spirits, and his ministers a flame of fire. ⁸ **But unto the Son he saith, Thy throne, O God**, is for ever and ever: a sceptre

---

[370] Carden, Paul, ed. *World Religions Made Easy*. Peabody, MA: Rose Publishing, 2018, 9.

of righteousness is the sceptre of thy kingdom.
⁹ Thou hast loved righteousness, and hated iniquity; therefore God, even thy God, hath anointed
thee with the oil of gladness above thy fellows.
(Heb. 1:1–9)

This passage says that Jesus is better than the angels. How can
He be better than the angels if He is an angel Himself? It also says
God has never called an angel Son. Jesus is called the Son multiple
times (Matt. 3:17, 17:5). How can Jesus be an angel if He is called
Son, and no angel has ever been called Son? This passage also reveals
that the angels worship Jesus. Why would the angels worship another
angel? And finally, Jesus is called God in verses eight and nine. How
can an angel be God? So clearly Jesus is not an angel. He is God. The
JWs use their "New World Translation" of the Bible to "correct" the
supposed errors in other translations. Here is John 1:1 in the Bible,
"In the beginning was the Word, and the Word was with God, and
the Word was God" (John 1:1 KJV).

And now the New World Translation: "In the beginning was
the Word, and the Word was with God, and **the Word was a god**"[371]
(John 1:1 NWT).

The Bible says that Jesus is God. Not only does the Bible say
this, but this has been the orthodox Christian belief since the beginning of the Church. The JW translations says Jesus is *a god*. They
translate it to fit their theology. This verse says Jesus was in the beginning meaning He has no beginning; He is uncreated, yet JWs say He
is created. Marvin Jones says,

> There is a parallel concept between Genesis
> 1:1 and John 1:1 as a "beginning" is referenced in
> both verses. However, the "beginning" that John
> refers to precedes the creation account. Genesis

[371] *New World Translation of the Holy Scriptures*. Wallkill, NY: Watch Tower Bible and Tract Society of New York, Inc, 2013. (All New World Translation quotations taken from here).

> 1:1 refers to the beginning of creation but John
> 1:1 refers to an epoch before creation (com-
> monly called "eternity past")… This "beginning"
> provides a cosmological background in order to
> interpret the person of Jesus Christ. The use of
> the preposition "in" establishes the existence of
> the Lord—He was not the beginning or from
> the beginning but existed "in" the beginning.
> The eternal nature of the Lord is further demon-
> strated by the word "was."[372]

Jesus has always been. If He has always been, He is God; not just "a god." The JW argument for their rendering of "a god," they say, is based on the Greek. Where John 1:1 says, "and the Word was with God," the word translated "God" is the Greek "ton theon." The Greek word *ton* means "the." The word *theon* means "God." Where John 1:1 says, "the Word was God," the Greek word used for God is *theos*, and it does not have an article preceding it. Because of this, JWs argue these words mean two different things—the word *theon* speaking of God the Father as the Almighty God and the word *theos* speaking of Jesus as a "lesser god." Their logic is flawed. The two words used for "God" are not two different words, but rather differ-ent parts of the sentence, which is why they have different endings. That is how the Greek language works.

Plus, the reason the second "God" does not have a definite arti-cle is because it is not needed when placed in its context. If one applies the JW translation to other parts of the Bible, it refutes their whole argument. James White says, "If one is to dogmatically assert that any anarthous noun must be indefinite and translated with an indefinite article, one must be able to do the same with the 282 other times [theos] appears anarthously. For example, of the chaos that

[372] Jones, Marvin. Recovering Historical Christology for Today's Church. Eugene, OR: Wipf and Stock Publishers, 2019, 34–35.

would create, try translating the anarthous [theos] at 2 Corinthians 5:19 (i.e., 'a god was in Christ')."[373]

Here is 2 Corinthians 5:19 (KJV): "To wit, that **God was in Christ**, reconciling the world unto himself, not imputing their trespasses unto them; and hath committed unto us the word of reconciliation."

Now apply the JW theory of "theos" to this verse: "That is, that **a god was in Christ** reconciling the world to Himself, not imputing their trespasses to them, and has committed to us the word of reconciliation" (2 Cor. 5:19 NWT).

If we apply the JW theory to this verse, it completely refutes itself. Translated this way, it says "a god was in Christ," but when speaking of John 1:1, they say "a god" refers to Jesus. So according to them this verse in 2 Corinthians means, "Jesus was in Jesus." Does that make sense? Not at all. Now, in verse 3 of John chapter 1 it says, "All things were made by him; and without him was not any thing made that was made" (John 1:3). The direct context says Jesus is Creator, not created. And what does it mean for Jesus to be "a god"?

The JWs are so strongly opposed to the Trinity because they believe it is pagan and polytheistic, yet they believe in two gods! They believe in the Father as God and Jesus as another god. One plus one equals two. That makes two gods. That is not monotheism. It is polytheism. So, while JWs accuse Christians of being polytheists for believing in the Trinity, they are actually polytheists themselves for portraying Jesus as some type of lesser god. Another verse JWs love to refer to is Colossians 1:15 which says, "[Jesus] is the image of the invisible God, the firstborn of every creature" (Col. 1:15).

They focus on the word "firstborn" and claim this means Jesus is a created being. Ironically, this is the same verse Arius appealed to back in the fourth century to prove his false teaching of Arianism (which was declared a heresy in AD 325 by the Church). As the

---

[373] White, James R. *The Forgotten Trinity.* Bloomington, MN: Bethany House Publishers, 1998, 52–53.

Scripture says, "there is no new thing under the sun" (Eccles. 1:9). Returning to Colossians, Marvin Jones writes,

> The meaning of "firstborn" seems to imply position. The emphasis on the prefix "first" would naturally convey the idea of "first-in-line," which indicated position or succession. However, the word also has the meaning of "kind." The idea of "kind" not only refers to a position but to a hierarchical order. The issue of hierarchy refers to the idea of "supremacy in kind." Thus, the word "firstborn" [prototokos] describes the Lord's relationship to The Father. Danny Akin states, "The idea is not that Christ was ever somehow 'born' to God but rather that in his relationship to the Father in the Trinity he enjoys all of the rights and privileges the Father bestows upon him." The word "firstborn" [prototokos] also informs Christ's relationship to creation. The concept is that Jesus has the sovereign right to rule creation as the Creator. It is difficult to imagine that Paul would want the Colossians to embrace the idea that Jesus is the created firstborn who in turn created everything else.[374]

Jesus being the "firstborn" means He is the Supreme Being. He is first overall. He has a special relationship to the Father. Paul was writing to people in Colossae who were known for worshipping false gods and had many false beliefs. Marvin Jones says, "The church was in grave danger of losing the biblical identity of Jesus Christ by blending him with the heretical streams of Judaism, Hellenism, and Gnosticism."[375]

---

[374] Jones, 11.
[375] Jones, 6.

The Apostle Paul wanted the Colossians to know that Jesus is the "firstborn" over all those false gods and false teachings, meaning He is supreme and above all. This makes sense in the direct context since verses sixteen and seventeen say Jesus created all things! How can a creation be the Creator? Jesus as the "firstborn" means He is the Lord overall and has always been from everlasting to everlasting. James White says,

> That *firstborn* came to be a title that referred to a position rather than a mere notion of being the first one born is seen in numerous passages in the Old Testament. For example, in Exodus 4:22 God says that Israel is "My son, My first-born." Obviously Israel was not the first nation God "created," but is instead the nation He has chosen to have a special relationship with Him... But certainly the most significant passage, and the one that is probably behind Paul's usage in Colossians, is Psalm 89:27: "I also shall make him My firstborn, the highest of the kings of the earth." This is a highly messianic Psalm (note v. 20 and the use of the term "anointed" of David), and in this context, David, as the prototype of the coming Messiah, is described as God's pro-totokos, the "firstborn." Again, the emphasis is plainly upon the relationship between God and David, not David's "creation." David had preemi-nence in God's plan and was given leadership and authority over God's people. In the same way, the coming Messiah would have preeminence, but in an even wider arena.[376]

The Septuagint (Greek Old Testament) uses the same word "protokos" (firstborn) to refer to David as the New Testament does

---

[376] White, 112.

for Jesus. David was not literally God's firstborn—God's literal "first-born" would be the first angel He created or humanly speaking His "firstborn" would be Adam. David being God's "firstborn" simply meant he was in close relationship to God, and he had authority from God over all. JWs also reject the idea that the Holy Spirit is a person, "Witnesses believe the "holy spirit" is not God, but rather an impersonal, invisible, active force—the "energy" Jehovah projects to accomplish his will."[377]

They do not believe the Holy Spirit is a person. Like the Arian heresy that was refuted long ago (AD 325), a heresy known as mace-donianism was refuted as well (AD 381). Macedonians rejected the deity of the Holy Spirit, just like JWs do today. Besides the facts of history, the Bible clearly teaches that the Holy Spirit is a person separate from the Father and Son. John says, "But the Comforter, which is the Holy Ghost, whom the Father will send in my name, **he** shall teach you all things, and bring all things to your remembrance, whatsoever I have said unto you" (John 14:26 KJV).

The New World Translation says, "But the helper, the holy spirit, which the Father will send in my name, **that one** will teach you all things and bring back to your minds all the things I told you" (John 14:26 NWT).

Notice how the JW translation takes away the personhood of the Holy Spirit. When Jesus refers to the Holy Spirit, He refers to Him as "He," not "it" or "that one." A few chapters later, Jesus says, "Howbeit **when he, the Spirit of truth, is come, he will guide you into all truth**: for he shall not speak of himself; but whatsoever he shall hear, that shall he speak: and he will shew you things to come" (John 16:13 KJV).

The JW translation says, "However, when **that one comes, the spirit of the truth, he will guide you into all the truth**, for he will not speak of his own initiative, but what he hears he will speak, and he will declare to you the things to come" (John 16:13 NWT).

[377] Carden, Paul, ed. *World Religions Made Easy*. Peabody, MA: Rose Publishing, 2018, 10.

The Bible, once again, refers to the Holy Spirit as a person using the word *he*. The New World Translation once again translates it to call the Holy Spirit "that one." The interesting part is that directly following that, it calls the Holy Spirit "he." So even in the JW translation of the Bible, the Holy Spirit is referred to as a person. To see the full Biblical and historical teaching on the Trinity, see the sections titled "The Plurality of God in the Old Testament" in the Judaism chapter and "The Trinity" in the chapter titled "Primitive Christianity."

CONCLUSION

Similar to Mormons, I have a respect for Jehovah's Witnesses. They spend a lot of time spreading their message which puts most Christians to shame. Most Christians are too lazy and/or scared to spread the message of the Bible. I commend the Jehovah's Witnesses for their dedication. But just like the Mormons and the other groups discussed in this book, JWs have false beliefs. I pray they turn to Jesus!

JEHOVAH'S WITNESSES REFUTED

1. JWs teach that Jesus is a created being, but the Bible says He is God and Creator (John 1:1–3, Col. 1:16–17).
2. JWs teach that Jesus is an angel, but the Bible says Jesus is higher than the angels and that the angels worship Him (Heb. 1:1–9).
3. JWs teach that the Holy Spirit is not a person, but the Bible says He is (John 14:26, 16:13).

CHAPTER 11

HEBREW ISRAELISM

INTRODUCTION

I remember after I came to Christ in 2018, a former high school football teammate began posting on social media about black people being God's people. This did not make much sense to me. "I thought God loved all people?" I remember asking myself. I had only been studying the Scriptures for a short time, but from what I had read it was clear that God came to save all people regardless of skin color, ethnicity, or nationality. This former teammate was also posting about how we should not be eating pig or shellfish or celebrating Christmas and Easter, etc.

What was this type of "black Judaism" that my former teammate was subscribing to? I knew it was not Christianity. The New Testament was clear on all these issues. Come to find out this group calls themselves the "Hebrew Israelites." They claim to be true people of God and they also claim that the Jews of today are imposters. I had to find out what this group was and what exactly they believed. The Hebrew Israelites are probably one of the hardest groups to address because one, they are fairly new and two, they do not have much material explaining their official beliefs. Their main platform is YouTube. The only real way to understand their beliefs is by piecing together different videos and a few books they have. Knowing this, I want to address some of the main beliefs of this group. It should be noted that the Hebrew Israelites are not a monolith. There are many different sects of Hebrew Israelites and they do not all believe the same things. The main group of Hebrew Israelites that I will be focusing on is the 1West group.

ORIGINS

The starting date for Hebrew Israelism is somewhat difficult to pinpoint. On November 8, 1896, a man named William Saunders Crowdy started the Church of God and Saints of Christ. According to the Church's website, Crowdy's supposed revelation led him to the main tenets of his new found faith which were, "The Sabbath (Saturday), the Passover, the Hebrew Calendar, the Day of Atonement, and above all, the Ten Commandments of the Sinai Revelation."[378]

From these beliefs, it's evident that this newly founded religion is a type of Judaism. The ironic part about this founding is that the original followers of Crowdy were white![379] This group that demonizes white people actually traces back to originally having white followers! In 1900, a man named Warren Roberson followed suit founding the Temple of the Gospel of the Kingdom in Virginia (which was later moved to Harlem in 1917). In 1917, F. S. Cherry founded the Church of God in Philadelphia. Wentworth Matthews founded the Commandment Keepers in Harlem in 1919. Arnold Josiah Ford started the Beth B'nai Abraham congregation in 1930, which later joined with the Commandment Keepers.

One of the most well-known groups of Hebrew Israelism is known as 1West based on the street at 1 West 125th in Harlem. A man named Abba Bivens, a student of Wentworth Matthews, eventually left the Commandment Keepers to start his own sect. Instead of just subscribing to the Old Testament, Bivens held the New Testament to be for them as well. He started the Israelite School of Torah in

---

[378] Malone, Vocab. *Barack Obama VS the Black Hebrew Israelites: Introduction to the History & Beliefs of 1West Hebrew Israelism.* Phoenix, AZ: Thureos Publishing, 2017, 27.

[379] Malone, 28.

1969. Now I want the reader to hear one of the strangest beliefs of this group. Abba Bivens's followers believed he was John the Baptist *reincarnate*.[380] Never did I expect a supposed monotheistic religion to subscribe to reincarnation. The Bible says, "And as it is appointed unto men once to die, but after this the judgment" (Heb. 9:27). We die and then we are judged.

There is no Scripture that ever even hints at us being reincarnate. After the death of Bivens, a successor by the name of Arieh predicted the second coming of Christ to be in the year 2000. Obviously, this prediction did not come to pass. This is what God has to say about false prophets:

> But the prophet, which shall presume to speak a word in my name, which I have not commanded him to speak, or that shall speak in the name of other gods, even that prophet shall die. [21] And if thou say in thine heart, How shall we know the word which the LORD hath not spoken? [22] When a prophet speaketh in the name of the LORD, **if the thing follow not, nor come to pass, that is the thing which the LORD hath not spoken**, but the prophet hath spoken it presumptuously: thou shalt not be afraid of him. (Deut. 18:20–22)

According to God, if a person prophesies falsely, he is to die. He is lying. God did not speak to him. Remember how Bivens was said to be John the Baptist reincarnate? Years later, a leader in the church started by Bivens's successors named Mashah, was believed to be King David reincarnate.[381] Note: Like stated before, not all Hebrew Israelite groups think the same, but I will mostly be addressing the "1West" line of Hebrew Israelites. I do not want to misrepresent any-

---

[380] Malone, 23.
[381] Malone, 24.

body, so the reader must keep this in mind: not all these beliefs apply to every single Hebrew Israelite group.

WHO IS GOD?

The so-called Hebrew Israelites are very intrigued with the name of God similar to the Jehovah's Witnesses. Except these so-called Hebrew Israelites do not like the name "Jehovah" either. They also claim that the name "Jesus" is wrong as well. And to that I say God does not only speak one language. Whatever language we call on Him in, He knows, and He will save us. I am not going to get into the name of God in this work, but the reader should be aware this group does not call Jesus "Jesus."

What I really want to focus on in this section is the doctrine of God. This group rejects the Trinity. For the biblical view of the Trinity, read the section titled "The Plurality of God in the Old Testament" in the Judaism chapter as well as the section titled "The Trinity" in the chapter titled "Primitive Christianity." I could not find an official statement of faith from the 1West groups, but Israel of God has a statement available. The reader must remember that the Israel of God group is not the same as the 1West groups.

The 1West groups are the more hostile groups seen on the street corners. Israel of God still has false doctrines but are not hostile. While this statement of faith is from Israel of God, most Hebrew Israelite groups believe the same regarding the godhead (although some may differ slightly). Instead of a Trinity, Israel of God seems to believe in a Biunity or something like it. Their website says, "Jesus of Nazareth is the Christ, the Son of God, the Holy One of Israel. He was the prophesied Messiah of the Old Testament and is described in the New Testament as being God in the Flesh. **As the second member of the Godhead, He has existed throughout eternity as the 'Word.'**"[382]

---

[382] "About Us." The Israel of God, March 2, 2020. https://theisraelofgod.come/about-us/.

According to Israel of God, Jesus is part of the Godhead, but the Holy Spirit is not. Vocab Malone quotes them, saying,

> **The Holy Spirit is not the third part of the "Trinity." There are currently only two members in the Godhead, The Father and His Son, Jesus Christ.** The Holy Spirit can be manifested to man in many forms. One form is an Angel sent from God to bring to remembrance what Jesus has told us in His Holy Word (another form of His Spirit).[383]

According to the "Hebrew Israelites," the Holy Spirit is not part of the godhead. This is similar to what the Jehovah's Witnesses believe, except they don't believe Jesus is part of the godhead either, while the "Hebrew Israelites" do. This view of the Holy Spirit is problematic since He is called God in the Bible (Acts 5:1–4) and referred to as a distinct Person (John 16:13).

WHO CAN BE SAVED?

Hebrew Israelites generally believe white people to be descendants of Esau or in other words, they are "Edomites." Dalton JR. says,

> There are many teachings and theories about what the Edomites looked like in Biblical times and who are the Edomites today. Many theories suggest that Edom is the white man. Other theories suggest that Edom was the twin Albino brother of Jacob. This theory goes off the fact that Jacob and Esau's uncle (and father-in-law by Leah and Rachel) was named "Laban

---

[383] Malone, 20.

(Lavan)" which in Hebrew means "white" or "to become white.[384]

Likewise, Christian apologist Vocab Malone says,

These groups, though slowly developing doctrines different from one another, all agree that true Jews are "myelinated peoples," and that Genesis 25:25 proves that "Edomites" are white (they claim white people are the actually red, as their blood shows through their face due to a lack of melanin).[385]

Hebrew Israelites generally draw their teaching of Esau being the white man based on Scripture that says he was "red" (Gen. 25:25). Since white people often get red, this must mean white people are descendants of Esau (Edomites). That is their line of reasoning. Vocab Malone easily refutes their argument, "It has been noted many times that the Hebrew word used in Genesis 25:25 to describe Esau as "red" is also used to describe David in 1 Samuel 16:12."[386] King David was also described as "red." Surely the Hebrew Israelites will not claim David was an Edomite seeing how numerous verses claim he is of the line of Judah (Matt. 1:1–17, Rev. 5:5); not to mention, former Hebrew Israelites believed the leader Mashah was King David reincarnate. Now, why would a "Hebrew Israelite" be reincarnate as an Edomite (whom they claim are a cursed people)? It would not make sense.

Let us assume that the so-called Hebrew Israelites are right, and all white people are Edomites. Does it matter? No. God says, "Thou shalt not abhor an Edomite; for he is thy brother: thou shalt not abhor an Egyptian; because thou wast a stranger in his land" (Deut. 23:7). God says not to abhor an Edomite. Edomites are still

---

[384] Dalton JR., Ronald. *Hebrews to Negroes: Wake Up Black America!* G Publishing, 2014, 308.
[385] Malone, 25.
[386] Malone, 25.

to be treated with respect! The Hebrew Israelites have fundamentally missed one of the main points of the New Testament—there is neither Jew nor Greek. Jew or Gentile does not matter. God came to save all races, ethnicities, and nationalities. Galatians says, "There is neither Jew nor Greek, there is neither bond nor free, there is neither male nor female: for ye are all one in Christ Jesus" (Gal. 3:28). We are all one! There is no separation! Ephesians says,

> For he is our peace, who hath made both one, and hath broken down the middle wall of partition between us; [15] Having abolished in his flesh the enmity, even the law of commandments contained in ordinances; for to make in himself of twain one new man, so making peace; [16] And that he might reconcile both unto God in one body by the cross, having slain the enmity thereby: [17] And came and preached peace to you which were afar off, and to them that were nigh. [18] For through him we both have access by one Spirit unto the Father. (Eph. 2:14–18)

God has made Jews and Gentiles one together in Christ! Christ surpasses all ethnic and/or racial boundaries. We are all one! There is no segregation in heaven! When the Apostle John had a revelation of heaven he said, "After this I beheld, and, lo, a great multitude, which no man could number, of **all nations, and kindreds, and people, and tongues**, stood before the throne, and before the Lamb, clothed with white robes, and palms in their hands" (Rev. 7:9). In heaven, there are people of all nations, tribes, peoples, and tongues! God is no respecter of persons (Acts 10:34–35). What about the story of Jonah? God sent Jonah to preach repentance to the Gentile city of Nineveh so they would be saved (Jon. 1:1–2). The interesting part of the story of Jonah is that his attitude somewhat resembled that of the Hebrew Israelites. Jonah did not want the Ninevites to be saved because they were Gentiles and he thought they were wicked. When Jonah finally preached repentance in Nineveh after being chastised by the Lord, chapter 4 says,

> But it displeased Jonah exceedingly, and he was very angry. [2] And he prayed unto the LORD, and said, I pray thee, O LORD, was not this my saying, when I was yet in my country? Therefore I fled before unto Tarshish: for I knew that thou art a gracious God, and merciful, slow to anger, and of great kindness, and repentest thee of the evil. [3] Therefore now, O LORD, take, I beseech thee, my life from me; for it is better for me to die than to live. [4] Then said the LORD, Doest thou well to be angry? (Jon. 4:1–4).

Jonah was angry with God because He was merciful and gracious to the Ninevites—who were Gentiles. Even in the Old Testament God showed mercy to Gentiles. What about Acts chapter 10?

> While Peter yet spake these words, the Holy Ghost fell on all them which heard the word. [45] And they of the circumcision which believed were astonished, as many as came with Peter, because that on the Gentiles also was poured out the gift of the Holy Ghost. [46] For they heard them speak with tongues, and magnify God. Then answered Peter, [47] Can any man forbid water, that these should not be baptized, which have received the Holy Ghost as well as we? [48] And he commanded them to be baptized in the name of the Lord. Then prayed they him to tarry certain days. (Acts 10:44–48)

In this passage, the Gentiles received the Holy Spirit! If a person has the Holy Spirit, they are in the family of God (Rom. 8:14). This means Gentiles are in the family of God! Paul said, "I say then, Have they stumbled that they should fall? God forbid: but rather through their fall **salvation is come unto the Gentiles**, for to provoke them to jealousy. [12] Now if the fall of them be the riches of the world, and the diminishing of them the riches of the Gentiles; how much more their fulness?" (Rom. 11:11–12).

Paul makes it clear that salvation is offered to Gentiles! This very statement appears in the book of Acts, "Be it known therefore unto you, that the salvation of God is sent unto the Gentiles, and that they will hear it" (Acts 28:28). The Bible is clear that salvation is offered to Gentiles! Hebrew Israelites say the opposite. Whom should I believe? Examine Paul's trial in Acts: "Then Agrippa said unto Paul, Almost thou persuadest me to be a Christian. [29] And Paul said, I would to God, that not only thou, but also all that hear me this day, were both almost, and altogether such as I am, except these bonds" (Acts 26:28–29).

As Paul was standing before Agrippa and the other Romans, he said he wished they would all be Christians as he was! Now it is widely known that the Romans were Gentiles! If Gentiles cannot be saved, why did Paul say he wanted them to be saved? Because Gentiles can in fact be saved! It is true that Jesus started His ministry focused on the Jews (Matt. 15:24), but that was because He had a specific order of doing things and was fulfilling the promises given to the Israelites. After His ministry, He commanded His disciples to go into all the world and preach the gospel to everybody (Matt. 28:19). He chose Paul specifically to go to the Gentiles (Acts 9:15–16). Not to mention, Jesus healed Gentiles in His ministry (Matt. 15:25–28).

Paul said, "For if thou [Gentiles] wert cut out of the olive three which is wild by nature, and wert grafted contrary to nature into a good olive tree: how much more shall these, which be the natural branches, be grafted into their own olive tree?" (Rom. 11:24). The Gentiles were part of their own wild olive tree, but God grafted them into His olive tree (the family of God)!

So we see that Gentiles throughout the New Testament were healed and saved by God. Not only Cornelius (Acts 10:44–48) and Lydia (Acts 16:14–15), but how about church leaders? According to the so-called Hebrew Israelites, a person is an Israelite based on their father's seed. Vocab Malone says, "For example, reggae artist Bob Marley is considered an "Edomite" because his father was not black."[387]

So according to the so-called Hebrew Israelites, a person must be able to trace their lineage back to Israel through their father. If the mother is an Israelite, but the father is not, they are not considered an Israelite and thus are unsaved Gentiles. If this reasoning is true, what do we make of Timothy? Acts says, "Then came [Paul] to Derbe and Lystra: and, behold, a certain disciple was there, named Timothy, the son of a certain woman, which was a Jewess, and believed; but his father was a Greek" (Acts 16:1). Timothy was a leader in the church whom Paul wrote two epistles (1 and 2 Timothy) to. Timothy's mother was, in fact, a Jew, but his father was Greek! His father was a Gentile! According to the Hebrew Israelites, this would make Timothy a Gentile!

So if Gentiles cannot be saved, why did Paul appoint Timothy to be a church leader? What sense would that make? The answer is because Gentiles can be saved. And even if white people really are Edomites, that would still make them children of Abraham (through Isaac). Paul said, "Know ye therefore that they which are of faith, the same are the children of Abraham. [8] And the scripture, foreseeing that **God would justify the heathen through faith**, preached before the gospel unto Abraham, saying, In thee shall all nations be blessed. [9] So then they which be of faith are blessed with faithful Abraham" (Gal. 3:7–9).

God justifies Gentiles (the heathen) in the same way He justifies Jews—by faith!

HOW TO BE SAVED

The so-called Hebrew Israelites are modern-day Judaizers. They believe one must keep the law of Moses to be saved. Vocab Malone says, "1West Hebrew Israelites believe salvation is procured by law-keeping. Sabbath-observance, dietary restrictions, and a

---

[387] Malone, 40.

certain outward appearance (beards and fringes) are marks of spiritual understanding and holiness."[388] In other words, they're like the Pharisees. They think they will be justified by the deeds of the law! Paul said, "Christ is become of no effect unto you, whosoever of you are justified by the law; ye are fallen from grace" (Gal. 5:4).

According to Paul, the so-called Hebrew Israelites have fallen from grace! They attempt to be justified by keeping the law, but "by the works of the law shall no flesh be justified" (Gal. 2:16). Nobody can be justified by the works of the law! Another thing that was mentioned in their beliefs is keeping the Sabbath. They argue one must observe the Sabbath! That is strange since Jesus worked on the Sabbath:

> And it came to pass, that he went through the corn fields on the sabbath day; and his disciples began, as they went, to pluck the ears of corn. 24 And the Pharisees said unto him, Behold, why do they on the sabbath day that which is not lawful? 25 And he said unto them, Have ye never read what David did, when he had need, and was an hungred, he, and they that were with him? 26 How he went into the house of God in the days of Abiathar the high priest, and did eat the shewbread, which is not lawful to eat but for the priests, and gave also to them which were with him? 27 And he said unto them, **The sabbath was made for man, and not man for the sabbath**: 28 Therefore the Son of man is Lord also of the sabbath. (Mark 2:23–28)

When the Pharisees confronted Jesus for working on the Sabbath, He made it clear that the Sabbath was made for us. We were not made for the Sabbath! In other words, the whole point of the Sabbath was to give people rest, not to be some legalistic thing.

---

[388] Malone, 38.

The rest the Sabbath gave was only a shadow of the true rest, which is found in Christ (Matt. 11:28–30). Paul makes it clear that we don't have to keep the Sabbath in the manner of the Old Covenant saying, "Let no man therefore judge you in meat, or in drink, or in respect of a holyday, or of the new moon, or of the sabbath days: ¹⁷ Which are a shadow of things to come; but the body is of Christ" (Col. 2:16–17). The Sabbath was just a shadow of Christ! Now that Christ has come, we are no longer obligated to keep it as the Jews did. Paul also said,

One man esteemeth one day above another: another esteemeth every day alike. Let every man be fully persuaded in his own mind. ⁶ He that regardeth the day, regardeth it unto the Lord; and he that regardeth not the day, to the Lord he doth not regard it. He that eateth, eateth to the Lord, for he giveth God thanks; and he that eateth not, to the Lord he eateth not, and giveth God thanks. ⁷ For none of us liveth to himself, and no man dieth to himself. ⁸ For whether we live, we live unto the Lord; and whether we die, we die unto the Lord: whether we live therefore, or die, we are the Lord's. ⁹ For to this end Christ both died, and rose, and revived, that he might be Lord both of the dead and living. ¹⁰ But why dost thou judge thy brother? or why dost thou set at nought thy brother? for we shall all stand before the judgment seat of Christ. ¹¹ For it is written, As I live, saith the Lord, every knee shall bow to me, and every tongue shall confess to God. ¹² So then every one of us shall give account of himself to God. ¹³ **Let us not therefore judge one another any more: but judge this rather, that no man put a stumblingblock or an occasion to fall in his brother's way.** (Rom. 14:5–13)

Paul says that some people esteem certain days above another, and some think all days are the same. Either way, we have the liberty as Christians to keep the Jewish Sabbath or not and to celebrate holidays we want. We are not supposed to judge fellow Christians based on what holidays they observe.

This leads into the next point which is food. The so-called Hebrew Israelites also believe we must keep the dietary laws—not eat shellfish or swine, etc. Once again, the dietary laws were just a shadow of things to come (Col. 2:16–17). We are not obligated to keep those laws anymore. In fact, Paul said, "For every creature of God is good, and nothing to be refused, if it be received with thanksgiving: 5 For it is sanctified by the word of God and prayer (1 Tim. 4:4–5). All food we eat is sanctified by prayer! I can eat a bacon cheeseburger if I want or a lobster tail dinner! Praise God! Returning to the passage in Romans,

> **For one believeth that he may eat all things: another, who is weak, eateth herbs. 3 Let not him that eateth despise him that eateth not; and let not him which eateth not judge him that eateth: for God hath received him.** 4 Who art thou that judgest another man's servant? to his own master he standeth or falleth. Yea, he shall be holden up: for God is able to make him stand. 5 One man esteemeth one day above another: another esteemeth every day alike. Let every man be fully persuaded in his own mind. 6 He that regardeth the day, regardeth it unto the Lord; and he that regardeth not the day, to the Lord he doth not regard it. **He that eateth, eateth to the Lord, for he giveth God thanks; and he that eateth not, to the Lord he eateth not, and giveth God thanks.** (Rom. 14:2–6)

Just like with holidays and holy days, we have the liberty as Christians to eat what we want! Now, some Christians may have more sensitive consciences which means they might not want to eat shellfish or swine or anything like it. That is their choice. But it does not mean the rest of us cannot eat those things. We have the liberty to do so. Paul also said,

> Howbeit there is not in every man that knowledge: for some with conscience of the idol unto this hour eat it as a thing offered unto an idol; and their conscience being weak is defiled. **8** But meat commendeth us not to God: **for neither, if we eat, are we the better; neither, if we eat not, are we the worse.** **9** But take heed lest by any means this liberty of yours become a stumblingblock to them that are weak. **10** For if any man see thee which hast knowledge sit at meat in the idol's temple, shall not the conscience of him which is weak be emboldened to eat those things which are offered to idols; **11** And through thy knowledge shall the weak brother perish, for whom Christ died? **12** But when ye sin so against the brethren, and wound their weak conscience, ye sin against Christ. **13** Wherefore, if meat make my brother to offend, I will eat no flesh while the world standeth, lest I make my brother to offend.
> (1 Cor. 8:7–13)

We have so much liberty in Christ that Paul even says we can eat foods sacrificed to idols! That is pretty extreme! Granted, this is more of a cultural situation as we in the twenty-first century are not normally presented with food sacrificed to idols, but nonetheless it shows how much liberty the Christian has. The only situation in which we should not eat something is if it hurts our brother's conscience. For example, if my brother thinks a certain food should not be eaten for biblical reasons, I will not eat it around him out of respect for his conscience. It is like not drinking alcohol around a former alcoholic. It is for their protection and out of love for them.

Besides a situation like that, we are at liberty to eat whatever we want if we pray over it! The truth is food means nothing! Jesus said, "Not that which goeth into the mouth defileth a man; but that which cometh out of the mouth, this defileth a man" (Matt. 15:11). God is not concerned with us keeping a certain diet. He is concerned with the state of our hearts!

The last legalistic doctrine that the so-called Hebrew Israelites stress is the outward appearance regarding things like beards and their clothing. But does outward appearance matter? Jesus said, "Judge not according to the appearance, but judge righteous judgment" (John 7:24). Judging according to appearance is wrong. After Samuel looked at David's brother and assumed he was the anointed one based on his outward appearance, God said to him, "Look not on his countenance, or on the height of his stature; because I have refused him: for the LORD seeth not as man seeth; for man looketh on the outward appearance, but the LORD looketh on the heart" (1 Sam. 16:7). God is not focused on the outward appearance. That is superficial. God sees the contents of our hearts.

DEUTERONOMY 28

One of the biggest passages that "Hebrew Israelites" appeal to as being a prophecy of black people is Deuteronomy chapter 28. Supposedly, this chapter is speaking of the transatlantic slave trade. Here is the passage:

> **And it shall come to pass, if thou shalt hearken diligently unto the voice of the LORD thy God, to observe and to do all his commandments which I command thee this day, that the LORD thy God will set thee on high above all nations of the earth: ² And all these blessings shall come on thee, and overtake thee, if thou shalt hearken unto the voice of the LORD thy God. ³ Blessed** shalt thou be in the city, and blessed shalt thou be in the field.

⁴ Blessed shall be the fruit of thy body, and the fruit of thy ground, and the fruit of thy cattle, the increase of thy kine, and the flocks of thy sheep. ⁵ Blessed shall be thy basket and thy store. ⁶ Blessed shalt thou be when thou comest in, and blessed shalt thou be when thou goest out. ⁷ The LORD shall cause thine enemies that rise up against thee to be smitten before thy face: they shall come out against thee one way, and flee before thee seven ways. ⁸ The LORD shall command the blessing upon thee in thy storehouses, and in all that thou settest thine hand unto; and he shall bless thee in the land which the LORD thy God giveth thee. ⁹ The LORD shall establish thee an holy people unto himself, as he hath sworn unto thee, if thou shalt keep the commandments of the LORD thy God, and walk in his ways. ¹⁰ And all people of the earth shall see that thou art called by the name of the LORD; and they shall be afraid of thee. ¹¹ And the LORD shall make thee plenteous in goods, in the fruit of thy body, and in the fruit of thy cattle, and in the fruit of thy ground, in the land which the LORD sware unto thy fathers to give thee. ¹² The LORD shall open unto thee his good treasure, the heaven to give the rain unto thy land in his season, and to bless all the work of thine hand: and thou shalt lend unto many nations, and thou shalt not borrow. ¹³ **And the LORD shall make thee the head, and not the tail; and thou shalt be above only, and thou shalt not be beneath; if that thou hearken unto the commandments of the LORD thy God, which I command thee this day, to observe and to do them:** ¹⁴ And thou shalt not go aside from any of the words which I command thee this day,

to the right hand, or to the left, to go after other gods to serve them. (Deut. 28:1–14)

In summary of these verses, God will bless the children of Israel if they obey Him. It is as simple as that. Now onto the "curses" section of this chapter:

But it shall come to pass, if thou wilt not hearken unto the voice of the LORD thy God, to observe to do all his commandments and his statutes which I command thee this day; that all these curses shall come upon thee, and overtake thee: [16] Cursed shalt thou be in the city, and cursed shalt thou be in the field. [17] Cursed shall be thy basket and thy store. [18] Cursed shall be the fruit of thy body, and the fruit of thy land, the increase of thy kine, and the flocks of thy sheep. [19] Cursed shalt thou be when thou comest in, and cursed shalt thou be when thou goest out. [20] The LORD shall send upon thee cursing, vexation, and rebuke, in all that thou settest thine hand unto for to do, until thou be destroyed, and until thou perish quickly; because of the wickedness of thy doings, whereby thou hast forsaken me. [21] The LORD shall make the pestilence cleave unto thee, until he have consumed thee from off the land, whither thou goest to possess it. [22] The LORD shall smite thee with a consumption, and with a fever, and with an inflammation, and with an extreme burning, and with the sword, and with blasting, and with mildew; and they shall pursue thee until thou perish. [23] And thy heaven that is over thy head shall be brass, and the earth that is under thee shall be iron. [24] The LORD shall make the rain of thy land powder and dust: from heaven shall it

come down upon thee, until thou be destroyed.
(Deut. 28:15–24)

Just as God promised blessings for obedience, He promised
curses for disobedience. The next few verses read, "The LORD shall
cause thee to be smitten before thine enemies: thou shalt go out one
way against them, and flee seven ways before them: and shalt be
removed into all the kingdoms of the earth. ²⁶ And thy carcase shall
be meat unto all fowls of the air, and unto the beasts of the earth, and
no man shall fray them away" (Deut. 28:25–26).

Many Hebrew Israelites will claim this is talking about black
people and slavery, but this has already been fulfilled in the Bible!
Jeremiah says, "And I will make void the counsel of Judah and
Jerusalem in this place; and I will cause them to fall by the sword
before their enemies, and by the hands of them that seek their lives:
and their carcases will I give to be meat for the fowls of the heaven,
and for the beasts of the earth" (Jer. 19:7).

> Thou shalt betroth a wife, and another man
> shall lie with her: thou shalt build an house, and
> thou shalt not dwell therein: thou shalt plant a
> vineyard, and shalt not gather the grapes thereof.
> ³¹ Thine ox shall be slain before thine eyes, and
> thou shalt not eat thereof: thine ass shall be vio-
> lently taken away from before thy face, and shall
> not be restored to thee: thy sheep shall be given
> unto thine enemies, and thou shalt have none to
> rescue them. ³² Thy sons and thy daughters shall
> be given unto another people, and thine eyes
> shall look, and fail with longing for them all the
> day long; and there shall be no might in thine
> hand. (Deut. 28:30–32)

Verse 30 explains how the children of Israel would have their
belongings and family members taken from them. The Hebrew
Israelites often argue this is talking about what happened to black

people in the transatlantic slave trade. But this is directly fulfilled in the prophets, "Therefore will I give their wives unto others, and their fields to them that shall inherit them: for every one from the least even unto the greatest is given to covetousness, from the prophet even unto the priest every one dealeth falsely" (Jer. 8:10). Amos says, "Forasmuch therefore as your treading is upon the poor, and ye take from him burdens of wheat: ye have built houses of hewn stone, but ye shall not dwell in them; ye have planted pleasant vineyards, but ye shall not drink wine of them" (Amos 5:11).

Zephaniah says, "Therefore their goods shall become a booty, and their houses a desolation: they shall also build houses, but not inhabit them; and they shall plant vineyards, but not drink the wine thereof" (Zeph. 1:13). Haggai says, "Ye have sown much, and bring in little; ye eat, but ye have not enough; ye drink, but ye are not filled with drink; ye clothe you, but there is none warm; and he that earneth wages earneth wages to put it into a bag with holes" (Hag. 1:6). These were punishments for disobedience that God promised back in Deuteronomy. In sum, they would not reap the fruit of their labor.

This was fulfilled in the Bible, not hundreds of years later in the transatlantic slave trade! Verse 32 speaks of sons and daughters being taken. Second Chronicles says, "For, lo, our fathers have fallen by the sword, and our sons and our daughters and our wives are in captivity for this" (2 Chr. 29:9). Once again, this passage in Deuteronomy is fulfilled in the Bible.

"The LORD shall bring thee, and thy king which thou shalt set over thee, unto a nation which neither thou nor thy fathers have known; and there shalt thou serve other gods, wood and stone" (Deut. 28:36).

Deuteronomy says the Israelites and the king they put over themselves would go into a foreign nation and serve foreign gods. Hebrew Israelites argue this is speaking of black people being stolen out of their homelands and forced into Christianity (apparently the wood represents the cross). But is this what the passage is speaking of? First, the king that is being spoken of is the king that was leading Israel when they went into captivity. Originally, Israel had no king because they were led directly by God, but they eventually asked for a king and God granted their request (1 Sam. 8).

Serving foreign gods does not refer to Christianity but rather pagan religions such as that of the Babylonians. Daniel says, "They [the Babylonians] drank wine, and praised the gods of gold, and of silver, of brass, of iron, of wood, and of stone" (Dan. 5:4). This is exactly what was prophesied in Deuteronomy 28:36. So this verse in Deuteronomy cannot be referring to Christianity and the wooden crosses or anything like it. It is clearly speaking of the foreign gods which were present in Israel's captivity. Daniel also says, "Therefore at that time, when all the people heard the sound of the cornet, flute, harp, sackbut, psaltery, and all kinds of musick, all the people, the nations, and the languages, fell down and worshipped the golden image that Nebuchadnezzar the king had set up" (Dan. 3:7).

The passage later says, "There are certain Jews whom thou [King Nebuchadnezzar] hast set over the affairs of the province of Babylon, Shadrach, Meshack, and Abed-nego; these men, O king, have not regarded thee: they serve not thy gods, nor worship the golden image which thou hast set up" (Dan. 3:12). Right after the Israelites went into Babylonian captivity, they were being forced to worship these foreign gods. That is what the passage in Deuteronomy is talking about. It has nothing to do with black people being forced into Christianity.

"The LORD shall bring a nation against thee from far, from the end of the earth, as swift as the eagle flieth; a nation whose tongue thou shalt not understand" (Deut. 28:49).

Many Hebrew Israelites claim this "nation" that would destroy Israel is actually America, especially since it displays it as an eagle and that's the symbol of America. Hosea identifies this eagle as Assyria, "Ephraim also is like a silly dove without heart: they call to Egypt, they go to Assyria" (Hos. 7:11). "Set the trumpet to thy mouth. He [Assyria] shall come as an **eagle** against the house of the LORD, because they have transgressed my covenant, and trespassed against my law" (Hos. 8:1). The next chapter of Hosea says, "They [Israel] shall not dwell in the LORD's land; but Ephraim shall return to Egypt, and they shall eat unclean things in Assyria" (Hos. 9:3). Isaiah says, "Of a truth, LORD, the kings of Assyria have laid waste all the nations, and their countries" (Isa. 37:18).

So-called Hebrew Israelites also argue that black people could not understand the language of America as they were brought over here. While that may be true, it does not prove that the people spoken of are black slaves from the transatlantic slave trade. That is a horrible and fantastical interpretation. The nation being described that would be judged is Israel/Judah. The nations that would come and judge Israel/Judah are Assyria/Babylon. Assyria and Babylon being the nations with a different tongue is explained all throughout the Bible. Isaiah says, "For with stammering lips and another tongue will he speak to this people" (Isa. 28:11).

A few chapters later, Isaiah says, "Thou shalt not see a fierce people, a people of a deeper speech than thou canst perceive; of a stammering tongue, that thou canst not understand" (Isa. 33:19). Jeremiah says, "Lo, I will bring a nation upon you from far, O house of Israel, saith the LORD: it is a mighty nation, it is an ancient nation, a nation whose language thou knowest not, neither understandest what they say" (Jer. 5:15).

"A nation of fierce countenance, which shall not regard the person of the old, nor shew favour to the young" (Deut. 28:50).

This passage is speaking of Babylon as is evident in many places. Isaiah says, "Come down, and sit in the dust, O virgin daughter of Babylon, sit on the ground: there is no throne, O daughter of the Chaldeans: for thou shalt no more be called tender and delicate... I was wroth with my people, I have polluted mine inheritance, and given them into thine hand: thou didst shew them no mercy; upon the ancient hast thou very heavily laid thy yoke" (Isa. 47:1, 6). The passage in Deuteronomy explained how this nation does not "regard the person of the old" and Isaiah 47:6 explains that Babylon laid a yoke on the "ancient," which refers to older people.

Second Chronicles says, "Therefore [God] brought upon them the king of the Chaldeans, who slew their young men with the sword in the house of their sanctuary, and had no compassion upon young man or maiden, old man, or him that stooped for age: he gave them all into his hand" (2 Chr. 36:17). The verse in Deuteronomy explained that this nation would not have compassion on the young or the old and this verse in 2 Chronicles describes the Chaldeans/ Babylonians as doing just that. This is a direct fulfillment of the verse in Deuteronomy twenty-eight.

"And thou shalt eat the fruit of thine own body, the flesh of thy sons and of thy daughters, which the LORD thy God hath given thee, in the siege, and in the straitness, wherewith thine enemies shall distress thee" (Deut. 28:53).

Part of the judgment that came upon God's people was famine and starvation leading to cannibalism. Jeremiah says, "And I will cause them to eat the flesh of their sons and the flesh of their daughters, and they shall eat every one the flesh of his friend in the siege and straitness, wherewith their enemies, and they that seek their lives, shall straiten them" (Jer. 19:9).

Lamentations says, "The hands of the pitiful women have sodden their own children: they were their meat in the destruction of the daughter of my people" (Lam. 4:10). Ezekiel says, "Therefore the fathers shall eat the sons in the midst of thee, and the sons shall eat their fathers; and I will execute judgments in thee, and the whole remnant of thee will I scatter into all the winds" (Ezek. 5:10).

Soon after Ezekiel says, "A third part of thee shall die with the pestilence, and with famine shall they be consumed in the midst of thee: and a third part shall fall by the sword round about thee; and I will scatter a third part into all the winds, and I will draw out a sword after them" (Ezek. 5:12). Second Kings describes all of this in more detail:

> And it came to pass after this, that Benhadad king of Syria gathered all his host, and went up, and besieged Samaria. [25] And there **was a great famine in Samaria**: and, behold, they besieged it, until an ass's head was sold for fourscore pieces of silver, and the fourth part of a cab of dove's dung for five pieces of silver. [26] And as the king of Israel was passing by upon the wall, there cried a woman unto him, saying, Help, my lord, O king.

[27] And he said, If the LORD do not help thee, whence shall I help thee? out of the barnfloor, or out of the winepress? [28] And the king said unto her, What aileth thee? And she answered, This woman said unto me, **Give thy son, that we may eat him to day, and we will eat my son to morrow.** [29] **So we boiled my son, and did eat him**: and I said unto her on the next day, Give thy son, that we may eat him: and she hath hid her son. [30] And it came to pass, when the king heard the words of the woman, that he rent his clothes; and he passed by upon the wall, and the people looked, and, behold, he had sackcloth within upon his flesh. (2 Kings 6:24–30)

Deuteronomy 28:53 is obviously speaking of something that happened in the Bible. This verse cannot be applied to black people or the transatlantic slave trade in any way. Sure, black slaves were obviously not fed well, but they did not eat their own children.

And ye shall be left few in number, whereas ye were as the stars of heaven for multitude; because thou wouldest not obey the voice of the LORD thy God. [63] And it shall come to pass, that as the LORD rejoiced over you to do you good, and to multiply you; so the LORD will rejoice over you to destroy you, and to bring you to nought; and ye shall be plucked from off the land whither thou goest to possess it. [64] And the LORD shall scatter thee among all people, from the one end of the earth even unto the other; and there thou shalt serve other gods, which neither thou nor thy fathers have known, even wood and stone. (Deut. 28:62–64)

Hebrew Israelites often argue that this description fits black people because they are few compared to other people groups in the world and are scattered among all nations. This may be true, but that does not prove this passage is talking about them. Almost any minority group could claim this passage is speaking about them by that logic. That is a huge stretch. The children of Israel were scattered because of their idolatry and unfaithfulness to God. Ezekiel explains how they would be scattered saying, "A third part of thee shall die with the pestilence, and with famine shall they be consumed in the midst of thee: and a third part shall fall by the sword round about thee; and **I will scatter a third part into all the winds**, and I will draw out a sword after them" (Ezra 5:10).

Nehemiah says, "Remember, I beseech thee, the word that thou commandest thy servant Moses, saying, **If ye transgress, I will scatter you abroad among the nations**" (Neh. 1:8). This scattering occurred with the captivity of Israel and Judah by Assyria and Babylon, not with the transatlantic slave trade.

> And among these nations shalt thou find no ease, neither shall the sole of thy foot have rest: but the LORD shall give thee there a trembling heart, and failing of eyes, and sorrow of mind: [66] And thy life shall hang in doubt before thee; and thou shalt fear day and night, and shalt have none assurance of thy life: [67] In the morning thou shalt say, Would God it were even! and at even thou shalt say, Would God it were morning! for the fear of thine heart wherewith thou shalt fear, and for the sight of thine eyes which thou shalt see. (Deut. 28:65–67)

The Hebrew Israelites argue these verses describe the life of minorities perfectly. They say minorities are constantly persecuted, have no rest, and are in fear for their lives constantly! While it may be true that black people have been persecuted, this passage is clearly speaking of the Israelites going into captivity, which took place in the eighth/sixth centuries BC. The Jews were highly oppressed in captivity and have been throughout history. This passage is in no way, shape, or form speaking of black people/minorities in America.

"And the LORD shall bring thee into Egypt again with ships, by the way whereof I spake unto thee, Thou shalt see it no more again: and there ye shall be sold unto your enemies for bondmen and bond-women, and no man shall buy you" (Deut. 28:68).

This is the last verse of the chapter and the verse that many Hebrew Israelites claim definitively proves this chapter is speaking of black people and the transatlantic slave trade. Hebrew Israelites claim "Egypt" is symbolic for America because Egypt is used symbolically throughout the Bible as a representation of places of bondage. And since black people have been oppressed in America, Egypt must be a representation of America (according to them).

It also says the Israelites would be sent in ships! This must be speaking of the transatlantic slave trade, right? Wrong. Egypt could very well be symbolic for any place the Israelites were kept in bondage and oppressed rather than literal Egypt, but this still does not prove this is speaking of America. That is a stretch. And this verse also says they will be sent in "ships." Now the Hebrew Israelites will claim this means literal ships! Yet they claim "Egypt" is symbolic. Do you see the inconsistency of their interpretation? If Egypt is symbolic, these "ships" could very well be symbolic as well. They also argue that this must be speaking of the transatlantic slave trade because it says the Israelites will be sold to their enemies and we all know that is what happened in the slave trade.

There is one major problem with their interpretation. They neglect the last part of the verse, which says, "and no man shall buy you." Now how can one be sold if nobody bought them? That does not quite make sense. The point of emphasis is the term "ye shall be sold." To us, this sounds like one party sold the Israelites to another party. But from the context, that is not what this is saying. In biblical times, slavery was often the result of debt/poverty. Nehemiah makes this point clear:

> There were also that said, We have borrowed
> money for the king's tribute, and that upon our
> lands and vineyards. ⁵ Yet now our flesh is as the
> flesh of our brethren, our children as their chil-

dren: and, lo, we bring into bondage our sons and our daughters to be servants, and some of our daughters are brought unto bondage already: neither is it in our power to redeem them; for other men have our lands and vineyards. (Neh. 5:4–5)

This gives more insight as to what the last verse of Deuteronomy 28 is actually saying. Regarding this verse, the abolitionist Theodore Dwight Weld said,

> And there ye shall be sold unto your ene-mies for bond-men and bond-women and no man shall buy you." How could they "*be sold*" without *being bought*? Our translation makes it nonsense. The word *Makar* rendered "be sold" is used here in the Hithpael conjugation, which is generally reflexive in its force, and, like the mid-dle voice in Greek, represents what an individ-ual does for himself, and should manifestly have been rendered, "ye shall *offer yourselves* for sale, and there shall be no purchaser." For a clue to Scripture usage on this point, see 1 Kings xxi. 20, 25—"Thou hast *sold thyself* to work evil.[389]

So it is evident that the term "be sold" should actually be "offer yourselves" or something of the sort. The English makes this confus-ing, but not the original language. So this verse and this whole chap-ter of Deuteronomy 28 is not talking about black people and the transatlantic slave trade. It is talking about the Israelites going into Assyrian/Babylonian captivity and persecutions which took place in the eighth/sixth centuries BC. In sum, the prophecy of Deuteronomy twenty-eight has already been fulfilled in the Bible itself. It was not fulfilled hundreds of years later in the transatlantic slave trade.

---

[389] Weld, Theodore Dwight. *The Bible Against Slavery*, 1838, chapter 1.

CONCLUSION

Being a person of color, the "Hebrew Israelites" stood out to me the most. Many of my fellow people of color have joined this group. My heart goes out to them. I pray for their salvation! This belief leads to a wrong understanding of the world and who Jesus is. John said, "Whosoever hateth his brother is a murderer: and ye know that no murderer hath eternal life abiding in him" (1 John 3:15)! It is not godly to have hatred for people. All people are equal in the eyes of God and we can all be saved in the same way regardless of race, ethnicity, or nationality.

HEBREW ISRAELITES REFUTED

1. Hebrew Israelites reject that the Holy Spirit is a distinct person apart of the godhead, but the Bible says He is (John 14:26, 16:13; Acts 5:1–4).
2. (Most) Hebrew Israelites teach that only descendants of Israel can be saved, but the Bible says Jews and Gentiles can be saved (Acts 28:28; Gal. 3:28).
3. (Most) Hebrew Israelites teach that you must keep the law of Moses to be saved, but the Bible says nobody can be justified by the works of the law (Gal. 2:16).
4. Deuteronomy 28 speaks of events that were fulfilled in the Bible (Babylonian/Assyrian captivity), not the transatlantic slave trade which happened centuries later.

CHAPTER 12

JUST A MAN FROM SIXTH STREET

BIBLE COLLEGE, HERE I COME

In my third semester of college around October or November of 2019, I began looking at Bible Colleges online. I knew that I loved reading the Bible and talking about God. It was also around this time that I healed from my heartaches and finally started to become secure in who I was. By the time I reached my fourth and final semester of community college, I had become completely secure in who I was as a child of God. I no longer placed my worth in sports, fitness, women, or anything else. My worth and security was in Christ.

That semester, I took a public speaking class. I gave two speeches on Christianity, and I loved it. I felt so at home telling others about Jesus. I felt like it was what God called me to do. He has called me to spread the gospel in some way, shape, or form. That semester I also gave a message for a Christian group on campus. I loved that as well. That semester I was just planning on transferring to a four-year school to continue my undergraduate degree in Health and Sports Science. I figured I would just do ministry later in life.

But I realized one major thing: I did not want to study anything else besides the Bible and subjects related to it. I did not want to spend hours in a science textbook when I could spend hours studying the living words of Almighty God and His Church. Not to mention, after hearing the messages/speeches I gave this semester, many people told me I should work in ministry. That truly encouraged me. One major reason that I was going to put off Bible College (besides the money) was because I did not know if I could do it. Spreading the gospel is hard. You get hate. You get attacked, not only from other people, but from demons. Spiritual warfare takes place (Eph. 6:12). But I truly believe God has called me to some type of ministry whether it be serving in Church leadership or something much simpler like writing books like this.

Because of that, I began looking into Bible colleges once again. During March of 2020, the whole world basically shut down. I ended up coming across a Bible college that was affordable. I called them, discussed it, and decided to enroll. I graduated that semester from my community college, May of 2020, with my associate's degree (in health and sports science). God allowed me to find a second job to save up enough money to pay off my tuition for Bible college. I officially started Bible college in June of 2020.

THE TRUTH SHALL SET YOU FREE

There you have it. That is my journey of faith. These are the reasons for the hope that is in me (1 Pet. 3:15). I chose the degree "Biblical Apologetics" for Bible college. Apologetics is the defense of the faith. This is very important to me. I did not just choose this degree to argue with people (although that is much of what it is). Defending the faith is extremely important to me because it is my whole life. It is where my security is. It is where my hope is. It is where my everything is. Apologetics is also important to me because I never want to be that kid in the sixth grade who could not explain his faith in class. Or that same kid who could not give a reason as to why evil happens to the people we love. I never want to be that kid again. I want to have the answers to the questions people have that nobody could answer for me. I want to be able to lead people out of confusion and into clarity. I want to lead people out of the dark and into the light. Many times, through these years I asked God "why?"

Many times, I felt angry at God. I felt like He was not protecting me from these afflictions. Looking back, I believe God put me through these events to shape my character. James says, "My brethren, count it all joy when ye fall into divers temptations; ³ Knowing this, that the trying of your faith worketh patience. ⁴ But let patience have her perfect work, that ye may be perfect and entire, wanting nothing" (James 1:2–4).

And in another place, "And not only so, but we glory in tribulations also: knowing that tribulation worketh patience; ⁴ And patience, experience; and experience, hope" (Rom. 5:3–4).

God used these events to shape me as a man and a follower of His. Just like Joseph said to his brothers who sold him into slavery, "But as for you, ye thought evil against me; but God meant it unto good, to bring to pass, as it is this day, to save much people alive" (Gen. 50:20). God used these events for my own good. And I also know that "all things work together for good to them that love God, to them who are called according to his purpose" (Rom. 8:28).

God used everything that happened to me to shape me for my own good. I truly believe I had a lot of potential as an athlete. And if I would have never battled all those injuries, I believe I would've gone on to play somewhere in college. But if I had gone on to play sports in college, I probably would not have sought God and I probably wouldn't have gone to Bible College. I believe God kept me from being successful in sports to make me successful in His ministry. I believe He kept me from being successful in sports so He could use me as a laborer for Him. The Scripture says, "Then saith [Jesus] unto his disciples, The harvest truly is plenteous, but the labourers are few; ³⁸ Pray ye therefore the Lord of the harvest, that he will send forth labourers into his harvest. (Matt. 9:37–38).

God needs laborers. He needs people to work for Him and spread His message. God had to close one door to open another. God worked in my life and He worked in my heart until finally I said, "Here am I; Send me" (Isa. 6:8). So I will become a fool for Christ (1 Cor. 4:9–13). I could live alone and still be content with the Lord

Jesus Christ. I could be single my whole life and still be content with the Lord Jesus Christ. As the Apostle Paul said to the Philippians,

> But I rejoiced in the Lord greatly, that now at the last your care of me hath flourished again; wherein ye were also careful, but ye lacked opportunity. [11] Not that I speak in respect of want: for I have learned, in whatsoever state I am, therewith to be content. [12] I know both how to be abased, and I know how to abound: every where and in all things I am instructed both to be full and to be hungry, both to abound and to suffer need. [13] I can do all things through Christ which strengtheneth me. (Phil. 4:10–13)

I can do all things through Christ. I can be content in every circumstance if I have Him. To me, apologetics means defending God. That is why I take it so seriously. If somebody attacks my God, they attack me. I will stand for God if it kills me. I do not care about people's opinion of me. When I was insecure only a year or so ago, I cared deeply about what others thought of me. But once I put my value and security into the Lord Jesus Christ, I stopped caring about opinions of me. I do not seek to please men. If I sought to please men, I would not be a bondservant of Christ (Gal. 1:10). The only things I seek to do now are love God, love my neighbor, and defend "the faith which was once delivered unto the saints" (Jude 3).

And now as I look back at that kid from sixth street, I see how pitiful he was. I see how lost he was. I see how empty he was. I was starving for so long. I was like Lazarus begging for crumbs (Luke 16:20–21). I just needed something to fulfill me; something to fill my hunger. But hallelujah! Once I came into the comfort of the Lord's bosom, I was filled with the Bread of Life! And he who eats this bread will never hunger again (John 6:35)! Sure, I still go through struggles. I still have bad days. I still go through trials and tribulations. But these present sufferings are nothing compared to the glory we will have (Rom. 8:18). Through the sufferings I always have hope. As Paul said,

> Therefore being justified by faith, we have peace with God through our Lord Jesus Christ: [2] By whom also we have access by faith into this grace wherein we stand, and rejoice in hope of the glory of God. [3] And not only so, but we glory in tribulations also: knowing that tribulation worketh patience; [4] And patience, experience; and experience, hope: [5] And hope maketh not ashamed; because the love of God is shed abroad in our hearts by the Holy Ghost which is given unto us. (Rom. 5:1–5)

I still fight temptations. I still mess up. I still go through storms. But being a Christian does not mean you will not go through storms. Being a Christian means you will never be alone in the storms. And as God answered my questions regarding all these other religions/worldviews, He answered that vital question I asked at the beginning of my journey: **"What is truth?"** After much study, prayer, trials, tribulations, and even some doubting, the answer to that question was only a few chapters prior: "Thomas saith unto him, Lord, we know not whither thou goest; and how can we know the way? [6] Jesus saith unto him, **I am the way, the truth, and the life**: no man cometh unto the Father, but by me" (John 14:5–6).

What is truth? **Jesus is the truth!** But not just any old, generic Jesus like other groups believe in. The **truth** is the Jesus of the Bible. The Son of God and God the Son. The One who was with God and was God at the same time (John 1:1). Jesus—the second person of the Trinity. He is the truth forever and always. And what does that truth do? "And ye shall know the **truth**, and the **truth** *shall make you free*" (John 8:32). Jesus is the **Truth**, and He has set me free! And He can set us all free! I have sought truth my whole life and have been called crazy for it. Consider the book of Acts. "And as [Paul] thus spake for himself, Festus said with a loud voice, Paul, thou art beside thyself; much learning doth make thee mad. ²⁵ But he said, I am not mad, most noble Festus; but speak forth the words of truth and soberness" (Acts 26:24–25).

The Apostle Paul was seen as crazy for his proclamation of the truth. Why is this? Because truth sounds crazy in a world full of lies. Satan is the father of lies (John 8:44), and this is his world (2 Cor. 4:4). Truth is called hate in society. Why? Because those who practice evil hate the light—a.k.a. the truth (John 3:20). Jesus said, "The world cannot hate you; but me it hateth, because I testify of it, that the works thereof are evil" (John 7:7).

Jesus was hated. Why was He hated? For speaking the truth. The saying goes, "Truth sounds like hate to those who hate the truth." Many people in this world have "changed the truth of God into a lie, and worshipped and served the creature more than the Creator, who is blessed for ever. Amen" (Rom. 1:25). But those who know God know love (1 John 4:8), which means they speak the truth because love rejoices in the truth (1 Cor. 13:6).

True love is not tolerating lies and wrongdoing. Jesus said, "As many as I love, I rebuke and chasten: be zealous therefore, and repent" (Rev. 3:19). Jesus corrects those whom He loves because that is true love. Parents correct their children because they love them, not because they hate them. Love and truth go hand in hand. You cannot have one without the other. We must all become lovers of the truth.

> And then shall that Wicked be revealed, whom the Lord shall consume with the spirit of his mouth, and shall destroy with the brightness of his coming: ⁹ Even him, whose coming is after the working of Satan with all power and signs and lying wonders, ¹⁰ And with all deceivableness of unrighteousness in **them that perish; because they received not the love of the truth, that they might be saved**. ¹¹ And for this cause God shall send them strong delusion, that they should believe a lie: ¹² **That they all might be damned**

who believed not the truth, but had pleasure in unrighteousness. (2 Thess. 2:8–12)

Those who do not love the truth will be deceived and will ultimately be damned. So we must love Jesus who is Himself the truth, and we must love His Church, which is "the pillar and ground of the truth" (1 Tim. 3:15). Jesus did not start the Baptist church and the Methodist church and the Lutheran church and the "nondenominational" church, etc. He started *one* Holy, Catholic, and Apostolic Church like He prayed for (John 17:20–23) because He "is not the author of confusion, but of peace" (1 Cor. 14:33). Like Ignatius (the bishop of Antioch) said around AD 110, shortly after the Apostle John's death, "Wherever Jesus Christ is, there is the Catholic Church."[390]

Jesus is truth and Satan is a liar. Satan is a deceiver (Rev. 12:9), and the confusion in the world comes from him. Two plus two equals four. It cannot equal five, six, seven, or anything else besides four. Two plus two equals the Catholic Church. It doesn't equal the Methodist church or the Lutheran church or Islam or Mormonism or atheism, etc. Two plus two equals the Catholic Church founded by the truth Himself—Jesus Christ. So since Jesus is the Truth and we must love the Truth to be saved, it is fitting to say, "**If any man love not the [Truth], let him be Anathema Maran-atha**" (1 Cor. 16:22).

---

[390] Ignatius. *The Ante-Nicene Fathers: Epistle to the Smyrneans.* Chapter VIII. Edited by Alexander Roberts, James Donaldson, and Arthur Cleveland Coxe. I. Vol. I. X vols. New York, NY: Cosimo Classics, 2007, 90.

BIBLIOGRAPHY

"About Us." The Israel of God, March 2, 2020. https://theisraelof-god.com/about-us/.

Akin, Jimmy. *The Fathers Know Best: Your Essential Guide to the Teachings of the Early Church.* El Cajon, CA: Catholic Answers Inc., 2010.

Athenagoras. *The Ante-Nicene Fathers: A Plea for the Christians.* Edited by Alexander Roberts, James Donaldson, and Arthur Cleveland Coxe. II. Vol. II. X vols. New York, NY: Cosimo Classics, 2007.

Beus, Stephen G. *The Vaudois: Last Faith Standing.* Pittsburgh, PA: Harmony Street Publishers, 2018.

Bickel, Bruce, and Stan Jantz. *World Religions & Cults 101.* Eugene, OR: Harvest House Publishers, 2002.

Book of Mormon; Doctrine and Covenants; Pearl of Great Price. Salt Lake City, UT: The Church of Jesus Christ of Latter-day Saints, 1981.

Carden, Paul, ed. *World Religions Made Easy.* Peabody, MA: Rose Publishing, 2018.

Catechism of the Catholic Church. Citta del Vaticano: Libreria Editrice Vaticana, 1994.

Chute, Anthony L., Nathan A. Finn, and Michael A. G. Haykin. *The Baptist Story: From English Sect to Global Movement.* Nashville, TN: B&H Publishing Group, 2015.

Clement of Alexandria. *The Ante-Nicene Fathers: The Instructor.* Edited by Alexander Roberts, James Donaldson, and Arthur Cleveland Coxe. I. Vol. I. X vols. New York, NY: Cosimo Classics, 2007.

Clement of Rome. *The Ante-Nicene Fathers: The First Epistle of Clement.* Edited by Alexander Roberts, James Donaldson, and Arthur Cleveland Coxe. I. Vol. I. X vols. New York, NY: Cosimo Classics, 2007.

Cyprian. *The Ante-Nicene Fathers: Letter LVIII.* Edited by Alexander Roberts, James Donaldson, and Arthur Cleveland Coxe. V. Vol. V. X vols. New York, NY: Cosimo Classics, 2007.

Cyprian. *The Ante-Nicene Fathers: Letter LXXI.* Edited by Alexander Roberts, James Donaldson, and Arthur Cleveland Coxe. V. Vol. V. X vols. New York, NY: Cosimo Classics, 2007.

Cyprian. *The Ante-Nicene Fathers: Letter LXXII.* Edited by Alexander Roberts, James Donaldson, and Arthur Cleveland Coxe. V. Vol. V. X vols. New York, NY: Cosimo Classics, 2007.

Cyprian. *The Ante-Nicene Fathers: Letter LXXV.* Edited by Alexander Roberts, James Donaldson, and Arthur Cleveland Coxe. V. Vol. V. X vols. New York, NY: Cosimo Classics, 2007.

Cyprian. *The Ante-Nicene Fathers: On the Lord's Prayer.* Edited by Alexander Roberts, James Donaldson, and Arthur Cleveland Coxe. V. Vol. V. X vols. New York, NY: Cosimo Classics, 2007.

Cyprian. *The Ante-Nicene Fathers: On the Unity of the Church.* Edited by Alexander Roberts, James Donaldson, and Arthur Cleveland Coxe. V. Vol. V. X vols. New York, NY: Cosimo Classics, 2007.

Didache: The Teaching of the Apostles. Coppell, TX, 2020.

Dalton JR., Ronald. *Hebrews to Negroes: Wake Up Black America!* G Publishing, 2014.

Ehrman, Bart D. *Did Jesus Exist?: The Historical Argument for Jesus of Nazareth.* New York City, New York: HarperOne, an imprint of Harper Collins Publishers, 2013.

Estep, William R. *The Anabaptist Story: An Introduction to Sixteenth-Century Anabaptism.* Grand Rapids, MI: Wm. B. Eerdmans Publishing Co., 1996.

Eusebius. *The Church History.* Translated by Paul L. Maier. Grand Rapids, MI: Kregel Publications, 2007.

Ferguson, Everett. *Church History: From Christ to the Pre-Reformation.* 1. Vol. 1. Grand Rapids, MI: Zondervan Academic, 2013.

Habermas, Gary R., and Mike Licona. *The Case for the Resurrection of Jesus.* Kregel Publications, 2004.

Ham, Ken, and A. Charles Ware. *Darwin's Plantation: Evolution's Racist Roots.* Green Forest, AR: Master Books, 2007.

Ham, Ken. *The New Answers Book 1: Over 25 Questions on Creation/ Evolution and the Bible.* Edited by Ken Ham. Green Forest, AR: Answers in Genesis, 2006.

Hinckley, Gordon B. The Church of Jesus Christ of Latter-Day Saints: The Father, Son, and Holy Ghost. Accessed February 24, 2021. https://www.churchofjesuschrist.org/study/ensign/1986/11/the-father-son-and-holy-ghost?lang=eng.

Hippolytus. *The Ante-Nicene Fathers: Against Plato, On the Cause of the Universe.* Edited by Alexander Roberts, James Donaldson, and Arthur Cleveland Coxe. V. Vol. V. X vols. New York, NY: Cosimo Classics, 2007.

Hippolytus. *The Ante-Nicene Fathers: Discourse on the Holy Theophany.* Edited by Alexander Roberts, James Donaldson, and Arthur Cleveland Coxe. V. Vol. V. X vols. New York, NY: Cosimo Classics, 2007.

Hippolytus. *The Ante-Nicene Fathers: Fragment from the Commentary on Proverbs.* Edited by Alexander Roberts, James Donaldson, and Arthur Cleveland Coxe. V. Vol. V. X vols. New York, NY: Cosimo Classics, 2007.

Hippolytus. *On the Apostolic Tradition.* Translated by Alistair C. Stewart. 2nd ed. Yonkers, NY: St Vladimir's Seminary Press, 2015.

Hodge, Bodie. *Glass House: Shattering the Myth of Evolution.* Edited by Ken Ham and Bodie Hodge. Green Forest, AR: Answers in Genesis, 2018.

Hunter, Braxton. *CORE FACTS.* Bloomington, IN: AuthorHouse, 2014.

Ignatius. *The Ante-Nicene Fathers: Epistle to the Ephesians.* Edited by Alexander Roberts, James Donaldson, and Arthur Cleveland Coxe. I. Vol. I. X vols. New York, NY: Cosimo Classics, 2007.

Ignatius. *The Ante-Nicene Fathers: Epistle to the Magnesians.* Edited by Alexander Roberts, James Donaldson, and Arthur Cleveland Coxe. I. Vol. I. X vols. New York, NY: Cosimo Classics, 2007.

Ignatius. *The Ante-Nicene Fathers: Epistle to the Smyrneans.* Edited by Alexander Roberts, James Donaldson, and Arthur Cleveland Coxe. I. Vol. I. X vols. New York, NY: Cosimo Classics, 2007.

Ignatius. *The Ante-Nicene Fathers: Epistle to the Trallians.* Edited by Alexander Roberts, James Donaldson, and Arthur Cleveland Coxe. I. Vol. I. X vols. New York, NY: Cosimo Classics, 2007.

Irenaeus. *The Ante-Nicene Fathers: Against Heresies.* Edited by Alexander Roberts, James Donaldson, and Arthur Cleveland Coxe. I. Vol. I. X vols. New York, NY: Cosimo Classics, 2007.

Irenaeus. *The Ante-Nicene Fathers: Fragments of Irenaeus.* Edited by Alexander Roberts, James Donaldson, and Arthur Cleveland Coxe. I. Vol. I. X vols. New York, NY: Cosimo Classics, 2007.

Jones, Marvin. *Recovering Historical Christology for Today's Church.* Eugene, OR: Wipf and Stock Publishers, 2019.

Josephus, Flavius. *The Complete Works.* Translated by Whiston William. Nashville, TN: Thomas Nelson Inc, 1998.

Luther, Martin. *The Ninety-Five Theses.* Eastford, CT: Martino Fine Books, 2018.

Malone, Vocab. *Barack Obama VS The Black Hebrew Israelites: Introduction to the History & Beliefs of 1West Hebrew Israelism.* Phoenix, AZ: Thureos Publishing, 2017.

Jeremias, Joachim. *Infant Baptism in the First Four Centuries.* Eugene, OR: Wipf and Stock Publishers, 1960.

Justin Martyr. *The Ante-Nicene Fathers: Dialogue with Trypho.* Edited by Alexander Roberts, James Donaldson, and Arthur Cleveland Coxe. I. Vol. I. X vols. New York, NY: Cosimo Classics, 2007.

Justin Martyr. *The Ante-Nicene Fathers: The First Apology.* Edited by Alexander Roberts, James Donaldson, and Arthur Cleveland Coxe. I. Vol. I. X vols. New York, NY: Cosimo Classics, 2007.

McDurmon, Joel. *Manifested in the Flesh.* Powder Springs, GA: American Vision Inc, 2007.

Morris, Henry M. *Many Infallible Proofs: Evidences for the Christian Faith.* El Cajon, CA: Master Books, 1974.

Nash, Ronald H. *The Gospel and the Greeks*. Phillipsburg, NJ: P&R Publishing Company, 2003.

New World Translation of the Holy Scriptures. Wallkill, NY: Watch Tower Bible and Tract Society of New York, Inc, 2013.

'Omar, Amatul Rahman, and 'Abdul Mannan 'Omar, trans. *The Holy Qur'ān: Arabic Text—English Translation*. Hockessin, DE: Noor Foundation International Inc., 2010.

Origen. *The Ante-Nicene Fathers: De Principiis*. Edited by Alexander Roberts, James Donaldson, and Arthur Cleveland Coxe. IV. Vol. IV. X vols. New York, NY: Cosimo Classics, 2007.

Pappas, C. H. *In Defense of the Authenticity of 1 John 5:7 Second Edition*. Bloomington, IN: WestBow Press, 2016.

Patterson, Roger. *Glass House: Shattering the Myth of Evolution*. Edited by Ken Ham and Bodie Hodge. Green Forest, AR: Answers in Genesis, 2018.

Polycarp. *The Ante-Nicene Fathers: Martyrdom of Polycarp*. Edited by Alexander Roberts, James Donaldson, and Arthur Cleveland Coxe. I. Vol. I. X vols. New York, NY: Cosimo Classics, 2007.

Purdom, Georgia. *The New Answers Book 1: Over 25 Questions on Creation/Evolution and the Bible*. Edited by Ken Ham. Green Forest, AR: Answers in Genesis, 2006.

Rhodes, Ron. *Answering the Objections of Atheists, Agnostics, & Skeptics*. Eugene, OR: Harvest House Publishers, 2006.

Riddle, Mike. *The New Answers Book 1: Over 25 Questions on Creation/Evolution and the Bible*. Edited by Ken Ham. Green Forest, AR: Answers in Genesis, 2006.

Rivera, Jennifer Hall. *Glass House: Shattering the Myth of Evolution*. Edited by Ken Ham and Bodie Hodge. Green Forest, AR: Answers in Genesis, 2018.

Smith Jr., Joseph. The Church of Jesus Christ of Latter-Day Saints. The King Follet Sermon. Accessed February 24, 2021. https://www.churchofjesuschrist.org/study/ensign/1971/04/the-king-follett-sermon?lang=eng.

Strobel, Lee. *The Case for the Real Jesus*. Grand Rapids, MI: Zondervan, 2008.

Tatian. *The Ante-Nicene Fathers: Address to the Greeks.* Edited by Alexander Roberts, James Donaldson, and Arthur Cleveland Coxe. II. Vol. II. X vols. New York, NY: Cosimo Classics, 2007.

Tertullian. *The Ante-Nicene Fathers: Against Praxeas.* Edited by Alexander Roberts, James Donaldson, and Arthur Cleveland Coxe. III. Vol. III. X vols. New York, NY: Cosimo Classics, 2007.

Tertullian. *The Ante-Nicene Fathers: Against Marcion.* Edited by Alexander Roberts, James Donaldson, and Arthur Cleveland Coxe. III. Vol. III. X vols. New York, NY: Cosimo Classics, 2007.

Tertullian. *The Ante-Nicene Fathers: Answer to the Jews.* Edited by Alexander Roberts, James Donaldson, and Arthur Cleveland Coxe. III. Vol. III. X vols. New York, NY: Cosimo Classics, 2007.

Tertullian. *The Ante-Nicene Fathers: Apology.* Edited by Alexander Roberts, James Donaldson, and Arthur Cleveland Coxe. III. Vol. III. X vols. New York, NY: Cosimo Classics, 2007.

Tertullian. *The Ante-Nicene Fathers: On Baptism.* Edited by Alexander Roberts, James Donaldson, and Arthur Cleveland Coxe. III. Vol. III. X vols. New York, NY: Cosimo Classics, 2007.

Tertullian. *The Ante-Nicene Fathers: On the Resurrection of the Flesh.* Edited by Alexander Roberts, James Donaldson, and Arthur Cleveland Coxe. III. Vol. III. X vols. New York, NY: Cosimo Classics, 2007.

Theophilus. *The Ante-Nicene Fathers: To Autolycus.* Edited by Alexander Roberts, James Donaldson, and Arthur Cleveland Coxe. II. Vol. II. X vols. New York, NY: Cosimo Classics, 2007.

Vermes, Geza, trans. *The Complete Dead Sea Scrolls in English.* Penguin Books, n.d.

Ware, Timothy. *The Orthodox Church: An Introduction to Eastern Christianity.* New ed. Penguin Books, 1963.

Webster, Merriam. "Empiricism." In *Merriam-Webster*, n.d. https://www.merriam-webster.com/dictionary/empiricism.

Webster, Merriam. "Epistemology." In *Merriam-Webster*, n.d. https://www.merriam-webster.com/dictionary/epistemology.

Webster, Merriam. "God." In *Merriam-Webster*, n.d. https://www.merriam-webster.com/dictionary/god.

Weld, Theodore Dwight. *The Bible Against Slavery*, 1838.

White, James R. *The Forgotten Trinity*. Bloomington, MN: Bethany House Publishers, 1998.

Woodbridge, John D., and Frank A. James III. *Church History: From Pre-Reformation to the Present Day*. 2. Vol. 2. Grand Rapids, MI: Zondervan Academic, 2013.

Wright, N. T. *Evil and the Justice of God*. Downers Grove, IL: InterVarsity Press, 2006.

Wylie, J. A. *The History of the Waldenses*. Coppell, TX: Cassell and Company, 1860.

ABOUT THE AUTHOR

Derrick (DJ) Robinson was born on May 14, 2000, in Oklahoma City, Oklahoma. He played football and basketball growing up. In high school, he planned on going to college to pursue a degree in writing. Prior to graduation, his passion for sports developed into a passion for lifting weights. He then switched his career plan from writing to personal training. He came to Christ in 2018 after graduating high school. He earned an associate degree from Rose State College in health and sports science and a bachelor's degree from Trinity College of the Bible and Theological Seminary in biblical apologetics. His main goal in life is to spread the gospel of Jesus Christ and to defend the faith once delivered to the saints.

CPSIA information can be obtained
at www.ICGtesting.com
Printed in the USA
LVHW102350080622
720762LV00003B/86

9 781638 745914